ASSISTED LIVING 2000

*Practical Strategies
For The Next Millennium ...
... How to **Survive** & **Succeed** in
This Large, But Complex Market*

JIM MOORE

Based in part on the column
"Assisted Living/Senior Housing" appearing monthly in
Contemporary Long Term Care Magazine.

Assisted Living 2000
Practical Strategies For the Next Millennium

First Printing, July, 1998

Westridge Publishing
Fort Worth, Texas

Copyright © 1998 by Jim Moore
All rights reserved $40.00

No part of this book may be reproduced without written permission from the author or publisher, except for the brief inclusion of quotations or other attribution to the author in reviews and industry briefs or technical documents. Requests for permission or further information should be directed to Jim Moore at 817-731-4266.

TABLE OF CONTENTS

ABOUT THE AUTHOR — *i*

INTRODUCTION — *ii*

ACKNOWLEDGMENTS — *iv*

SECTION ONE - Developing a Solid Foundation

CHAPTER

1	**Market Positioning for Assisted Living** *Strategic Focus vs. Market Myopia*	1
2	**The Four Market Models** *The Competitive Battlefield Gets Defined*	11
3	**Ten Major Trends Impacting Assisted Living** *Operators Must Develop Strategic Responses to Inevitable Trends*	18
4	**Hospitals and Nursing Homes Are Getting Into Assisted Living** *Everybody is Getting Into Everybody Else's Business*	28
5	**Effectively Addressing Aging in Place** *Should You Embrace or Avoid a "Naturally Occurring Assisted Living Community?"*	37
6	**Developing the Foundation for a New Assisted Living Project** *Successful Outcomes Require Correctly Answering Ten Key Questions*	45
7	**Controlling the Referral Pipeline** *If You Don't, Someone Else Will!*	53

Table of Contents

CHAPTER

8	Managed Care Impacts *There's a Future Role for Assisted Living*	57
9	The Role of Home Health in Assisted Living *Beware of Oversimplified Approaches*	65

SECTION TWO - Physical Design Strategies

CHAPTER

10	Market - Driven Design Strategies for New Assisted Living Communities *You Really Get Only One Chance to do it Right !*	72
11	Adaptive Reuse for Assisted Living *Conversion Dreams Turned Into Nightmares*	89
12	Investing for Improvements *Physical Plants Also Experience Aging in Place*	104

SECTION THREE - Financial Considerations; Capital Costs and Operating Expenses

CHAPTER

13	Developing a Realistic Capital Budget *The Lifeblood of a Successful Project*	114
14	Realistic Approach to Determining Operating Expenses *Properly Evaluating All Costs is Critical When Projecting Expenses*	124

Table of Contents *Page 3*

CHAPTER

15	Assisted Living Cost Creep Can be a Fatal Disease *Many Sponsors Are in For a $1 Million⁺ Wake-Up Call*	142
16	Getting Creative With Capital Investment *Four Simple Steps That Can Produce Dramatic Results*	150
17	The Agony and Ecstasy of Financing Assisted Living *Refinancing is Easy - But Financing New Projects is More Complex*	156
18	Benchmarking Assisted Living *Not Just an Industry Buzzword, a Sound Business Strategy*	165

SECTION FOUR - Pricing & Affordability

CHAPTER

19	Creating an Optimum Pricing Structure *Win - Win Pricing Strategies for Financial Success*	172
20	Myths & Realities of Serving the Gap Income Group *Can We Deliver Affordable Assisted Living?*	187
21	Finding New Ways to Pay *Creative Uses of Home Equity Can Lower the Qualifying Income Bar and Increase Assisted Living Affordability*	200

SECTION FIVE - Special Market Niches and "Carve-Outs"

CHAPTER

22	Special Care Alzheimer's/Dementia *A "Carve-Out" Market Niche* *Whose Time Has Come*	212
23	Competing With Nursing Homes for Market Share *The Turf Battle of the New Millennium*	220
24	Branching Out Into the Community *Before Offering Community-Based Services,* *Answer Five Crucial Questions*	229
25	The Adult Child Decision Influencer *The Sandwich Generation Caught* *in a Squeeze*	236

SECTION SIX - Strategic Considerations

CHAPTER

26	Making the Case for Multi-Facility Consolidation *Senior Housing Operators Are Finding* *Strength in Numbers*	245
27	Single Facility Operators Face New Challenges *They Must Maintain a Sharply* *Focused Attention to Detail*	252
28	Managing Assisted Living *Internal Resource or* *Third-Party Contract?*	259
29	"I *Was* Somebody Once" *The Real Issue is Resident Quality of* *Life . . . Not Just Resident Satisfaction*	270

Table of Contents

SECTION SEVEN - The Future is Not What it Used to Be

CHAPTER

30	Preparing for a Market Correction *An Ounce of Prevention is* *Worth (More Than) a Pound of Cure*	277
31	Turning Around Troubled Communities *What to Do When Things Go Wrong*	285
32	The Top Ten Assisted Living Issues to Address in the Next 12 Months *A "Back to Basics" Checklist for Success*	291
33	Game Plan for Growth *How to Turn Four Key* *Challenges Into Opportunities*	298
34	These May Be the Good Old Days *Times Are Good, But it Will Take Work* *to Keep Them That Way*	304

Appendices

A	Overview of Market & Financial Feasibility	310
B	Mortgage Loan Constants	322
C	The Capitalization Rate Concept	324

About the Author

Jim Moore is president and founder of Moore Diversified Services, Inc. For the past 27 years, Jim's company has been heavily involved in market feasibility studies, detailed financial pro forma analysis, marketing consulting, strategic planning and investment advisory services.

Jim has over 35 years of industry experience and has personally conducted over 1,500 major Senior housing and health care consulting engagements in over 475 markets in 46 states – experience that is unmatched in the industry today. He has also conducted major consulting engagements in Japan, Australia, Canada, Europe and Mexico. As part of his consulting practice, he has lived in over 30 retirement and assisted living communities. His clients include a broad spectrum of national leaders and small organizations – with a balanced mix of both for-profit and not-for-profit clients.

As a recognized national expert, his courtroom testimony as an expert witness is frequently in demand across the U.S. He has provided expert witness support and testimony in over 35 cases at the local, state and national levels. He is the author of several hundred industry technical papers and trade journal articles. Jim has also authored a regular weekly business column for two major newspapers and for the past 7 years has authored a monthly column entitled, **"Assisted Living/Senior Housing"** for *Contemporary Long Term Care Magazine* – a leading industry trade periodical. He is the author of several previous books on senior housing, including *Assisted Living – Pure & Simple Development and Operating Strategies."*

Jim is past president of the National Association of Senior Living Industry Executives – NASLIE is a major industry trade association. He is active in five other industry trade associations and serves on the Advisory Boards of ten senior housing and health care organizations. He is on the Board of Directors of a public senior living company traded on the New York Stock Exchange.

Jim holds a Bachelor of Science degree in Industrial Technology from Northeastern University in Boston and an MBA in Marketing and Finance from Texas Christian University in Fort Worth, Texas.

INTRODUCTION

This book is being released during a period that could well be a major turning point in our exciting industry (July, 1998). History may record that from this point forward *"Assisted Living's Future Is Not What It Used To Be!"* This book does not cover *everything* you need to know about assisted living. No single book can. But, the 34 chapters address the most relevant issues facing our industry as we approach the new millennium. *Assisted Living 2000* covers leading edge information on strategies, tactics, industry benchmarks, rules of thumb, current trends and future marketplace impacts. I've attempted to present pure and simple winning strategies and money making ideas communicated with sophisticated simplicity. Real world problems are identified and cost-effective, practical solutions are provided.

Portions of this book are based on my column series entitled **"Assisted Living/Senior Housing"** published monthly by *Contemporary Long Term Care Magazine* – a leading industry periodical. The column has been appearing in *Contemporary Long Term Care Magazine* for over seven years.

I've tried to provide "random access" for the reader. This means that you can scan the detailed table of contents and jump to the chapter addressing the issue of interest to you on any given day. I've also tried to strike a delicate balance between leading edge ideas and theories combined with proven experience and trends observed consistently in the marketplace. These observations are the culmination of a 16 year odyssey where I've been in an average of three senior housing markets a week; 50 weeks each year. During my work, I've lived briefly in over 30 senior living communities in an attempt to get as close as possible to the residents, the front line staff and the local competition.

Introduction

A unique feature of the book is the detailed profiling of a typical 80-unit assisted living community; using today's industry comparables and financial factors that are representative of existing projects in approximately 75 percent of the U.S. markets in the 1998 time frame. Financial factors are presented in 1998 dollars using the prevailing interest rates of this time period. A word of caution – each individual project in each market is unique; the quantitative examples in this book should be used for guidance purposes only and must be appropriately adjusted for each individual situation.

For the experienced senior housing professional and their staff, this book can be a useful checklist of appropriate strategies and initiatives. For those who are new to our industry, it can act as a strategic planning handbook. I wish you much success in your endeavors to better serve seniors and their families.

ACKNOWLEDGMENTS

Assisted Living 2000 reflects the consolidated input of literally thousands of professionals, industry colleagues and senior consumers. I merely acted as a facilitator to translate their collective knowledge into a usable format. What I said in my previous book, ***Assisted Living – Pure & Simple Development and Operating Strategies*** needs repeating. I am deeply indebted to the professional staffs at hundreds of senior living communities that have taken valuable time from their very busy schedules to allow me to both help them and to expand my base of knowledge and experience. I have tremendous respect for these professionals who provide endless love, care and patience to their residents; much of it accomplished in a time sensitive, stressful environment.

Over 10,000 residents and senior consumers, in formal focus groups and informal conversations, took the time to share their personal experiences with me. They discussed both the good life and the challenges of growing older. Hundreds of clients, sponsors and owner/operators allowed me into their communities and boardrooms to exchange strategic ideas. Industry colleagues openly shared their ideas, experiences and strategies.

I would like to specifically thank **Contemporary Long Term Care Magazine** for helping make this book possible. Elise Nakhnikian, Editor-in-Chief, has a remarkable talent of reworking my thoughts and ideas. In short, she is largely responsible for my column's tenure and long term success.

My professional team at MDS played a tremendous role in creating this book; especially Mary Ann Baltzer, Kim Jimenez and Jeff Moore. I'm deeply indebted to Sue Bregenzer, who somehow found time to provide enormous assistance in coordinating my column for the past seven years and producing the manuscript for this book during one of the busiest periods of our company's 27-year history.

Finally, to my wife Gerry who, as a management professional, has provided unbelievable understanding, support and patience with my long days and busy travel schedule.

SECTION ONE

Developing A Solid Foundation

CHAPTER 1

MARKET POSITIONING FOR ASSISTED LIVING

Strategic Focus vs. Market Myopia

State-of-the-art assisted living has become one of the most appropriate alternative living options for many seniors. While perhaps slightly overstated, many industry observers say that assisted living has literally taken the senior housing and health care markets by storm.

The reasons are very simple. Assisted living responds very effectively to the need-driven, health-related concerns of the senior. It is also a cost-effective and emotionally acceptable alternative for many caregivers; adult children faced with a growing family dilemma involving complex emotional and financial decisions. For both seniors and their adult children, assisted living has a simple but very powerful market positioning statement:

> **"The surprisingly affordable living alternative offering ambience, dignity and maximum independence for many seniors in their later stages of life"**

In spite of the potential for very favorable market positioning, the concept of assisted living is still largely misunderstood by many owner/operators and the consumer marketplace. While effective market positioning has proven to be very successful for many sponsors, others either ignore or are not aware of the value of positioning strategies.

Many experienced owner/operators are still attempting to explain assisted living as another form of independent living or a vague variation of nursing care. This positioning in the marketplace is lacking from two major perspectives:

1. Attempting to explain assisted living as a variation of independent living results in a consumer education problem in most markets. This is because the concept of independent retirement living is largely misunderstood by many seniors who have not yet decided to seriously investigate such living arrangements.

2. Relating assisted living to nursing stirs up the *dreaded nursing home syndrome* in the minds of seniors and their families. Regardless of how nice a nursing home might be and how high the last inspection scores were, it is still the *dreaded nursing home* to most senior consumers and their caring, guilt-ridden children. This is not an indictment of the nursing home industry – it is a marketplace fact of life!

Chapter 2 defines the four basic assisted living market models that currently exist. These models should be carefully reviewed because they form a solid foundation for future market positioning strategies.

Strategic Market Positioning

An ideally conceived assisted living facility is not just bricks and mortar. It is also far more than just shelter, quality food service, housekeeping and health care. A second powerful market positioning statement is:

> **"Assisted living must have a strong, but largely invisible, medical basis as the solid foundation for its internal operating philosophy and external market positioning strategy."**

The strategic advantages of freestanding assisted living are subtle, but pervasive, and are largely overlooked by many owner/operators.

Assisted living gradually became the senior consumer's decision option by-pass of the 1990s (refer to Figure 1-1). One of the most common marketing objections to independent retirement community marketing is *"I'm not ready yet."* Astute marketing professionals have responded to this objection by reminding prospects that they may fail the stringent health and frailty admission requirements of independent living retirement communities if they continue to delay their decision. The marketers urge them to be "pre-planners" and make timely decisions *now*.

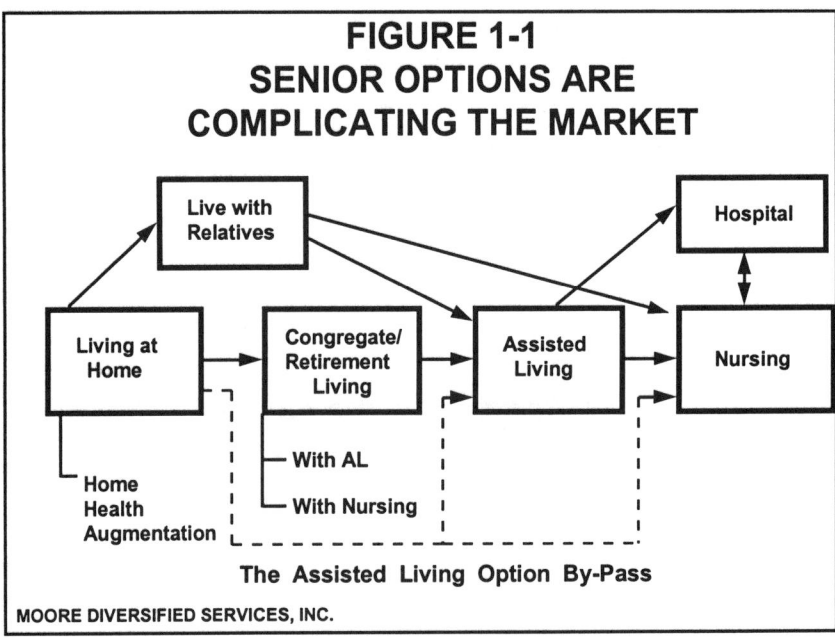

Now, seniors and their caregiver children are realizing that they have a legitimate hedging option that can stretch this difficult move decision even further out in time. In many markets, seniors need not worry about qualifying for acceptance under independent living and CCRC admission criteria because they can wait and still qualify under more frail conditions for state-of-the-art freestanding assisted living.

Three Market Positioning Mistakes

Unfortunately, there are three fundamental positioning mistakes being made consistently in the business:

- Many owner/operators do not recognize (or understand) what they have or how to effectively communicate their community in the competitive marketplace

- Owner/operators focus too heavily on shelter and food service and do not recognize that they are truly in the sophisticated health care business

- Health care providers and many not-for-profit sponsors are creating a health care or institutional assisted living model when the market really wants a residential/social model

Positioning Assisted Living vs. Nursing

Assisted living can frequently be positioned as a surprisingly affordable, more attractive alternative to nursing. Obviously, not every senior who might otherwise opt for nursing can be accommodated in assisted living. However, there is emerging evidence that anywhere from 10 to 15 percent (sometimes up to 20 percent) of existing private pay nursing home patients might be accommodated in various levels of well-conceived assisted living. However, the potential of this transfer alternative is trending downward as patient acuity levels in nursing homes continue to increase due to emerging managed care market forces and subtle changes in Medicare and Medicaid entitlement criteria. Some assisted living operators are now dealing with incontinence, middle stages of dementia and relatively high acuity levels hoping for lower resident turn-over and their share of the lower acuity nursing market.

With the exception of some experimental Medicaid waiver programs and local entitlements, there are currently very few third party payors for assisted living. However, with the advent of long term care insurance, a new wave of benefits is likely to be offered to fund at least a portion of future assisted living service fees. Insurance underwriters and actuaries are quickly recognizing assisted living as a more cost-effective payor benefit for those who can be adequately served in this environment. But today, assisted living is still fundamentally a private pay living option.

Properly conceived, assisted living has important – and relatively rare – dual market positioning points:

> **ASSISTED LIVING IS BOTH:**
>
> ● <u>**NEED**</u>**-DRIVEN (SENIOR CONSUMER)**
>
> **AND**
>
> ● <u>**MARKET**</u>**-DRIVEN (DECISION INFLUENCER)**

The future of assisted living appears bright, but not without some future marketplace and regulatory turbulence. Astute operators will discover they can expand their market areas by communicating more effectively with adult children who are separated from their aging parents. Hospitals will get into assisted living as they look for ways to expand their horizons, by moving away from heavy concentrations of acute care and creating more comprehensive vertical integrated networks.

Market Sector Overlap

Figure 1-2 shows how assisted living clearly overlaps into the traditional business sectors of independent living and nursing.

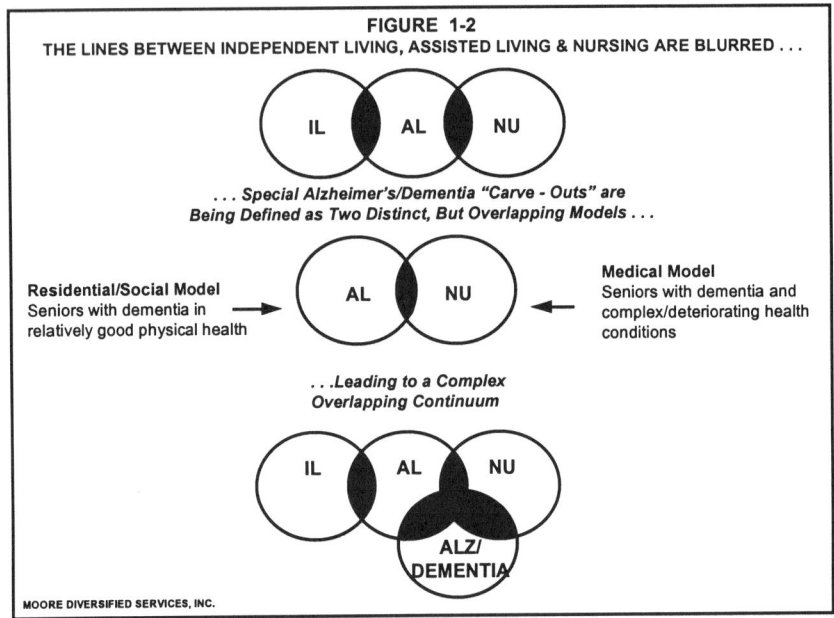

Special Care Alzheimer's/Dementia "Carve-outs"

These market sector overlaps are further complicated by the rapidly emerging trends of special care carve-outs. Special care Alzheimer's/dementia is being addressed by special purpose-built living options within traditional assisted living communities. See Chapter 22 for additional details.

> **Special Care Alzheimer's/Dementia "Carve-Outs" Are Being Defined as Two Distinct, But Overlapping Models:**
>
> - **Residential/Social Model** – Seniors with dementia but in relatively good physical health
>
> - **Medical Model** – Seniors with dementia and complex/deteriorating health conditions

These carve-out market niches lead to a complex, overlapping continuum as illustrated in Figure 1-2. These market positioning changes caused by the maturing assisted living business sector are subtle but pervasive; you must respond by making market positioning an integral part of your development and operating strategies.

Other Trends and Impacts

Assisted living also provides the potential for other revenue enhancement business spin-offs such as home care agencies, expanded rehabilitation services, respite care, and adult day care.

Assisted living is a cost-effective response and alternative to growing home care entitlement costs, especially when the senior needs continuous assistance. Some home health costs up to $80 for less than a one hour in-home visit. For that same $80, assisted living can provide 24 hours care *plus* housing and shelter services. Home health care is a very viable service delivery system for short-run needs. The concept becomes less efficient as needs increase.

Consider this market positioning:

> **"It is far more efficient to deliver 24-hour home care into 80 residences on one five-acre campus than it is to provide the same services into 80 randomly distributed single family homes throughout a metropolitan area."**

Eventually health care cost containment efforts will likely result in a total restructuring of home health care entitlements – possibly placing more emphasis and priority on assisted living.

Despite the changing trends that are complicating assisted living, the concept can still be positioned to be one of the most practical solutions to long term care in the future; containing costs while successfully responding to the needs and desires of the senior consumers and their families.

CHAPTER 2

THE FOUR MARKET MODELS
The Competitive Battlefield Gets Defined

There are four fundamental assisted living market models: 1) integrated with independent living, 2) freestanding facilities, 3) integrated with nursing and 4) assisted living as an integral part of a hospital campus. Each model offers unique marketplace opportunities and challenges. Figure 2-1 illustrates these four models.

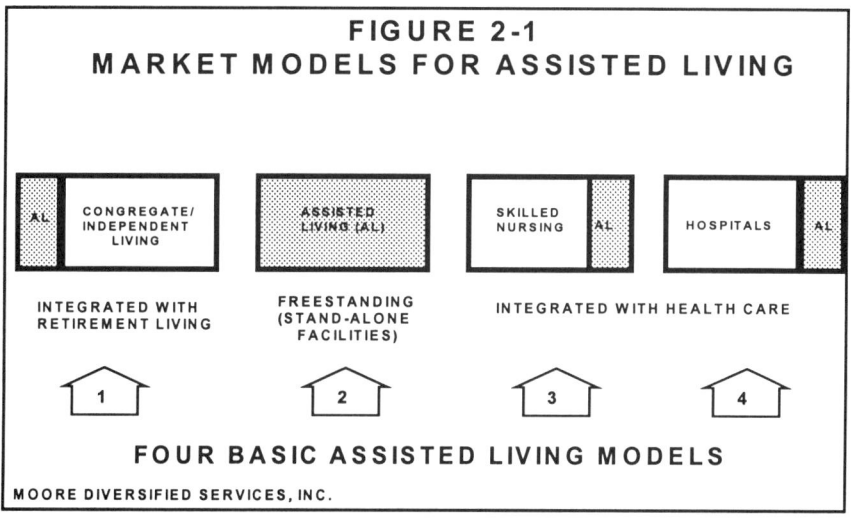

***Assisted living, integrated with independent living –** The first market model* has proven to be one of the best "cures" for a slow-moving independent living retirement community. The reasons for this are quite simple. In reality, most seniors do not want to move into even the nicest retirement community until a truly need-driven circumstance gives them a "wake-up call" and pushes them over the decision threshold. Faced with moving out of their homes, seniors want to avoid two other future situations: 1) having to move again and 2) facing the nursing home as their only other future option. Seniors are more willing to make the difficult move to independent living – as long as they know there is still another acceptable living option on the campus.

In competitive markets, those retirement communities offering either a full continuum of care, or at least a combination of independent and assisted living, have consistently performed better across the United States. In the 1980s, many owner/operators, and particularly those in the for-profit sector, initially hedged their decision about getting into assisted living. For the most part, they have paid a heavy price for this procrastination. The ultimate addition of assisted living is frequently one of the top three corrective action strategies for a slow-moving or severely distressed retirement community that previously offered only independent living.

Freestanding assisted living – The second market model is really the new product of the 1990s and offers unique challenges and opportunities. Assisted living integrated with either independent living or health care allows the sponsor's marketing flanks to be covered and provides some inherent cross-referral potential. This allows some maneuverability and hedging of risks in the marketplace. But freestanding assisted living sometimes becomes the lost patrol of health care marketing warfare. It is either right on target and takes the market by storm, or it flounders and gets lost due to marketplace ambivalence, rejection or confusion.

Assisted living integrated with nursing – The third market model provides nursing home operators with enhanced economies of scale, diversification and marketplace flexibility. For these operators, expanding into assisted living draws a wider pool of potential patients and residents while providing increased efficiencies and economies of scale from their existing base of operations. These benefits include expanded utilization of the "back of the house" core operations such as the commercial kitchen, laundry and maintenance functions. There is also the possibility of some staff sharing and the co-mingling of other resources between the separated yet integrated nursing and assisted living operations.

Many nursing homes across the United States are still enjoying strong occupancies. Some actually turn away potential business daily while maintaining waiting lists. Couple these occupancy trends with significant private pay ratios in some markets and the addition of assisted living becomes a very powerful business strategy.

But others are experiencing sagging occupancies and increased competition from some new assisted living operators who are offering services to high acuity level residents. Adding assisted living in these situations can be an imperative for survival. Assisted living permits cross-referrals of residents on a campus; the net effect can be increased overall occupancy and revenue enhancement.

Assisted living on hospital campuses – The fourth market model – Approximately 50 percent of my firm's assisted living consulting engagements directly or indirectly involve hospitals. Due to managed care trends and forces, many hospitals are now being measured by the *vacancy* of the acute care beds. Most are experiencing shortened average length of stay and a decline in total patient-days. Revenue enhancement from other related sources is now the name of the game for many organizations. Hospital CEOs and CFOs are asking the pragmatic question, **"Why should we continue to make courtesy assisted living referrals when we could be in the business?"**

Nursing homes and hospitals can now respond to a broader spectrum of health care needs, while serving more patients (residents) in a less intense, lower cost medical service delivery environment. They will be able to do this while maintaining optimum resource utilization (higher occupancies). Intracampus transfers between subacute care, nursing and assisted living are becoming quite commonplace. Chapter 4 provides more insight into the current trends of health care providers getting into assisted living.

Despite these potential advantages, it sometimes becomes difficult for a quality nursing home or hospital provider to effectively position, communicate, market and operate assisted living. The stronger their acute care reputation, the more difficulties many have in effectively positioning assisted living away from being just another form of expensive institutionalized health care. Some operators get caught up in their own culture and tradition; their strong reputations can actually become a major disadvantage. Moreover, their staff mentality and health care organizational culture inadvertently creates a strong medical model for a living arrangement that should be sending just the opposite signals to the consumer marketplace.

The Four Major Components of Assisted Living

Assisted living service delivery for the new millennium is comprised of four major components:

1. Real Estate (bricks and mortar)

2. Hospitality Services (shelter)

3. Restaurant (meal service)

4. Health Care (assistance with ADL's)[1]

To be truly successful, you must execute each one in an integrated, *seamless* manner. And each component is significantly different when applied to assisted living as contrasted with the individual and conventional market sectors outlined above.

---

[1] Activities of Daily Living

Special "Carve-Outs" or Market Niches

Any of the four models can be further modified or enhanced by adding specialized services offering diversification and revenue enhancement. These additional market niches include, but are not necessarily limited to, the following:

- Special Care (Alzheimer's/Dementia)
- Respite Care
- Adult Day Care
- Rehabilitation
- Home Health
- Community-Based Services

Many of these are discussed in other chapters.

Unfortunately, the discreet blocks illustrated in Figure 2-1 do not do full justice to the real complexity of the continuum which is, in reality, blurred and overlapping as shown in Figure 1-2 in Chapter 1.

Service Delivery Models

There are two basic service delivery models:

- ***Service Provider*** – Typically, the owner/operator's permanent staff provides meals, housekeeping, laundry, activities, ADL assistance, health monitoring and medical emergency response.

The Four Market Models 17

- *Home Health* – In this model, the owner/operator generally provides "shelter" type services and the home health agency focuses on medically related services such as ADL assistance, case management and health management. (See Chapter 9 for more details.)

Figure 2-2 depicts these two basic service delivery models. A word of caution; the combination of service provider and third party home health agency should appear seamless to the senior and their families. Cost recovery and pricing must be equitable, understandable and reasonably affordable. Chapter 19 addresses this important issue in more detail.

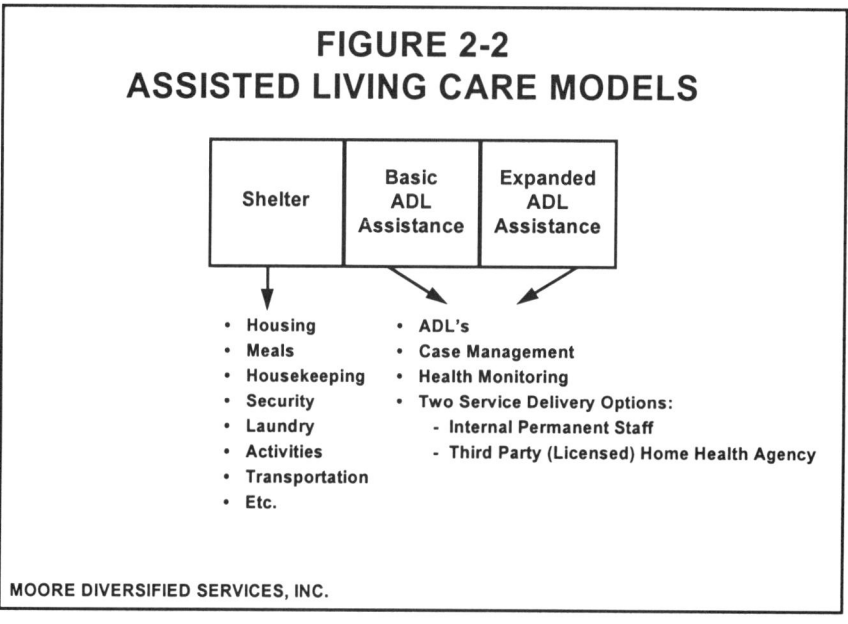

CHAPTER 3

TEN MAJOR TRENDS IMPACTING ASSISTED LIVING

Operators Must Develop Strategic Responses to Inevitable Trends

Assisted living has a number of favorable attributes: the concept is cost-effective, it serves a clearly defined need for a growing market segment, and it is generally "user friendly." Assisted living is also positioned well for future growth as managed care spreads throughout our health care system. There is considerable debate on how managed care will ultimately interface with long term care, but assisted living's cost-effective and efficient method of delivering services appears quite compatible with the fundamental cost containment philosophies and objectives of managed care.

Ten "Unexpected" Trends

Notwithstanding favorable industry hype and market responsiveness, assisted living has proven to be a constantly moving target; and no one definitive success strategy has emerged. Investors and operators in this field have encountered some surprises in recent years, and there may be more to come. If you don't pay attention to some increasingly evident trends, you will pay a price. I would propose my personal "top ten."

These ten unexpected trends are forcing sponsors and operators to constantly monitor their radar screens and re-evaluate their current operations.

1. *Increasing acuity levels and high resident turnover.* Many operators had visions that their residential/social model of assisted living would attract the moderately frail elderly; they hoped these residents could be cared for with relative ease and at modest cost. However, changing entitlement systems and managed care market forces are bringing higher acuity level patients into nursing homes, and the effect is filtering down through the continuum of care to assisted living. Add to that the natural effects of aging in place and it's not surprising that assisted living communities are finding themselves with an unexpectedly high number of residents in need of complex and expensive care. As a result, most assisted living sponsors are experiencing annual resident turnover rates of 40 to 50 percent. This translates to an average length of stay of approximately two and one-half years.

Many operators have responded by providing higher acuity services such as incontinence management and dementia care; services that weren't considered a few years ago. In fact, some organizations are becoming increasingly concerned about drifting into "gray areas" concerning nursing-type licensure. They are (or should be) keeping close watch on their state and local licensure requirements, which vary considerably from state-to-state. The licensure issue is one reason why nursing homes themselves, rather than fighting assisted living, are starting to join in; some 60 percent of nursing homes are estimated to be at least considering the assisted living alternative.

2. *Threat of regulation*. As acuity levels rise, assisted living care may well cross the line into the domain of licensed nursing. If this happens, the types of assistance offered, staffing levels, and resident care outcomes are likely to trigger competing trade association debates and a barrage of new state and federal regulations.

There is concern that the nursing OBRA experience not be repeated with assisted living. The question arises, though, that if Medicaid eventually becomes a major payor for assisted living, what sort of strings will be attached? How much regulation will be federal, how much state, and what will the regulation be like? For now, the most practical approach to the issue is to make sure that your facility is built in accordance with anticipated basic regulatory and fire/safety requirements – e.g., fire doors, appropriate corridor widths, sprinkler systems – that, while not required now, may well be in the near future. In short, make sure that at least your "bricks and mortar" are prepared for future government oversight.

3. *Cost creep – an insidious economic disease*. Residents want high ambience, non-institutional residential settings, but they will also need increased assistance in activities of daily living. These needs must be met through a strong, albeit largely invisible, medical structure. Satisfying these needs may not entail the significant expense of high-acuity nursing services, but increasing levels of care in assisted living are resulting in subtle increases in operating costs. These cost increases "trickle" through your financial statements in the form of overtime and additional staffing requests; and one day you may get that financial "wake-up" call. Implementing price changes with existing residents to compensate for the newly discovered cost creep is not a pleasant experience for front line professionals to initiate. Chapter 15 addresses cost creep impacts and strategies in detail.

4. *Complex pricing systems are emerging.* In response to cost creep, operators are implementing tiered, multilevel pricing policies. While these policies may seem rational, they can sometimes cause marketplace confusion.

Suddenly your community's nice, simple, easy-to-understand basic service fee schedule has evolved into a multi-level price structure. You start by increasing fees $200 to 300 a month for increasingly intense levels of assistance with the activities of daily living. Or perhaps you charge $8 to $12 for every 15-minute increment of additional hands-on care daily.

Existing residents and their families will go through a period of economic adjustment. New residents will likely understand this fee structure at the start and, presumably, will accept it. From an administrative standpoint, though, this requires more sophisticated record keeping and cost accounting systems – but that investment is usually an imperative and comes with the increasing complexity of this business. Chapter 19 addresses pricing in detail.

5. *Potential for market proliferation and possible saturation*. The current consumer demand that is assisted living's greatest strength may also be a major weakness in the near future. Inexperienced developer/operators eager to cash in on current demand may overbuild. This could result in a glut of poorly planned facilities and a tarnished reputation for the industry, as people unfamiliar with assisted living underestimate the complexities of resident care and the competitive marketplace.

Many large, public companies feel that they must have a multi-facility presence in most major metropolitan areas such as Atlanta, Boston, etc. As this book goes to press, this major market focus has not yet reached market saturation. But in assessing whether saturation is approaching, there are some important "vital signs" to watch for and questions to ask. Are occupancy levels in various neighboring facilities starting to sag? Why? And what about new project fill-up rates? Today's projects fill up, on average, at a rate of five-to-seven units a month, net of turnover. Anything slower than that over a reasonable period of time is cause for concern.

6. *Market area overlap is already occurring in some cities.* This is the ultimate marketing challenge for assisted living developers. Interestingly, in some market areas there is primary market overlap occurring within the *same* company's operations. Marketing manager A is competing with marketing manager B to fill units for the same multi-facility operator. And they are confronting consumers who are smart enough to attempt to make deals by pitting one sales manager against the other. The headquarters office, of course, just wants to see units filled, and may not be aware that the company is actually competing with itself to accomplish their objectives!

With firms that compete with one another, the situation resembles having two new service stations on opposite corners of the street. Suddenly they both notice that their business is turning markedly downward. Frequently, it's not so much that there isn't market size and depth to ultimately support the competing facilities, it's that they're both going through their critical market introduction and acceptance at the same time.

7. *You can't necessarily rely on future demographics to solve current overbuild problems.* In some respects, current assisted living growth patterns are analogous to the 1990's real estate version of *"if you build it, they will come."* Even if you're not filling up now, you might rationalize that, surely with the aging boom you'll have no problems by the year 2000. This summons up memories of the 1980s, when inflation was supposed to cover up many a real estate mistake. Unfortunately, tomorrow's demographics will not cover up serious assisted living project overbuilding mistakes that are made today.

8. *Managed care and entitlements may not have a significant short-run impact on assisted living*. There used to be the argument – and it still exists in some quarters – that since assisted living provides a less costly alternative to nursing home care, it will be very attractive to managed care organizations as they take hold in long-term care. Today I am less certain that this is true.

Acuity levels in nursing homes have increased to such an extent that relatively few residents today fit the ideal profile for assisted living. Two years ago one might have argued that at least 15 to 20 percent of nursing home residents could be appropriately relocated to assisted living (assuming, of course, that they could private-pay). Now, though, I think that we have two separate populations in these settings, with very little overlap – i.e., a nursing home population whom government largely supports but can ill-afford to pay for, and an assisted living population who, if they become Medicare- and/or Medicaid-qualified, are also too large a population sector to support. I would love to see assisted living become a major player in the entitlements market, but how can this work given the current numbers and budgetary restraints?

I don't see Medicare HMOs going beyond covering basic Medicare benefits anytime soon. Meanwhile, private long-term care insurance, which might be expected to use managed care to keep premiums under control, is still only a very small player in the market and is growing perhaps a little less rapidly than some might have anticipated five or six years ago.

For these reasons, we counsel all our clients that assisted living must be viewed primarily as a private-pay business. If there is ever an entitlements breakthrough, that will be a big plus for the industry – but don't count on it.

9. *Truly affordable assisted living is a moving target.* There is a lot of talk about "affordable" *assisted living.* Well intended individuals are making erroneous comparisons with the concept of affordable *senior housing.* Clearly, such federal programs as Section 8 and 202 have been very good for the economically disadvantaged Senior needing basic housing. But unfortunately, assisted living operates in an altogether different economic arena.

Let's look at the elementary costs involved in providing basic assisted living; shelter, food, reasonable assistance with ADLs. These operating expenses come to about $40 per resident day (if you're fortunate). Multiply this by 30.4 days per month, and the basic outlay is between $1,200 and $1,300 a month.

There is simply no escaping this. Even if someone were to *give* the developer or sponsor the land and the building, which seems unlikely, the basic operating costs must be covered each month for the operator to break even. Tax credit programs help the land and building cost challenge, but are certainly not the total solution to the affordability problem.

I wish there was a way to resolve this, because there are certainly large numbers of people in our society who need and deserve affordable assisted living services. But, as a practical matter, assisted living is and probably will continue to be private pay. From society's standpoint, that is our challenge – and dilemma – for the future.

10. *A Market Correction in the Future?* Recently my firm calculated that if all the projects announced by major companies in a particular market came on line during the next 18 months, the area's assisted living inventory would increase by over 23 percent. That is a huge increase, especially given current resident turnover rates. The combination of companies going public and the rising availability of capital are fueling the current 1998 boom which will impact the industry over the next two or three years. Is there a "boom/bust" potential here? The marketplace will provide answers fairly soon.

TEN MAJOR TRENDS IMPACTING ASSISTED LIVING

1. High acuity levels and resident turnover
2. Threat of regulation
3. Cost creep
4. Complex pricing systems
5. Potential for market saturation
6. Market area overlap
7. Overbuild not solved by demographics
8. Managed care impacts
9. Is there affordable assisted living?
10. A market correction?

Sponsors and operators seeking to respond to some or all of these trends must first understand the numbers associated with assisted living development. These numbers include demographics, capital costs, operating expenses, and the financial dynamics and consequences resulting from existing and future competition.

CHAPTER 4

HOSPITALS AND NURSING HOMES ARE GETTING INTO ASSISTED LIVING

Everybody is Getting Into Everybody Else's Business

Nursing homes are being battered on two economic fronts; hospitals are creating swing wings and getting into skilled nursing, rehabilitation and subacute care on one front while many assisted living operators are crossing the line offering quasi-nursing services on the other. Some industry analysts feel that assisted living could eventually replace hundreds of thousands of the 1.7 million nursing beds in operation today. I feel there will be an impact on nursing bed growth in the future, but the actual impact is currently difficult to quantify.

Nursing bed supply/inventory has seen only modest growth over the past five years as managed care impacts and the introduction of assisted living has changed the basic demand structure for new nursing beds. An indication of relative nursing bed supply is a ratio indicating the number of beds per 1,000 seniors age 85+. This ratio has declined from 650 beds per 1,000 85+ seniors in 1980 to approximately 400 beds in 1998. The changing ratio is the result of increasing numbers of age 85+ seniors while the nursing bed supply has remained essentially flat.

Who would have thought that a hospital's success would be measured by the *vacancy* of their acute care beds? That is exactly what is happening to some hospitals who sponsor and become payors of 65+ Medicare Risk HMOs and are under pressure to lower the health care costs (within the Medicare benefit structure) for seniors joining their HMOs.

Hospitals and nursing homes are fighting back. Both industries are placing assisted living right in the middle of their radar screens. Many hospitals and nursing home operators are seeking ways to enhance revenues by offering new services, achieving higher operational efficiencies and responding to evolving managed care initiatives. At the same time, they are being pressured to reduce costs by both the consumer private-pay marketplace and third party payors. In their search for a solution to this dilemma, some sponsors are finding assisted living a tempting, but perplexing, opportunity. Both nursing home operators and hospital CEOs are asking the complex question, *"Is the assisted living concept competitive or compatible with our future business strategies?"* A number of traditional health care sponsors see the opportunities, but very few truly understand the challenges.

Positioning for Success and Synergy

The hospital and nursing home industries can position themselves to benefit from assisted living operations synergy and market opportunities. But to do so successfully, many management philosophies, operating policies and organizational cultures must change dramatically.

For health care providers, assisted living can be a sound and synergistic diversification strategy by allowing their facilities to expand or complete the continuum of care they offer while enhancing revenues by serving a broader sector of the market. In addition, they can realize significant operational economies of scale; primarily in the areas of staffing, food service, housekeeping, laundry, maintenance, operations, and health service delivery. Assisted living also appeals to traditional health care providers because their traditional subcontracting, outsourcing and patient referral initiatives are gradually being replaced by revenue enhancing, internal service delivery strategies. But before they can diversify into assisted living, health care providers must adopt appropriate management philosophies, operating policies and create new organizational cultures.

Impacts of Reimbursement Systems

As 65+ Medicare and Medicaid Risk HMOs, Medicaid waivers and other managed care initiatives play a larger part in financing long term care, a third-party payor system for assisted living may eventually evolve. These providers and payors will be taking on increasing financial risks for the total health care of seniors, which means they will seek the common objective of integrated health service delivery at the lowest possible cost. For

Medicare and Medicaid policy makers as well, assisted living could prove to be the cost-effective missing link between existing entitlements involving institutionalism (acute, subacute, skilled nursing) at one end of the continuum and some inefficiencies of delivering home health care at the other end. **A word of caution; don't count on significant third party payors for assisted living in the short run. The existing Medicare and Medicaid budgets are being strained and *cutbacks*, not new *entitlements*, are the current topics of discussion with policy makers.**

Nursing Home Initiatives

For nursing home operators, reimbursement and third party payor programs are becoming more complex. High census rates no longer automatically lead to a strong financial position, and the threat of increased regulation has made long-range planning a difficult task. Approximately 70 percent of the total age 65+ nursing home patient-days are Medicaid reimbursed; private pay nursing patients are becoming a relatively rare resource. In addition, nursing homes in many markets are struggling to sustain a strong presence as a myriad of competing health care options emerge. Many facilities have room to grow, thanks to underutilized resources and excess land, and some wonder whether simply adding new skilled nursing beds is the best business strategy to pursue.

For nursing homes considering expansion, there are several innovative implementation strategies. One such strategy would be to add an assisted living wing or floor to an operating nursing home, thereby benefitting from the existing service core area or "back of the house" functional area. This would be a *medical model* of assisted living. Another strategy is to develop a new non-institutional free-standing assisted living building on the same site/campus (the *residential/social model*). Sometimes this new building is actually oriented away from the main entrance of the existing nursing home. This individualized sense of entrance can create a strong, favorable non-institutional first impression.

Hospital Initiatives

Meanwhile, hospitals are realizing that expanding the spectrum of health related services to seniors is a natural and sometimes necessary step. Not only are more than 50 percent of hospital patient days related to seniors, but average lengths of stay are declining and competition for outpatient services is intensifying. This makes assisted living an attractive revenue enhancement option for progressive hospitals planning for the future; especially those in suburban markets. In the past three years, approximately half of our assisted living feasibility studies and strategic planning engagements have directly or indirectly involved hospitals.

Expanding into assisted living is a relatively new initiative for hospitals, and one that usually remains a closely guarded secret during the exploratory phase. Typically, hospitals consider three options. The first option would be to convert existing space, which is generally best suited for the more institutional personal care, or a medical model of assisted living. Secondly, they can construct a new facility on the existing campus, creating a more residential/social model that can benefit from the hospital's economies of scale. Thirdly, they may develop a facility off-campus at a "satellite location." The latter is a popular option for joint ventures between a hospital and a developer or operating partner. It also allows a core area/inner city hospital to have a high-quality satellite presence in other suburban areas for both marketing visibility and service delivery.

Economies of Scale and Synergy

Both hospitals and nursing homes can realize significant economies of scale as they consider entry into the senior housing market. There are five major areas of potential economies of scale that could lead to synergistic growth opportunities. These include:

1. Staff and Management Resources – Some of the human resources that are already in place for a hospital or nursing home can lead to synergistic economies of scale when considering adding independent living and/or assisted living arrangements on or near their campus. Contrasted with the new assisted living community that is entirely "stand-alone," there are the benefits of inherent economies of scale if assisted living is integrated (but separated) within a comprehensive campus.

2. Food and Beverage Operations – Hospitals and nursing homes already have extensive commercial kitchens and mass purchasing power. While the food service menus and needs are different in senior housing and assisted living, there are some potentially significant dietary economies of scale that can be realized.

3. Delivery of Health Care Services – This is an obvious extension of something that most health care providers do quite well. Staff depth and the ability to rotate health care personnel can alleviate burnout and employee turnover.

4. Housekeeping, Laundry, and Maintenance Operations – In many instances, these existing operations have additional capacity and underutilized resources. Cost-effective expansion can be implemented with relative ease.

Diversification Pitfalls

All of this diversification sounds easy, but it should be emphasized that implementation of these growth strategies involves significant challenges. There are a number of pitfalls regarding health care providers entering the senior living market sector.

One of the pitfalls involves the inability of providers to adjust their philosophy of service delivery. Health care providers sometimes have difficulty recognizing that offering independent and assisted living is really a new and different business for them.

The differences center on several important areas critical to the overall success of a health care provider's strategy: market positioning, marketing approach, physical and aesthetic design, interior finish-out, furnishings, and day-to-day operations.

Of paramount importance is the clear recognition that providers must move away from a heavily institutionalized medical service model to one of satisfying more benefit-driven, but still complex, senior consumer needs and motivations.

Despite these challenges, the spin-off benefits for providers can be significant. For example, a hospital that develops a strong image by responding effectively to the senior market is more likely to enhance their capture of senior acute care admissions.

Like it or not, assisted living will be a major player in the overall health care arena. Many hospital and nursing home operators still resist entering the fray. But, in response to marketplace forces and the changing policies of third-party payors, astute providers are reviewing their five year strategic plans to see where assisted living might fit in.

Think of it this way, if you are either a hospital or nursing home provider currently *giving away* courtesy referrals to assisted living, should you rethink the process?

ASSISTED LIVING
OPPORTUNITIES AND CHALLENGES
FOR HOSPITALS AND NURSING HOMES

Opportunities	Challenges
1. Synergy of operations	1. Changing culture
2. Economies of scale	2. Mind-set of staff
3. Revenue enhancement	3. Serving different markets
4. Favorable response to managed care	4. Different cost structure
5. Expand the continuum	5. Must create a residential vs. institutional market model

CHAPTER 5

EFFECTIVELY ADDRESSING AGING IN PLACE

Should You Embrace or Avoid a "Naturally Occurring Assisted Living Community?"

A human drama is unfolding in senior living communities across the United States that will have an enormous impact on the future of the senior housing industry in general and assisted living in particular. Aging in place and the gradual deterioration of the health of seniors in senior living communities is one of the most predictable trends in senior housing today. Annual resident turnover rates range from 15 to 25 percent for independent living and 40 percent or higher for many assisted living communities. Yet, practical, effective and consistent responses to this dilemma have eluded even the most experienced sponsors.

This book primarily addresses "purpose-built" assisted living, but there are alternative ways to deliver assisted living. During the past ten years, the senior living industry has learned that the key to success is being market-driven; responding to the wants and needs of the senior consumer. And most owner/operators and sponsors now recognize that one of the most urgent needs they face is effectively addressing the aging in place of their residents. Meeting this enormous challenge is more than many initially bargained for when attempting to accommodate older, frailer seniors.

A relatively high level of confusion exists between the two fundamental conditions involving the health and aging of seniors:

- *Chronic Condition* – The natural and largely predictable changing health status of seniors as they age. The need for assistance with ADL's gradually increases with time – including addressing the special needs of these seniors experiencing various levels of Alzheimer/dementia.

- *Episodic Condition* – A sudden change in health status due to an "episode"; a hip fracture, stroke, etc. This usually triggers an abrupt increase in ADL needs and sometimes a permanent change in the need for sheltered living arrangements.

Medicare and Medicaid entitlement programs attempt to define these two conditions with each offering specific and unique entitlement challenges and opportunities.

Seniors age in place and develop chronic health conditions in a very predictable manner. This aging process has caused many older, conventional apartment buildings and condominiums to gradually transition into what is called a "NORC"; a Naturally Occurring Retirement Community. This same aging process can cause an independent living retirement community to evolve into a marginally efficient, defacto assisted living operation.

The Assistance in Living (AIL) Concept

Dealing with aging in place is, at best, extremely difficult and complex. There is a strong temptation to either procrastinate or to make shortsighted, short-run decisions. Many astute operators have created distinct living and care continuums that include active adult housing, independent living, assisted living, special Alzheimer/dementia units, and nursing. But others are implementing Assistance in Living (AIL) strategies; offering assistance with the residents' activities of daily living (ADL) in their existing independent living units.

In the short run, providing such services is good for the residents, solves an immediate and significant aging-in-place problem and, if properly priced, can provide the sponsor with a hedge against operating expense cost creep. But this short-run solution frequently leads to serious long-range problems.

Some sponsors are using licensed, third party home health agencies to deliver the "medical component" while they continue to focus on the "shelter component." Properly executed, this can be a viable concept. However, the strategy is frequently not market-driven or resident-centered. Many concepts and approaches are frequently not seamless and the additional charges to the resident become fragmented, excessive, inequitable and confusing.

Deliver this assistance into your independent living section long enough and most of your clients will become assisted living residents, with many experiencing various stages of

Alzheimer's. And to compound this challenge, the profile of new residents moving in will likely change. New prospects visiting communities that offer AIL services in their independent living units increasingly see the existing residents as "older, frailer people." These prospects and their families tend to make move decisions based on their observations of the existing resident population, often assuming that they're not ready for the community until they need as much help as the frail residents they observed. Thus, new move-ins tend to be the result of a *self-selective process;* they too are older and frailer, compounding and accelerating the aging in place process.

Ask and Answer Five Tough AIL Questions

To avoid getting in trouble down the line by delivering AIL services into existing independent living units, ask yourself five tough questions **now**, answering them from the perspective of the year 2001:

1. *What is my optimum resident profile, for both existing residents and new move-ins?*

2. *What will be my future business posture and market positioning; moderately need-driven independent living or fully need-driven assisted living? Or both?*

3. *Will I be able to properly measure care levels and cover my increasing service delivery costs?*

4. ***Will I be fully market-responsive if I charge residents for incremental increases in the assistance with ADLs as they age in place?***

5. ***As service needs intensify, can I still deliver assistance with ADLs cost-effectively to randomly distributed independent living units throughout my community?***

If your long-term prospects look dim under your current operating scenario, consider adding an *integrated but separated* assisted living section to your campus. With less individual living unit area and more services compared to the typical independent living unit, an assisted living unit is frequently the optimum way to deliver maximum service to your residents for a reasonable, affordable price. This can also be accomplished by converting existing space.

Before deciding which strategy is right for you, however, ask yourself three key planning questions:

1. *What is likely to be my least costly way of serving residents' varying and growing needs for assistance with ADLs?* To answer this question, make a detailed cost comparison between providing a dedicated assisted living section vs. delivering assistance with ADLs randomly distributed within your independent living units. Consider the likely impacts on cost and your resident profile now as well as five, seven, and ten years in the future. This is a tough, but very important, decision. The short-run path of least resistance option may not be the best long-run strategy.

2. How will three very important senior consumer groups and their adult children feel about the strategy you're about to adopt? These three groups are your existing residents who need assistance with ADLs, residents who are still relatively healthy, and potential new residents. The challenge is finding a service delivery system that will satisfy the first group without alienating the other two.

3. Will your residents actually move to the appropriate living arrangement at the appropriate time if you develop a state-of-the-art residential/social model assisted living section? Despite the best of intentions, a multi-level, full-service senior living community can experience mediocre performance because of resident noncompliance. To help ensure that residents are willing to move when the time comes, you must develop definitive and specific resident admission and discharge policies – and they must be tactfully and consistently enforced.

The Top Seven Strategies For Dealing With Aging in Place

Whichever route you follow, you must adopt certain strategies now in order to effectively plan for the future. These seven strategies represent imperatives when dealing with the aging in place issues:

1. Deal with the problem *now,* because it will surely intensify rather than diminish with time.

2. Resist simplistic "politically correct" approaches that accommodate individual residents in the short run but create extensive community problems in the long run.

3. Clearly define the circumstances under which a resident must move to another living arrangement.

4. Communicate policies, procedures, and admission criteria to new residents and their families.

5. Get your resident leadership involved in the acceptance of the difficult but necessary policy making processes, making the residents part of the *solution* and not part of a lingering *problem*.

6. Closely monitor each resident's health status on a continuing basis.

7. If you operate an older community, consider developing a second-generation independent living section that will replace the existing one as aging residents gradually convert the initial community into a NORC; a "Naturally Occurring Assisted Living Community."

Senior housing sponsors have an obligation to provide appropriate, cost-effective assistance with ADLs for their residents. But besides the satisfaction of knowing they're doing the right thing, there could be other significant payoffs for those that do so effectively. And communities that offer either full or modified life care contracts could lower their health care benefit costs by substituting assisted living and home health services for higher-cost nursing home admissions, where applicable.

CHAPTER 6

DEVELOPING THE FOUNDATION FOR A NEW ASSISTED LIVING PROJECT

Successful Outcomes Require Correctly Answering Ten Key Questions

When developing a new assisted living project, many owners and sponsors have been tempted to make situation-driven decisions, offering whatever they have to sell and hoping the marketplace will respond favorably. With luck this method can sometimes lead to success. But, more often than not, inadequate planning results in either total failure or a seriously distressed project. An example would be the independent senior living communities of the mid-'80s, in which the wrong products and services were offered or the right ones were improperly positioned or aimed at the wrong market.

The "Build it And They Will Come" Days Are Over

A better approach is to study the market and learn what is really needed both now and in the future and then provide the most appropriate product and service. This requires answering at least ten questions with the answers developed from a *market-driven* perspective rather than from an emotional *situation-driven* position.

The Ten Planning Questions

1. *Which assisted living market model will you provide?* The market currently favors a *"residential/social"* model developed within local building code restraints and current or anticipated state licensing regulations. Although this trend reflects a dramatic contrast to the older institutional *"medical model,"* appropriate medical care and significant assistance with activities of daily living (ADLs) must be made available to your residents. In answering this question, you should review the market positioning points covered in Chapter 1 and the description of market models addressed in Chapter 2.

2. *What is the expected resident profile?* A classic example of situation-driven thinking involves planning for residents who are old, but need minimal assistance with ADLs. Many well-intended, but naive, developers say, ***"You just don't understand, we are going to be different."*** This is a recipe for failure. Seniors who are responding to the market and opting for assisted living generally have relatively high levels of need, as is evident by current annual resident turnover rates of 40 to 50 percent.

3. *How will you deliver assistance with the Activities of Daily Living (ADLs)?* Underestimating residents' current and increasing ADL needs is the most significant situation-driven mistake being made by operators and sponsors. Some inexperienced sponsors assume residents will satisfy their own needs through individual relationships with home health agencies, but this oversimplified approach can frequently lead to fragmented care, uncoordinated service delivery, or a la carte costs that the resident cannot afford. Some experienced operators are successfully combining a basic shelter product wherein the residents have the option of buying additional services from licensed home health operators. But such plans must be carefully conceived and coordinated. They should appear relatively *seamless* to the senior consumer in terms of both service delivery and costs. For more details review Chapter 15 on cost creep and Chapter 9 dealing with home health care.

4. *What is the optimum project size?* While it's desirable to maximize the number of units to optimize revenues and spread capital and operating costs efficiently, it is equally crucial to avoid unacceptable marketplace risk by overbuilding. Industry experience indicates that the minimum size for a highly efficient stand-alone assisted living community should be approximately 60 to 80 units. Earlier minimum size criteria of 45 to 60 units has not consistently met current day cost-effectiveness tests. The unit count can be lower if your assisted living units are integrated with other independent living apartments and/or nursing beds, thereby creating acceptable operational efficiencies by spreading fixed costs across other revenue producing units. **Keep in mind the project size decision involves the classical trade-off between the cost-effectiveness of your internal operations and external marketplace risk.**

5. *What will be the design philosophy?* Assisted living units have evolved from modest "shotgun" studios of 275 to 300 square feet to slightly larger studios and alcove units of approximately 350 square feet. In the early 1990s, up to 20 percent of the assisted living units in new projects have been modest one-bedroom units with average living areas of 450 to 550 square feet; accommodating either single residents who can pay higher prices or couples in which at least one spouse needs assistance with ADLs. But recent trends indicate a growing market acceptance of an even larger concentration of one-bedroom units. Chapter 10 addresses this important issue in more detail showing that currently 60 percent or more of the assisted living units in some new projects are of the modest one bedroom design.

Elaborate common spaces are nice, but they can be expensive. For example, an 80 unit assisted living project design can have either conventional corridors and public spaces or several innovative "pods," also called "neighborhoods" or "clusters." These design features can increase common space in a typical community by up to 5,000 square feet. And with hard construction costs averaging about $85 per square foot in 1998, your project hard costs could increase by $425,000. Including the additional cost of furnishings, soft costs, utilities, and debt service results in approximately a $60 to $80 increase in monthly service fees for each resident[1].

---

[1] Considers added debt service or return on investment for the additional cost.

6. How will the project interface with the total continuum of care? When planning freestanding or stand-alone assisted living, consider whether the local competition offers a superior response to the *total* concerns of seniors and their families and the future objectives of managed care organizations. All are frequently looking for access to a total continuum of living arrangements. Review Figure 8-2, the "vertical (business) continuum" discussed in Chapter 8 and Figure 1-1, the "horizontal (consumer) continuum" shown in Chapter 1. Ask the further question, *"Will I be a legitimate player in this continuum?"* If not, how will other players impact your game plan?

7. What are the initial fill-up/absorption expectations? The early announcement of a new project generates significant initial enthusiasm, but little of this actually translates into future move-ins! While there might be an initial in-rush of move-ins of 10 to 15 percent, it is the *average net absorption over the life of the fill-up period that really counts.* A net absorption rate of between five and seven units per month, net after turnover, is a realistic goal and should be programmed into your financial pro formas.

8. How much staffing will the project require? Underestimating ADL requirements can lead to underestimating staffing needs. Remember that labor costs represent over 60 percent of total assisted living operating expenses. Progressive operators are using the "universal worker" approach to respond to the ADL needs of residents while keeping labor costs as low as possible. This involves cross-training certified nursing assistants and other entry level staff to also assist in areas such as food service delivery and housekeeping. Industry experience indicates that an 80 unit assisted living project generally requires between 36 to 44 total Full Time Equivalent Employees (FTEs) – or approximately 0.45 to 0.55 FTEs per resident.

9. *What will be the magnitude of the start-up losses?* There will be significant negative cash flow in the early months of a new project, as most of your costs are fixed and only about 20 to 25 percent of the operating expenses are truly variable (raw food, some utilities, housekeeping, some staff, etc.). A typical 80 unit assisted living project normally takes nine to eleven months to reach break-even cash flow. Break-even cash flow (after debt service) typically occurs at approximately 80 to 85 percent occupancy. During that fill-up period, the project may experience cumulative negative cash flows of $300,000 or more. See Chapters 14 and 15 for a more detailed analysis.

10. *How will you price your project?* Pricing must be competitive, market-driven, reasonably affordable, and compare favorably with the nursing alternative. Most importantly, pricing must be flexible to compensate for inevitable "cost creep" that results from residents' increasing chronic conditions and intensified ADL needs. More details are contained in Chapter 15 on cost creep. You cannot price your project in a vacuum. The senior and their families are fast becoming sophisticated, value-oriented, educated consumers.

The Assisted Living Industry is Maturing

As the assisted living industry continues to mature, two new trends are emerging:

1. The market is gradually becoming more educated with respect to alternative living arrangements and health care options.

2. The senior consumer and their families will give you very little credit or compassion for your mistakes and unacceptable trade-offs.

State-of-the-art assisted living can be a surprisingly affordable living arrangement and a viable alternative to nursing facilities. But your project is unlikely to succeed if you fail to answer these ten questions fully, honestly and appropriately during the planning phase.

Perhaps the most important question of all should be saved for last:

"When and under what conditions would my mother willingly, and with my support and blessing, move into this community?"

THE TOP TEN QUESTIONS TO ANSWER WHEN PLANNING ASSISTED LIVING

1. Which assisted living market model will you provide?
2. What is your expected resident profile?
3. How will you deliver assistance with ADLs?
4. What is the optimum project size?
5. What will be your design philosophy?
6. How will your project interface with the total continuum of care?
7. What are your initial fill-up/absorption expectations?
8. How much staffing will your project require?
9. What will be the magnitude of your start-up losses?
10. How will you price your project?

CHAPTER 7

CONTROLLING THE REFERRAL PIPELINE
If You Don't, Someone Else Will !

Just as in any successful business, we can become complacent and take our clients and customers for granted. In assisted living this can rapidly become a fatal flaw in an otherwise well conceived business plan. Figure 7-1 depicts typical resident referral patterns. Each community and market area would obviously have a unique resident origin referral profile.

Potential Changes in the Referral Pipeline

Your referral pipeline, as depicted in Figure 7-1, may change dramatically in the future for at least six reasons:

1. Hospitals are getting into the assisted living business. Just as they have rapidly encroached on the nursing home industry by developing special subacute care units, many hospitals are now diversifying into assisted living. Since hospitals represent approximately 15 percent of the traditional referrals into assisted living, it is reasonable to presume that an owner/operator's referral pattern could change in some markets in the future.

FIGURE 7-1
INPUTS TO THE REFERRAL PIPELINE

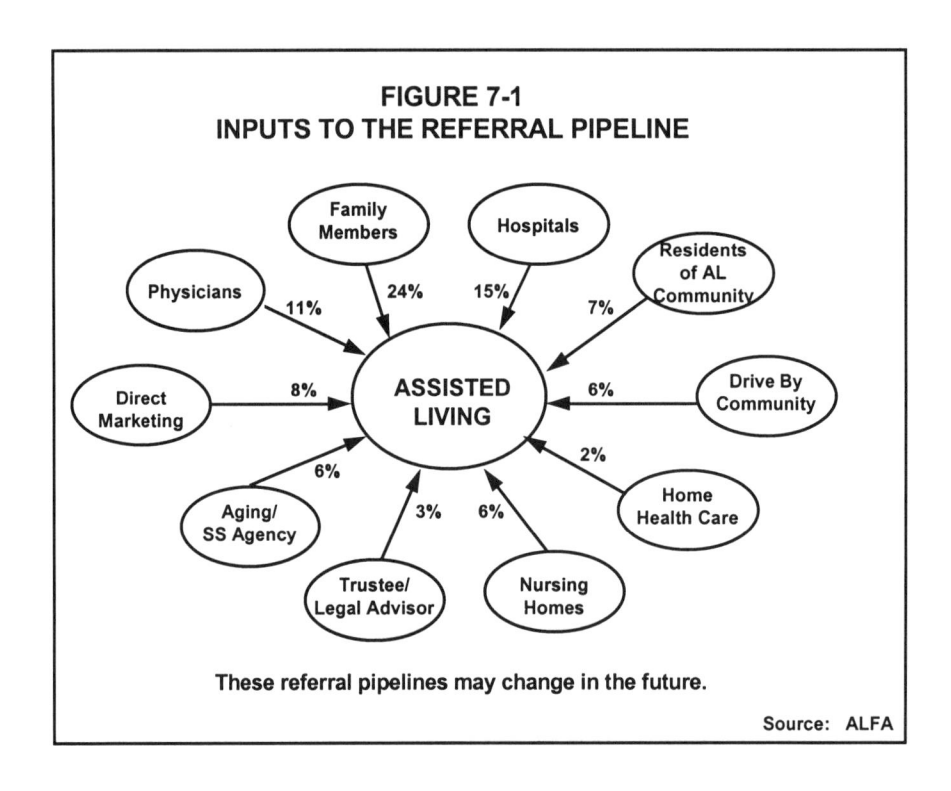

- Family Members: 24%
- Hospitals: 15%
- Residents of AL Community: 7%
- Drive By Community: 6%
- Home Health Care: 2%
- Nursing Homes: 6%
- Trustee/Legal Advisor: 3%
- Aging/SS Agency: 6%
- Direct Marketing: 8%
- Physicians: 11%

These referral pipelines may change in the future.

Source: ALFA

2. Nursing homes are creating a turf battle for assisted living residents. As outlined in Chapter 4, both hospitals and nursing homes are impacting the traditional referral patterns of assisted living. Nursing homes are integrating, but separating assisted living operations within their campuses. Many of these same nursing homes could also have substantial cross referral relationships with other hospitals and independent assisted living operators.

3. Independent living and continuing care retirement communities are expanding their assisted living emphasis. One of the most common growth strategies for both for-profit and not-for-profit campuses is to add assisted living; either within their community or on an adjacent/near-by tract of land. In the past, many residents would be discharged from their independent living community and referred to other assisted living options in the immediate area.

4. Managed care and Medicaid waiver trends may alter referral patterns in the future. While the jury is still out on the true role of managed care, Medicare and the Medicaid waiver system for assisted living, it is certainly reasonable to presume that some changes could take place in the future. Under those circumstances, communities would enter either a "preferred provider network" or a "Medicaid approved" status. Some existing assisted living operators could be part of the scenario while others might be excluded. This is best depicted in Figure 8-2 of Chapter 8; the vertical integrated network or continuum of care.

5. Many home health care agencies will be fighting for survival. As Medicare and Medicaid reimbursement changes and other competitive forces emerge, home health care agencies must develop new initiatives to serve their clients. This would, at the least, delay the entrance of some potential residents into a continuous sheltered living arrangement within assisted living communities. Chapter 9 addresses the role of home health in the future.

6. Emerging competition will change traditional patterns. As major markets become very active with new assisted living projects, the referral patterns of the past may not be projected into the future. Competition involving price, value, benefits and unique designs could dramatically alter the future referral patterns to an existing assisted living community developed by yesterday's competitive standards.

Couple all of these trends with the significant overlapping of sectors that has been outlined in Chapter 23, and it is easy to see that predictable referral pipelines for assisted living may be a thing of the past. Referring to Figure 7-1, it is conceivable that between 30 and 40 percent of "traditional referrals" may in fact be up for grabs in the new millennium.

Progressive assisted living sponsors must carefully evaluate each element of the referral pipeline and develop appropriate hedges and strategies to ensure that the negative impacts of the above mentioned trends will be minimized in the future.

CHAPTER 8

MANAGED CARE IMPACTS
There's a Future Role for Assisted Living

The current turbulence in the health care industry generates lead stories in the business press on a daily basis. Some typical headlines include: *"Managed care will result in integrated delivery systems," "Managed competition is becoming the model for cost containment,"* and *"Practitioners and health care providers are working harder and experiencing fewer financial rewards."*

Two other headlines that are likely to run in the future are: *"Seniors are joining 65+ Medicare Risk HMOs in record numbers"* and *"Retirement, nursing and assisted living communities are being gradually sucked into the industry turbulence of health care reform and managed care."* Like it or not, continuing care retirement community sponsors offering a complete continuum of living arrangements must ultimately participate in the managed care arena. The big unanswered question is, *"What role will assisted living play in future managed care initiates?"*

Medicare and Medicaid Risk HMOs and other managed care organizations define optimum provider performance as driving consumers out of costly acute care beds and down through the continuum as fast as possible. As a result, subacute care units, rehabilitation, outpatient services and home health agencies are multiplying rapidly. The average acuity level of patients in nursing units has soared in the last several years. Most states now give little recognition to the *intermediate* level of nursing care.

The Total Continuum of Care

As senior consumers are pushed down through the vertical continuum of care, more comprehensive living arrangements and levels of care are emerging on senior housing campuses. These include a sophisticated residential/social model of assisted living and special care units dealing with dementia and Alzheimer's care. In addition, rehabilitation, home health care, and community-based service delivery systems are also becoming better defined and more sophisticated.

Will Assisted Living Be the Catalyst of the Continuum?

There are actually two continuums of care:

- *The Vertical Continuum* – The way business and managed care professionals view the situation.

- ***The Horizontal Continuum*** – The consumer's perspective.

Current Trends Shift the Continuum

In the past, senior housing and health care professionals thought of the continuum that influenced their strategies as a *horizontal structure* with essentially exclusive emphasis on the senior consumer. At the left side was the senior's current residence, while the other end was typically anchored by a hospital; the ultimate in health care service delivery as indicated in Figure 8-1. But with the evolution of managed care industry consolidation and aggressive cost containment strategies, a new *vertical* continuum is now emerging as illustrated in Figure 8-2.

In the new structure, the hospital or other major health care provider is the gateway. After the acute care hospital comes subacute care, skilled nursing, special care/dementia units, assisted living, independent living, home health, community-based services and finally the senior's home.

Owner/operators now have two moving targets on their radar screens to track; the *horizontal* continuum in the consumer market and the *vertical* continuum in the business/managed care areas.

**FIGURE 8-1
THE HORIZONTAL CONTINUUM**

*Special Alzheimer's/Dementia Units

MOORE DIVERSIFIED SERVICES, INC.

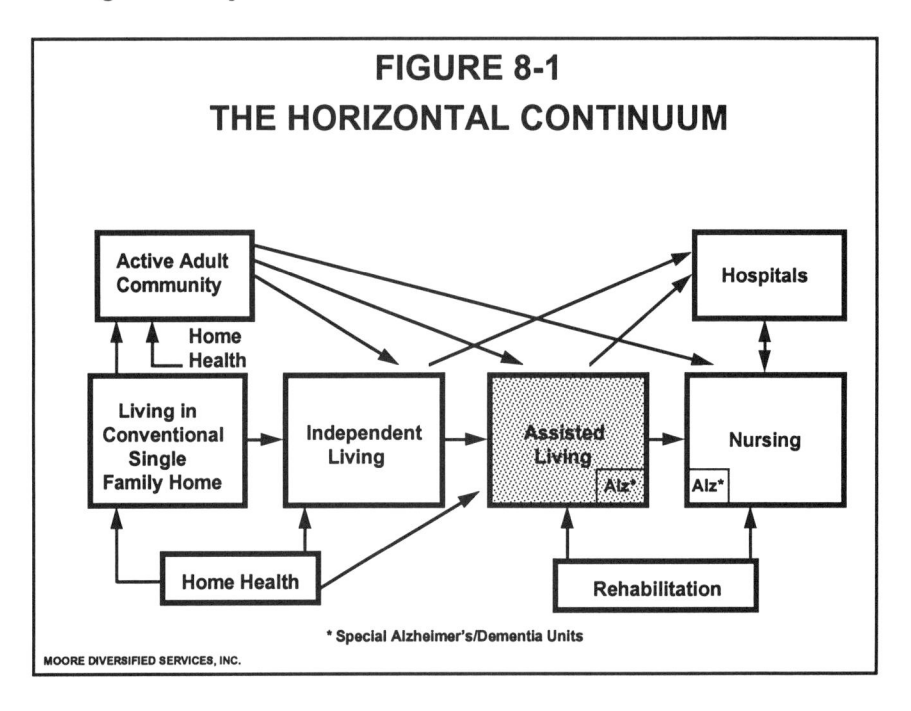

Shifting Payor Sources

Third party payors are gradually shifting to the managed care, vertical continuum model. States, meanwhile, are becoming increasingly responsible for the funding of health care programs for economically disadvantaged seniors. Some will rely more heavily on managed care organizations to implement innovative cost containment strategies. As a result, managed care organizations will gain significant economic and negotiating clout.

Managed Care Impacts 61

FIGURE 8-2
THE "VERTICAL" CONTINUUM OF CARE
Eventually capitation and cost pressures will "push" Seniors down through the "vertical continuum".

```
                    ┌──────────┐
                    │ Hospital │
                    └────┬─────┘
                         ▼
                  ┌───────────┐
                  │ Subacute  │
                  │   Care    │
   ╭─────────╮    └─────┬─────┘
   │Business │          ▼
   │Definition│   ┌───────────┐      ┌──────────────┐
   ╰─────────╯   │  Skilled  │◄─────│ Special Care │
                  │  Nursing  │      │ • Dementia   │
                  └─────┬─────┘      │ • Alzheimer's│
                        ▼            └──────────────┘
                 ┌──────────────┐
                 │ Personal Care│
                 │Assisted Living│
                 │Catered Living│
                 └──────┬───────┘
                        ▼
  ┌────────┐     ┌─────────────┐     ┌──────────────┐
  │ Active │────►│ Independent │◄────│ Home Health  │
  │ Adult  │     │   Living    │     │     and      │
  │ Living │     └──────┬──────┘     │Physician Care│
  └────────┘            ▼            └──────────────┘
                 ┌─────────────┐     ┌──────────────┐
                 │   Seniors   │◄────│  Community   │
                 │    Home     │     │    Based     │
                 └─────────────┘     │   Services   │
                                     └──────────────┘
```

21st Century Assisted Living Planning Must Be Consistent With New Evolving Managed Care Strategies and Imperatives

Moore Diversified Services, Inc.

Many assisted living community sponsors may feel they are shielded from managed care impacts, but a real-world example of what is actually happening in some parts of the country provides sobering, contradictory evidence.

Mrs. Jones – after very careful consideration – made the difficult decision to choose a state-of-the-art assisted living community in which to spend the rest of her life. She is paying the required fees that assure her a lifetime of comprehensive care on a beautiful campus, which included assisted living, nursing and a state-of-the-art rehabilitation unit. She capped off her prudent planning by also joining a 65+ Medicare HMO offered by a local health care provider network.

These relatively new HMOs administer the federal Medicare program at the local level by agreeing to care for a defined *risk pool* of seniors on a fixed cost or capitation basis for their defined Medicare benefits. Seniors in the HMO must use designated preferred providers in terms of both medical practitioners and health care service delivery systems. Members of these HMOs may also get a wide array of additional benefits, frequently at no increase in their traditional Medicare premiums.

Little did Mrs. Jones know that when she broke her hip and was hospitalized that she would have to recuperate in a strange, institutionalized nursing home across town; not the beautiful campus where she lived. How could this happen when she thought she had opted for a complete lifetime living arrangement? It turns out that her assisted living and nursing community was not part of the 65+ Medicare HMO preferred provider network. All of this may sound bizarre – but these situations are actually happening in some parts of the country where the senior 65+ HMO membership participation rate has exceeded 50 percent. In other areas of the country, the concept is relatively unknown.

A Look to the Future

These trends send the message that the vertical continuum will change the structure and economics of senior housing and health care markets of the future. Providers who deny this fact or procrastinate in dealing with it may be in for some unpleasant surprises. They, like thousands of medical practitioners who avoided managed care in the 1990s, may find themselves shut out of the managed care game – and before long, that may be the biggest game in town.

The bedrock of managed care is controlling costs and shifting the risk from payor to provider through strategies such as capitation. The ultimate in capitation is paying an individual provider to be totally responsible for a wide array of health care for a specific pool of senior lives. The operative words here are "individual provider" and " wide array." Managed care payors want turn-key, comprehensive provider networks to minimize contract administration costs and to contain financial risks within one provider network. The days of the totally private-pay, fee-for-service, freestanding health care provider are numbered.

Sponsors and owner/operators who become part of the new vertical integrated network will be pressured to lower prices for subacute care, nursing, rehabilitation, home health services and, ultimately, for assisted living. But operators who do not participate in the managed care game could find themselves at a much greater disadvantage. Chances are good that a hospital that provided steady referrals in the past will team up with another organization or create its own managed care integrated network, causing assisted living referrals to disappear overnight.

Assisted living is not currently a Medicare benefit, but nursing, rehabilitation and home health care are beneficiaries of current reimbursement programs. Relationships between assisted living and Managed Care Organizations (MCOs) could develop as the care option is proven to be more cost-effective. As a practical matter, assisted living is encroaching on nursing; making assisted living a more viable Medicare reimbursement alternative for short term recovery of an episodic event (hip fracture, stroke, etc.). Simply stated, there may eventually be a **Medicare** cross-over from nursing to assisted living similar to the evolving **Medicaid** trends.

All of this leads to a good news/bad news situation. The bad news is that managed care will eventually impact almost every senior housing and health care provider. The good news is that operators in most markets should have a window of opportunity to respond to the vertical continuum. Progressive operators will use this critical time window to form centrally controlled vertical continuums or integrated networks, either through direct ownership and control or through carefully conceived strategic alliances.

CHAPTER 9

THE ROLE OF HOME HEALTH IN ASSISTED LIVING
Beware of Oversimplified Approaches

Home health care performed within *appropriate limits* is a very viable service delivery system. Having said that, I see a number of dark clouds in the horizon which will likely change the plans for both senior consumers and assisted living sponsors.

In 1998, Medicare certified home health provided over 280 million visits serving over 4.7 million clients. The *total* number of agencies – both Medicare certified and others – encompassed approximately 19,000 organizations.

The Ominous Trends

Figure 9-1 summarizes the trends of an industry that has literally exploded over the past 10 years. The average annual growth in home health activities has far exceeded the growth in the senior population.

Many industry supporters disagree with a recent Government Accounting Office study that concluded that up to 40 percent of

FIGURE 9-1

THE TEN-YEAR HOME HEALTH EXPLOSION
(Medicare Certified Agencies Only)

Home Health Characteristics[1]	1988	1998 (Estimate)	Percent Change
• Number of Medicare Certified Agencies	5,785	9,200+	59%
• Number of Clients Served (1,000s)	1,580	4,755	200%
• Number of Visits (1,000s)	37,150	283,650	664%
• Average Number of Visits/Client	23.5	59.5	153%
• Total Expenditures ($ millions)	$2,033	$24,370	1,100%
• Average Cost per Visit	$54.00	$86.00	59%
• Average Cost per Client	$1,800	$4,600	156%

[1]Sources include: HCFA, Health Standards and Quality Bureau, Agency for Health Care Policy and Research (AHCPR)
The Moore Institute

home health services paid for by the government were "wasteful" – or even "fraudulent". Keep in mind that those ominous terms are the government's position; the senior consumer served by home health and their families have a diametrically opposing point of view. Regardless of your sentiments on this important issue, there are two sobering facts of life that we must face as we approach the new millennium:

1. We can't afford the home health entitlement system as it is currently structured.

2. Many very old and frail seniors are living at risk – alone in their homes – grasping for limited independence between home health visits that average less than one hour in direct personal attention.

General Criteria for Medicare Coverage

The American Association for Homes and Services of the Aged (AAHSA) reminds their members that there are five key criteria for home health services to be covered by Medicare:

1. *Services must be skilled:*

- Nursing services
- Physical therapy
- Speech therapy

Services must be provided under the supervision of a registered nurse, physical therapist or speech therapist. The following services also can be provided as long as the client requires at least one skilled service:

- Occupational therapy
- Medical social services
- Home health aide service
- Medical supplies

2. *The patient must be homebound.*

3. *The level of care must be part-time and intermittent.*

4. *A plan of treatment must be authorized by a physician with recent verification every 60 days.*

5. *The care must be medically reasonable and necessary.*

Note that these home services are primarily intended to respond to recovery from an *episodic event*.

Episodic Versus Chronic Needs

Most seniors would like to stay in their home full of love and memories until the day they die. But life is not that simple. As one senior told me, *"Life is what happens to you while you're making other plans!"* Home health care offers the hope (and frequently the reality) of staying in one's home longer. But there is growing evidence that we have crossed the line from cost-effective, quality, *periodic* care to providing fragmented, expensive care to seniors who should not live alone in an unsupportive environment 24 hours per day. Many seniors are living (sometimes just existing) in a high risk situation – as they carry out the human drama of trying to stay in the home as long as possible. They have irreversible *chronic* ailments; they are not recovering from an *episodic* event.

The Cost Issue

In recent years up to 74 percent of total home health costs were paid for by Medicare; 26 percent were from private pay or other sources. As Figure 9-1 illustrates, Medicare cost growth has been significant. This has masked the two sobering realities:

1. Many seniors receiving home health assistance might be better served in a service enriched, sheltered assisted living environment.

2. For the cost of about a one-hour home health visit (approximately $80), a senior can be provided *both* shelter (housing services) and assistance in living (care) 24 hours per day.

This is not an indictment of the home health industry; it is an economic and health related fact of life.

Home Health and Assisted Living

The relationship and roles of home health in an assisted living setting are appropriately addressed throughout this book. Many operators are using licensed home health agencies to deliver the care component of assisted living. Some are doing it because it solves some state regulation dilemmas; others do it so that they do not have to get into the health care business. Some sponsors carefully integrate *both* shelter and care services and cost to the consumer, while others seem to be looking the other way – hoping they can charge their fees for shelter and services and assuming the consumer will also pay the separate home health bills.

Figure 9-2 depicts a *seamless* approach to developing a win-win relationship with a quality home health agency. Home health agencies will be placing a *very* high priority on improving their private pay mix – and providing the care component of assisted living could be their new, significant market niche for the future.

As a sponsor, you *must* create a seamless relationship. I'd like to offer my four top success imperatives:

1. The resident should feel like it is all one operation.

2. All services should be consistent, coordinated and seamless.

3. Your total cost should ideally come in as close as possible to an all "in-house" staffing model – with total operating expenses per resident day competitive for your market area.

4. The pricing to the consumer should be consolidated wherever possible – or at least fair, understandable and competitive.

Finally, develop your home health partnering strategy from a consumer-driven perspective.

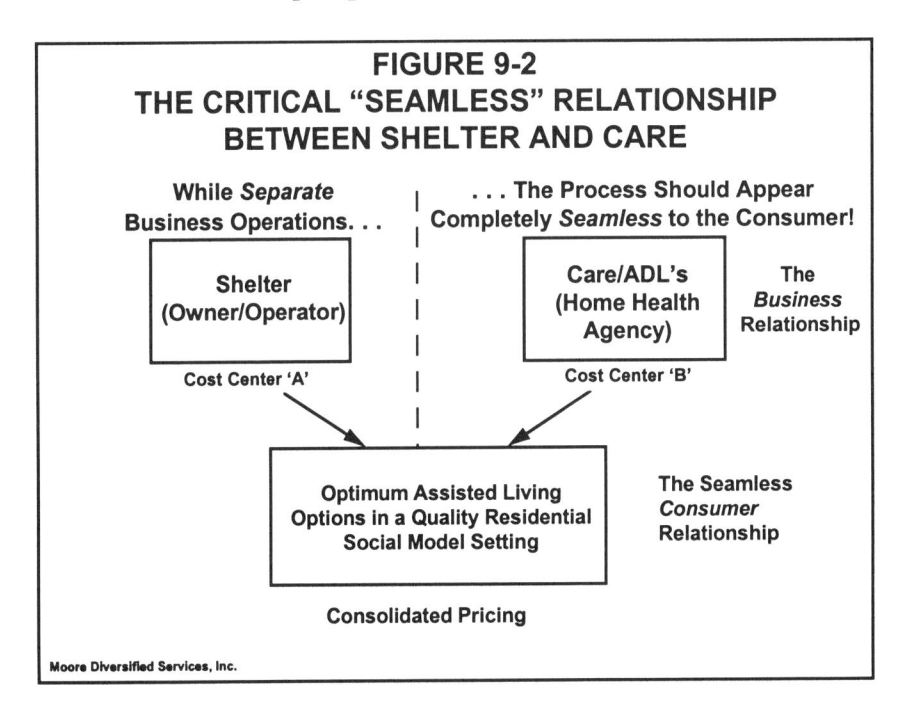

FIGURE 9-2
THE CRITICAL "SEAMLESS" RELATIONSHIP BETWEEN SHELTER AND CARE

While *Separate* Business Operations... | ...The Process Should Appear Completely *Seamless* to the Consumer!

- Shelter (Owner/Operator) — Cost Center 'A'
- Care/ADL's (Home Health Agency) — Cost Center 'B'

The Business Relationship

↓ ↓

Optimum Assisted Living Options in a Quality Residential Social Model Setting

The Seamless Consumer Relationship

Consolidated Pricing

Moore Diversified Services, Inc.

SECTION TWO

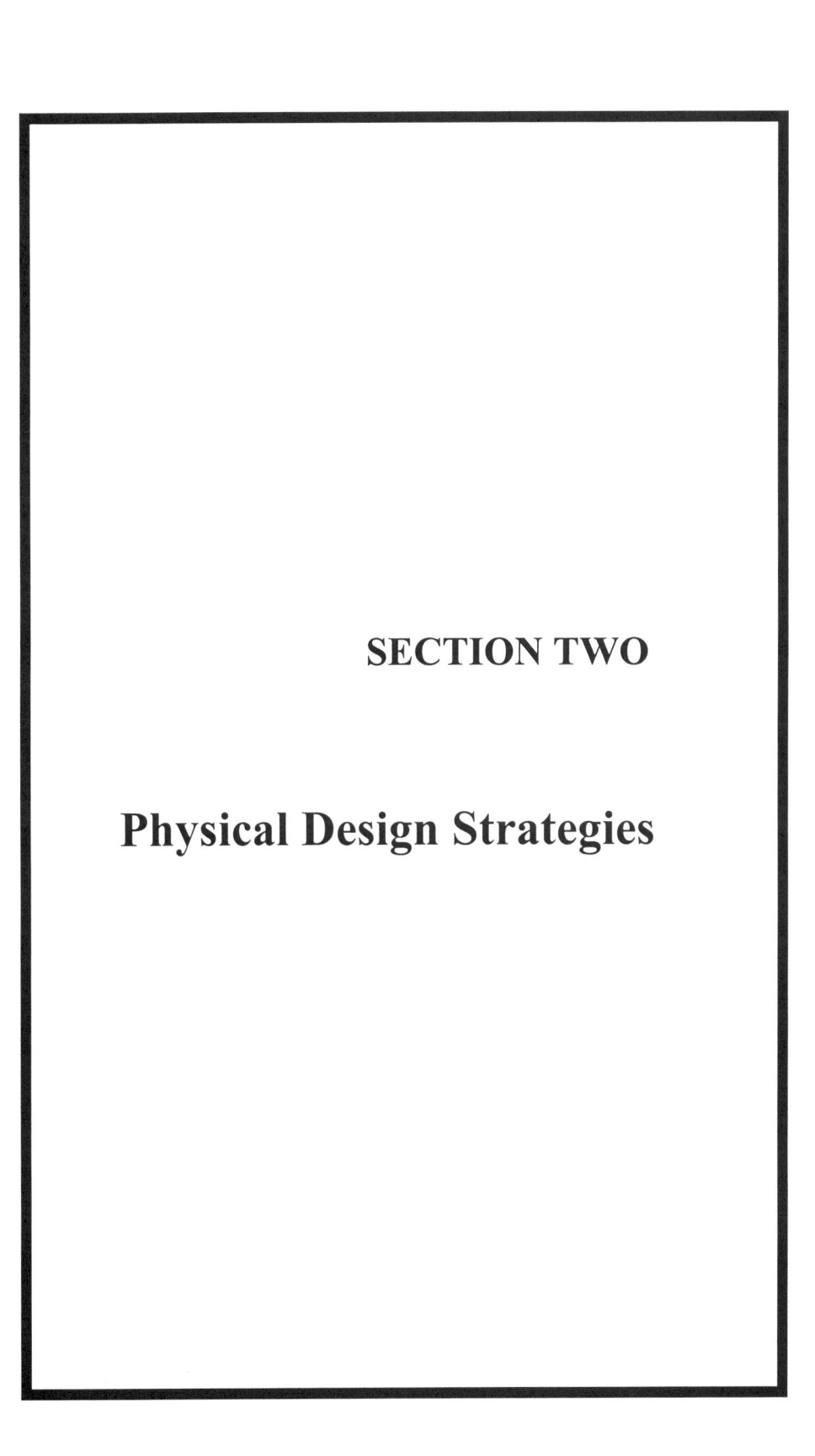

Physical Design Strategies

CHAPTER 10

MARKET-DRIVEN DESIGN STRATEGIES FOR NEW ASSISTED LIVING COMMUNITIES
You Really Get Only One Chance to Do it Right!

In Chapter 6, I identified 10 key questions which must be answered as you develop your new assisted living community strategies. Three of those 10 questions related specifically to market-driven *design* initiatives: 1) Which assisted living market model will you provide, 2) What is the optimum project size and 3) What will be the overall design philosophy?

The Residential/Social Market Model

The empirical evidence in the competitive marketplace clearly indicates that a "residential/social" design model is preferred by seniors and their families. This concept reflects a highly residential, purpose-built structure developed within local building code restraints and state licensing regulations. There is a major focus on a residential design flair; providing features and amenities such as:

- Carpeting in all areas
- Drapes and window treatments
- Aesthetically pleasing wall covering/treatments in public spaces
- Non-institutional furniture
- Artwork
- Significant millwork (door frames, moldings, baseboards, etc.)
- Ceiling heights consistent with total area and volume of a particular space
- Somewhat of a trend toward softer incandescent light fixtures (vs. fluorescents)

While certainly operated from a different perspective, the "look" of the spaces should take on the impression of a well-conceived country club or hotel by sending subtle signals of comfortable, moderate luxury. As indicated in Chapter 1, this market model must also be positioned as having *a strong, but largely invisible, medical basis.* For example, the traditional *nurses station* now looks like and is positioned as a *concierge desk.*

The Medical Market Model

There is obviously a role for the medical model assisted living design concept. The most common application today is providing an alternative living arrangement to nursing for seniors with complex health care needs or to serve advanced stage special care Alzheimer's/dementia residents. These seniors have complex, high acuity health care needs as well as requiring a special Alzheimer's/dementia sheltered living environment. The development of this model can be realized by:

- ***Conversion/adaptive reuse*** of existing space such as a nursing wing, etc.

- ***New construction*** on a comprehensive senior living campus that is expanding their overall continuum

New development and construction of the medical model of assisted living as a freestanding facility is relatively rare.

Optimum Size of an Assisted Living Community

Once you've decided to build an assisted living project, one of your key decisions is how many units to develop. Overbuild and many of your units will remain empty. Underbuild and you may doom yourself to marginal financial performance – or worse.

Financial sensitivity analysis indicates that a well-conceived freestanding assisted living community should contain at least 60 to 80 units. In fact, many of the current industry models encompass up to 100 units. While it will be more difficult to reach the financial break-even point with a small project as compared to a medium sized or large one, you can't just arbitrarily increase the unit count to make your operations more efficient. From a market feasibility perspective, you should generally not assume an individual project market penetration rate of more than five to seven percent. That means that your project should not require more than seven percent of the age and income qualified households in a properly defined primary market area; and that's after allowing for important factors such as existing and announced competition and resident turnover. This important decision represents a classical trade-off between establishing financial viability and avoiding excessive marketplace risk. Market and financial feasibility is addressed in more detail in Appendix A.

Initial Development vs. Ongoing Ownership Costs

Another challenge in realistically assessing market demand is keeping your monthly service fees high enough to stay in business, yet low enough to be competitive and attract residents. And that means focusing on how much you spend in two major categories: initial capital costs and ongoing operating expenses. Both of these financial areas have significant design implications.

Capital costs represent the money spent to design, develop, and furnish your project. It also provides funds for an effective sales and marketing program to bring the project to an initial stabilized occupancy of 93 percent. In 1998 and 1999, the total (all-in) capital costs for developing assisted living in most areas will typically range from $85,000 to $130,000 per unit. This includes land, hard construction and soft development costs and all other costs to bring your project to stabilized occupancy. A common definition is the total or all-in project costs divided by the number of living units or beds. This cost per unit range mentioned earlier probably encompasses approximately 75 percent of the current marketplace experience. The remaining 25 percent would indicate total costs per unit lower or higher than the range indicated.

Many of these costs are fixed and do not change in direct proportion to unit count. This makes it harder for smaller facilities to come up with an affordable monthly rate while covering all development costs. For example, spending $200,000 on landscaping, enhanced common areas, or funding a construction overrun could increase each resident's monthly service fees by about $25 for 60-unit community, but up to $50 for a 35-unit community. This is but one example of the challenge of spreading fixed capital costs to satisfy resulting debt service costs. Chapter 13 provides guidelines for developing a realistic capital budget.

Operating expenses are the funds needed to run the community on a continuing basis, not counting depreciation, interest, taxes or amortization. Assisted living operating expenses at stabilized occupancy typically range from $40 to $48 per resident day or about $1,215 to $1,460 per unit per month. These operating costs fall into one of three categories:

- **Fixed costs.** Examples would be certain salaries such as your executive director and some "core operations" such as your kitchen or laundry.

- **Semi-variable costs.** These costs do change with project size, but not in *direct* proportion to changing unit counts. Utilities, maintenance, and transportation, for example, may vary somewhat depending on how many occupied units you have, but a significant portion of these costs are included in the basic operations of the project and do not directly vary as a function of unit count.

- **Variable costs.** These costs generally change in direct proportion to the increases and decreases of the number of units. An example would be raw food expenditures. In a typical assisted living community, only about 25 percent of the operating expenses are truly variable.

Larger projects can more effectively spread fixed or semi-variable costs over more units; keeping an individual resident's monthly fees lower. Labor costs, for instance, are a semi-variable cost outlay representing more than 60 percent of most assisted living communities' total operating expenses. This is why new projects experience significant negative cash flow during fill-up and have a relatively high break-even cash flow (after debt service) of approximately 85 percent. This negative cash flow must be funded by your project's initial capital budget as indicated in Chapter 13.

It is worthwhile to make cost sensitivity comparisons between a relatively efficient 60-unit project vs. a marginal 35-unit project. (The purpose of this analysis is to demonstrate the desirability of operating between a *minimum* of 60 units and an *optimum* of 80 units.)

To see how labor costs can affect various sized communities, let's assume that you decide you need two additional entry-level employees (maybe because of the cost creep addressed in Chapter 15). With a direct compensation of about $8 per hour and a 22 percent fringe benefit factor, your cost per employee is about $20,300 per year. The two employees will cost you about $40,600 per year. To recover that expense over the *occupied* units in a 60-unit project, you'd have to raise each resident's monthly service fee by $61. In a smaller, 35-unit project, the increase would be $103 per unit per month.

A typical community could have a number of other cost considerations that must be passed on to the residents. When evaluating a typical detailed financial pro forma for both the 60 unit and 35 unit assisted living prototypes, two sobering observations emerge: 1) average total cost per unit, $100,000 vs. $113,000; a 13 percent differential, 2) operating expenses per resident day $40 vs $48; a 20 percent differential.

More importantly, the 60 unit project will require an average monthly service fee of $2,100 per month to maintain acceptable operating margins/financial ratios in a typical market, while the 35-unit project will require approximately $2,500 per month.

This differential also increases a resident's required annual qualifying income from approximately $39,000 to $47,000; assuming she can spend approximately 80 percent of her *after-tax cash flow income* for the service fee.

Five Effective Planning Strategies

There are five design concept considerations that can lead to a successful project:

1. Accurately and realistically determine the size and depth of your market so that you know how many units you can realistically launch into the competitive marketplace.

2. Value engineer your project with a passion (see Chapter 13). A small project usually can't tolerate "Cadillac" designs, cost overruns or inefficient operations.

3. Be aware that future operating expense cost creep can be a fatal disease for a modest sized community (see Chapter 15) so don't cut staff unrealistically.

4. Consider the practical financial economies of scale that might be realized if your new assisted living project will be an integral part of an existing continuing care or health care campus; resulting in more revenue-producing units to spread both fixed and semi-variable costs.

5. Study the possibility of orderly and prudent project phasing. This means master planning your community for additional units in the future; assuming a favorable initial market response to your project. Small scale projects do work. But they require realistic planning and laser sharp focused attention to detail.

Providers Are Offering One-Bedrooms in Addition to Studios

In the first half of the 1990s, conventional wisdom indicated that a 300 to 350 square foot studio or alcove unit was adequate and appropriate for assisted living; especially when compared to the alternative 200 to 225 square foot semi-private nursing room. But that assumption is changing fast as we approach the next millennium. Many providers now offer one-bedroom units with living areas of 450 to 550 square feet in addition to well-conceived studios and alcoves.

The pace of this trend has been surprising. In the past two years, I've seen the average mix in new assisted living facilities change from about 85 percent studios and 15 percent one-bedroom units to more of a 60/40 split (see Figure 10-1). And it's not unusual for a CCRC to design it's new assisted living section entirely of modest sized one-bedroom units.

FIGURE 10-1
TYPICAL UNIT TYPE/SPACE
ENVELOPE SCENARIOS

Unit Type	Size (s.f.)	"A"	"B"	"C"
• Studio/Alcove	325 - 350 s.f.	80%	40%	60%
• One Bedroom	450 - 550	20	60	40
		100%	100%	100%
• Special Care Alzheimer's/Dementia	325 - 350			

Moore Diversified Services, Inc.

Consumer Considerations

Fueling this development trend are consumer demand preferences and the promise of financial gain by sponsors and owner/operators. Consumer considerations involve three key factors:

1. What seniors and their families prefer – Seniors want to maintain their independence and dignity. Their families are coping with love, guilt and economic concerns among other emotions. One-bedroom assisted living units can satisfy many of these concerns assuming value and affordability expectations are also met.

2. What consumers can afford – The primary financial components of an 80-unit assisted living community with a base monthly service fee of $2,100 for studio units are comprised of approximately 60 percent operating expenses and 40 percent debt service and cash flow/profit. A one-bedroom unit might cost $2,500 per month; a $400 per month increase. Assuming Mrs. Barker can spend approximately 80 percent of her after-tax, disposable income on a monthly service fee, she needs to gross approximately $7,500 more per year for every $400 monthly increase in fees. One bedroom units are currently popular, but this economic reality of affordability will put bigger units beyond the reach of many seniors.

3. Health and acuity level – Some seniors would have difficulty in dealing with even the modestly larger space of a one-bedroom unit. As long as the assisted living industry attempts to slow its relatively high turnover rate by accommodating higher acuity levels, including the early stages of Alzheimer's, studio units will continue to play a key role.

Sponsor and Owner/Operator Considerations

From the sponsor or owner/operator's perspective, the studio vs. one-bedroom design considerations tend to focus heavily on financial issues. These issues include development costs, operating margins, cash flow and, for many public companies, earnings per share which impact stock price and price-earnings ratios.

- **_Operating expenses_** – For an assisted living community opening in 1998 or 1999, these expenses will probably be about $40 to $48 per resident day or $1,215 to $1,460 per month at stabilized occupancy. The incremental increase in operating expenses for a one-bedroom unit versus a studio is represented by elements of cost that make up approximately 25 percent of the operating expense statement; housekeeping, maintenance, utilities, taxes, insurance and an incremental management fee assessment. These expenses vary largely as a function of building square footage, and will likely add approximately $4 per resident day, or $125 per month, to the cost of a larger one-bedroom unit (vs. the studio).

- **_Capital costs_** – You will add approximately 175 square feet of space to the larger one-bedroom unit, which will increase your capital costs. Assisted living project hard construction costs in many areas of the U.S. average about $85 to $90 per square foot (1998 dollars). This cost index includes certain relatively expensive basic items found in every unit such as the bathroom, small tea/Pullman kitchen, front entrance and the heating and air conditioning system.

Your new, *incremental* costs in going from a studio to a one-bedroom will be an additional wall, door and window. There will also be expanded ceiling and floor space in both the living unit and the adjacent corridor. These incremental costs will probably total about $55 per square foot in hard costs, adding about $9,600 in hard costs to the unit. Note that the *incremental* costs per square foot for the extra room will not be as high as the *base* cost because certain relatively expensive items mentioned previously are not repeated.

- ***Soft costs*** – Certain soft development costs, including architectural, engineering, development and general conditions also vary as a percent of construction costs. Adding these increased soft costs to the hard costs results in a total additional cost of about $10,500 for a modest-sized, one-bedroom unit versus a studio unit. At nine percent interest, this yields an additional debt service cost per occupied unit of about $85 per month that must be passed on to Mrs. Barker.

Adding this cost to the increased operating expenses of $125 per month, brings the total cost increase of a 500-square-foot one-bedroom over a 360 square-foot studio to $210 a month. But due to increased perceived value, operators can usually charge substantially more than that for the larger units. In many markets, a one-bedroom unit commands a monthly service fee of about $2,500, while a studio goes for about $2,100. This gives the resident the luxury of a larger unit and allows the sponsor to realize higher financial returns. This positive synergy is demonstrated in Figure 10-2.

There is clearly a trend toward effectively designed one-bedroom assisted living units. But, even this apparent win-win solution must be approached with caution; don't forget, not every prospective resident can afford that monthly bump. But for those who can, larger one-bedroom units can be a very appealing option.

FIGURE 10-2

RUNNING THE NUMBERS . . .
. . . ASSISTED LIVING STUDIO VS. ONE BEDROOM UNIT SYNERGY

	Studio	vs.	1-BR	Percent Increase
• Living Area Square Footage	350		500	43%
• Cost per Unit	$90,000		$100,500	12
• Monthly Service Fee	$ 2,100		$ 2,500	19
• Operating Expenses per Resident Day	$40		$44	10
• Cash Flow:				
- <u>Before</u> Debt Service	$ 8,845		$ 11,845	34
- <u>After</u> Debt Service	$ 2,770		$ 5,065	83
• Resident's Qualifying Income	$39,000		$ 47,000	20

Moore Diversified Services, Inc.

How Many Stories?

The decision involving the number of stories in a new assisted living building is typically a function of a series of restraints and trade-offs: 1) local building codes, 2) optimizing "flow" and operational efficiency, 3) optimizing resident walk distances from the furthest assisted living unit to the dining room, 4) relative cost and 5) available land leading to required unit density. Another important factor is providing for safe and practical emergency evacuation of the residents.

Usually, all of the above factors and restraints dictate the ultimate configuration of a new assisted living building. Note that overall development and construction costs can vary as a function of the number of floors. As the number of levels increase, some costs go down (land, foundation, etc.), while other costs tend to increase (elevators, type of construction, etc.). For very preliminary planning purposes, you can typically count on the density (approximate number of units per acre) to range from 15 to 25 units per acre. This includes not only the building structure, but roadways, parking spaces and the overall site infrastructure.

Building Efficiency

Figure 10-3 summarizes the general space profile for an 80-unit community. This profile obviously must evolve from a detailed design and space planning effort. However, the "envelope" might look like that summarized in Figure 10-3.

Market-Driven Design Strategies
For New Assisted Living Communities

**FIGURE 10-3
A TYPICAL 80-UNIT ASSISTED LIVING
COMMUNITY SPACE PROFILE**

- Studio/Alcove   32 units @ 350 s.f.   11,200 s.f.
- One Bedroom   <u>48</u> units @ 500 s.f.   <u>24,000</u>
    Totals   80   35,200 s.f.
    Weighted average living area: 440 s.f.
    Common/public space @ 45%   <u>28,800</u> s.f.
    Total area under roof   64,000 s.f.

*Livable areas typically represent approximately
55% of the total area under roof.*

Moore Diversified Services, Inc.

Special Care/Alzheimer's/Dementia "Carve-Outs"

Unique designs are evolving for special care units. We are rapidly progressing up the learning curve with respect to helping seniors and their loved ones cope with these dreaded diseases by pushing the state-of-the-art in the following areas:

- Lowering excitement levels and optimizing security, while minimizing the use of chemical and physical restraints

- Providing cueing to compensate for loss of memory, cognitive skills and disorientation

- Offering higher levels of ambience in a secure, user-friendly environment

- Developing a more *holistic* approach to care and sheltered living

Purpose-built special care units are quickly becoming a separated, yet integrated, portion of many new assisted living designs. Special design features for this very important "market niche/carve-out" are included in Chapter 22.

When it comes to design, you have only one chance to get it right. And the cost-effective design of assisted living units represents one of the biggest challenges – and opportunities for the future.

CHAPTER 11

ADAPTIVE REUSE FOR ASSISTED LIVING
Conversion Dreams Turned Into Nightmares

Adaptive reuse or conversion of existing structures to assisted living has emerged as a commonly considered strategy. The most common initiatives involve conversion of apartments and moderately sized hotels and motels into assisted living projects. But the conversion of existing real estate into other uses involves delicate trade-offs, objective evaluations and marketplace risk. You must walk a very thin line between being emotionally influenced by inappropriate, situation-driven limitations and realizing the significant benefit-driven opportunities that can exist through the conversion of appropriate properties. Unfortunately the underlying motivation of the developer in many cases is, *"I have this old property (that I'm in love with) – now what do I do with it?"* A common rationalization is that, *"Surely the marketplace will understand what I went through to pull off this conversion!"* They may not.

Recent examples of adaptive reuse clearly indicate that while many successful conversions were based on a sound rationale, other projects experienced the agony not unlike that of a homeowner "fixing up that old house." Serious problems continue to emerge as you get deeper and deeper into the conversion activity; and you quickly get beyond the point of no return.

There are some economic and market realities which make adaptive reuse a very valid concept. From time to time sectors of our real estate markets become overbuilt – or as some say facetiously – under demolished. Properties are typically sold by lenders and owners for deep discounts. These market situations can lead to some interesting adaptive reuse opportunities. But along with these opportunities come significant pitfalls.

The Rules of the Adaptive Reuse Game

I have four fundamental rules of successful adaptive reuse. If these rules are broken or inappropriately stretched, your project may fail.

First, the site characteristics of the adaptive reuse candidate should be essentially irreplaceable in the immediate primary market area. If someone else can build a new, state-of-the-art product on a similar nearby site, the new project is likely to be far more competitive than an existing structure involving tradeoffs and compromises inherent in the conversion of an existing/older property.

Second, the building structure should be truly unique – with innovative, practical and cost-effective adaptive reuse potential. It could be a historical landmark or one with a favorable, memorable past.

Third, the total turn-key cost of acquisition, renovation and conversion should be moderately less than the alternative cost of a newly developed state-of-the-art assisted living community. But keep in mind that debt service cost recovery makes up only 25 to 30 percent of the resident's total monthly service fee. So saving on capital costs certainly helps; but be sure to quantify the real benefit in the competitive marketplace. With adaptive reuse, you must offer very competitive pricing. If the price/value relationship is not competitive, the cost vs. value perceptions in the consumer marketplace may quickly pick up this important economic issue.

Fourth, the consumer will give very little credit for some of the inevitable tradeoffs and compromises in the end product that typically result from adaptive reuse of an existing structure. The only thing that counts in the consumer marketplace is the perceived value and tangible benefits of the end product or service. Just as homeowners fall in love with the "quaint old home" that appears suitable for fix-up, some operators get involved in irrational love affairs with their newly acquired "bargain real estate."

The key to successful adaptive reuse is to facilitate a value-oriented match between the realistic adaptive reuse opportunities that are present in the conversion property and the benefits and demand-driven needs of the marketplace.

This means that the rework of a current site and building through adaptive reuse efforts must deliver an end product that is totally compatible with marketplace needs. The acid test of adaptive reuse feasibility is whether or not the fully converted community can effectively compete with new state-of-the-art products that do not have to deal with conversion trade-offs or compromises.

Three Traps to Avoid

There are three major traps that developers and owner/operators typically fall into when implementing adaptive reuse:

1. *Inappropriate design configuration* – Significant flaws frequently exist in either the basic building layout or footprint or within the existing living units.

2. *Mediocre Location* – The project location was not really unique and ideally situated. Determining suitability of the location is very similar to site selection for a completely new project. The margin for error is very narrow – and major compromises will likely lead to a troubled project.

3. *Undesirable Perceptions or Misconceptions of the Past* – Sometimes the history or past use of the structure or site casts a permanent negative perception on the new community.

Many different structures can offer good conversion options as long as the "footprint" and overall design configuration is compatible with the current state-of-the-art. Schools, hotels/motels, nursing homes, hospitals and religious facilities have been successfully converted under the right conditions.

Schools

Many elementary schools in mature neighborhoods are now "demographically obsolete." The neighborhoods are aging and the demand for large numbers of elementary classrooms has long since passed. These schools are sometimes located in good "in-fill" locations that can now serve seniors within high quality, mature neighborhoods. From a strategic standpoint, adaptive reuse of these facilities frequently involves less neighborhood opposition to planning and zoning approval requests as compared to attempting to get the same approvals on a vacant piece of land for a start-up development effort.

Some physical characteristics that make schools good candidates for conversion include:

1. Public spaces are adaptable:

    - Cafeteria converts into a dining room

    - Kitchen can be expanded/used as the commercial kitchen

2. Classrooms and hallways are generally of a configuration that can be converted to corridors with living units:

    - Load-bearing walls and columns are frequently relatively easy to deal with in the adaptive reuse process.

3. Schools typically have a rather flexible "building shell." That means the basic exterior shell stays in place, but a number of changes can be made inside the building with relative ease.

4. In several cases, the auditorium has been left largely in place and has been converted into a "senior village mall."

Hotels and Motels

A number of hotels and motels across the United States are facing depressed occupancy and some markets may be permanently overbuilt. Many of these facilities can make excellent adaptive reuse candidates, while others should be subjected to the wrecking ball. Many older lodging facilities have now been bypassed by the interstate and new highway/arterial systems. Depending upon the neighborhoods in which they reside, some of them can become excellent conversion candidates. Many are located in traditional, well-established neighborhoods representing excellent in-fill locations in both suburban or urban areas.

In terms of design, a number of futile attempts have been made to convert austere budget motels that do not have interior hallways or suitably configured sleeping rooms. These attempts are clearly situation-driven and miss the mark in the seniors marketplace by a wide margin. Conventional hotels with interior, double loaded corridors and adequate sleeping rooms might make a good conversion to assisted living – but it is highly unlikely that they could serve the independent living market that typically requires full function kitchens and larger living areas. An exception would be a suite hotel discussed later in this chapter.

Another challenge with the conversion of hotels and motels is sometimes the relatively large number of rooms. The resulting senior living unit count is frequently higher than the marketplace is likely to absorb in a reasonable time frame.

Hospitals and Nursing Homes

Complete conversion of older hospitals and nursing homes sometimes appear to work well, but the perceptions of past (institutionalized) use of that space can linger on when one suddenly tries to offer upscale, high ambiance retirement living.

The business base of hospitals – and, in some cases, nursing homes – is changing due to the evolving trends in managed care and the impacts of vertical integrated networks. Conversion of space within a hospital or reuse of a nursing home wing may provide good opportunities for adaptive reuse. But special caution must be exercised when converting existing health care facilities. This is frequently either the perception or reality of institutionalism. Some hospitals and nursing homes do have the potential for conversion to a residential/social model of assisted living, but most should probably focus on the medical model. The medical model conversion opportunities fall into two major business sectors:

- Conventional assisted living

- Special care Alzheimer's/dementia units

These medical market model concepts are discussed in detail in Chapters 2 and 4.

Apartments and Condominiums

The condominium and apartment markets are still in a recovery phase in some areas of the country. These too can be the subject of solid adaptive reuse considerations. As with hotels, these structures should have living units with interior loaded hallways. The typical shortcoming is likely to be inadequate common/public spaces whose requirements can represent 30 to 40 percent of the total area under roof for a senior living community.

The portion of the total area devoted to common space in a typical apartment or condo is frequently 15 percent or less. However, there are some compensating strategies to consider:

- Sometimes an added building appropriately connected to the apartment complex can satisfy the new common space requirements.

- For example a "u-shaped" apartment or condominium complex footprint can locate a commons building including a dining room, commercial kitchen and space for other services in the center of the footprint; connecting the two ends of the building.

Apartments and condos can make good conversion candidates for independent living because they typically have:

- Separate sleeping rooms

- Full-function kitchens

- Adequate living areas

- Interior loaded hallways (in many geographical areas)

Condos and apartments of a more modest design (studios, alcoves, etc.) have the potential of being more readily adapted to assisted living where livable space requirements are less demanding than for independent living

Specific Conversion Considerations

Living units that enter into the interior loaded hallways and projects that have adequate common space and public areas are key requirements when evaluating the overall suitability of an adaptive reuse candidate. Obviously, the building's exterior elevations and "external look" are also very important. Some characteristics to look for include:

- What is the exterior (first impression) look of the building?

- Are there patios and balconies?

- Are there aesthetically pleasing "breaks" in the contour of the vertical surfaces?

- Are there interesting building roof lines?

In other words, how appealing does the building look when one first observes it? Many facilities work functionally – but appear to be far too institutional from a consumer perspective.

Other design features such as the ability to meet current fire and safety codes and other licensing requirements must be carefully considered. It is amazing how experienced operators have overlooked codes and requirements that suddenly come into play as previous variances that were grandfathered no longer apply to the new owner. Asbestos has sometimes killed an otherwise sound project.

What They See is What They Pay For

The paramount consideration to keep in mind is that the senior consumer marketplace only sees and gives credit for the converted end product. Consumers really do not care what it took to get there or why some of the obvious tradeoffs or compromises are still highly visible. If there is well-conceived competition nearby for comparison purposes, the converted product gets even less credit for the necessary conversion compromises.

Conversion Success Stories

In spite of all of these cautions, there are numerous success stories. Some examples include the following:

1. *A relatively new suite hotel* with full function kitchens and separate living areas became a troubled property in an overbuilt hospitality market. It was converted to independent retirement living very easily because of its original configuration. The location was ideal and the property offered the opportunity to convert one floor to assisted living with relative ease. A new nursing section is also planned to be added to one end of the property; integrated with the original building.

2. *An aging hotel and convention center* was donated by the city to the local housing authority in order to serve modest gap income seniors. The gap group typically has annual incomes from between $12,000 to $25,000 and is an extremely difficult group to serve in a private-pay situation. This facility was able to avoid excessive capital costs and could offer reasonable congregate services at modest fees.

3. *A large hospital campus* decided to expand their service delivery systems into residentially oriented assisted living and more medically driven personal care. Through a combination of conversion of existing facilities and additional construction, both medical and residential-social models of assisted living were accomplished and integrated within the hospital campus.

4. *A demographically obsolete elementary school* in an established mature neighborhood was successfully converted to freestanding assisted living. The neighborhood's residents had actively opposed previous new development efforts involving nearby vacant land. The adjoining neighbors were less concerned about the approvals for the school's adaptive reuse because the owner/operators assured them that the "look and character" of the property would not change. It was a property that the neighborhood had become accustomed to over the past 30 years.

5. *A company in Paris has taken a different approach to adaptive reuse.* Paris is the epitome of urban density, yet this company finds urban sites of varying shapes and sizes and determines how many of their standard state-of-the-art living units can fit on the site. If this number is acceptable, they save the original building elevation/facades, demolish the existing structure and create a state-of-the-art structure with the original old European facades in place. The end result is the flavor of traditional Europe – with a state-of-the-art interior infrastructure – in a highly desirable location.

Each of these successful examples were the result of careful consideration of the ultimate end product design, the location and how the product would be perceived in the future by the senior consumer marketplace. Most importantly, none of the projects broke the four fundamental rules of adaptive reuse.

The successful approach to considering adaptive reuse is to consider what the marketplace needs and wants **first** and then determine whether the conversion candidate really meets those needs. While apparently simple, the reverse of this process is frequently undertaken. Remember that adaptive reuse works best if the site is irreplaceable and the ultimate turn-key cost is approximately 20 percent less than new replacement cost. This pricing advantage makes reasonable trade-offs easier to accept in the marketplace. This strategy can deliver a powerful product into the marketplace because it involves a unique location and excellent value at a surprisingly affordable cost for that particular market area. That is something that most consumers will notice. Absent of these advantages, adaptive reuse risk increases geometrically.

Adaptive reuse can play a significant role in delivering needed senior housing and health care while helping to balance an overbuilt real estate market. The strategy can also save classic structures from the wrecking ball.

ADAPTIVE REUSE - THE FOUR CRITICAL QUESTIONS TO ANSWER

1. Is the site truly irreplaceable in the primary market area?

2. Is the building truly unique - with practical and cost-effective adaptive reuse potential?

3. Is the total turn-key acquisition and conversion cost moderately less (approximately 20 percent) than the replacement cost of a newly developed state-of-the-art assisted living facility?

4. Will the consumer understand and give appropriate credit for the inevitable tradeoffs and compromises in the end product that typically result from adaptive reuse process?

CONVERSION DREAMS ?	**OR**	**PHYSICAL OR ECONOMIC NIGHTMARE ?**
The Right Approach		*The Wrong Approach*

- The site <u>was</u> irreplaceable

- Approvals obtained with relative ease

- You paid not more than 80% of alternative costs for:
    - Acquisition
        Plus
    - Renovation

- There were no major design trade-offs:
    - Suitable unit size and configuration
    - Appropriate building layout
    - Interior loaded hallways

- The site was really <u>not</u> unique

- You paid too much for:
    - Acquisition
    - Renovation

- You rationalized away serious design flaws:
    - No showers
    - Bedrooms too small
    - Very narrow corridors
    - Long walk distances to insufficient common areas
    - Asbestos
    - Inadequate HVAC system
    - Etc.

Focus on the practical realization of a good end product and <u>don't</u> fall in love with your real estate !

TYPICAL TYPES OF ADAPTIVE REUSE OPPORTUNITIES

- Hotel/Motel
- Suite Hotel
- Conventional Apartment
- Condominium
- Hospital
- Church
- Nursing Home
- School

CHAPTER 12

INVESTING FOR IMPROVEMENTS
Physical Plants Also Experience Aging in Place

While most of us are aware that *residents* age in place, we frequently overlook or ignore another insidious and chronic aging trend; the gradual deterioration of our *physical plants*. As the assisted living industry matures, significant and innovative improvements are being made in the functional physical design and ambiance of newer state-of-the-art assisted living communities; and this could become a major threat to the future viability of many older communities.

Owner/operator response to the aging process must now be in two important areas; the residents and the community itself. The two are very complex and interrelated with no clear-cut solutions, but the very survival of many owner/operators may be at stake. Sponsors must deal with these aging issues now.

Types of Improvements

This aging process of physical plants is analogous to a senior's increasing chronic illness. Both represent a gradually deteriorating, but highly predictable trend. Planning for appropriate physical plant capital investment is an imperative that must be executed in a pragmatic manner. Capital

Investing for Improvements 105

investment strategies are typically deployed in three general areas:

1. *Cosmetic wear and tear* – Examples are frayed or soiled upholstery, worn carpets, out of style drapes and cosmetic defects in the surfaces and finishes in your public areas.

2. *Physical plant deterioration* – Leaky roofs or chronic failures of the heating, ventilating and air conditioning (HVAC) system usually are tell-tale signs of deferred preventive maintenance.

3. *Functional obsolescence.* The most obvious impacts are kitchen and bathroom cabinets, plumbing fixtures and lighting in the individual living units. Also included would be dated furniture styles and electrical fixtures in the common areas. Outdated and drab interiors in public spaces can sometimes create negative first impressions that send unfavorable perceived value signals to potential residents and their families touring an older community.

Five Areas of Potential Improvements

There are five specific areas of physical plant improvements that frequently require capital investment (Specific capital investment strategies are addressed in Chapter 16):

1. *Enhanced first impressions of the community* through improvements in the external site characteristics, including signs, paving repair, lighting, and creating interesting visual impressions through innovative and well-maintained landscaping.

2. *Improved impressions of the building exterior,* including fresh paint, new color treatments and more interesting elevation facades and roof lines.

3. *Rejuvenation of interior public spaces* –This generally means using new materials and finishes to improve interior design accents, or adding new or renovated furniture.

4. *Back-of-the-house details,* including expanded and improved kitchen equipment or laundry facilities and energy-efficient heating, ventilating and air conditioning (HVAC) systems.

5. *Improvements to individual living units,* such as refinishing or replacing cabinetry, new carpeting, and refinishing vertical and horizontal surfaces. Individual living units are often improved on an attrition basis as they are vacated. These upgrade packages can also be offered to existing residents for a modest increase in monthly service fees.

Faced with an aging physical plant, you may wonder, ***"How did we get in this position in the first place?"*** The answer may relate to the concept of depreciation as a generally accepted accounting practice. Most buildings are depreciated each year over a 25- to 35-year period, using a conservative definition of useful life. But "writing off" depreciation allows you to satisfy your CPA or auditor on paper without actually investing any real cash in your aging community. This trap is called "unfunded depreciation," and it is creating major problems for many aging assisted living, senior housing and health care communities.

Capital Investment Planning – A Five-Step Process

To avoid that trap, answer the question, *"Now that we recognize the problem, how do we properly plan for the future?"* A pragmatic capital investment strategy must be deployed. A good technique is to combine your actual facility experience with available industry standards and guidelines. Here is a pragmatic five-step approach:

1. Create a revolving five-year plan, adding another 12 months with every year that passes.

2. Make a detailed list of components, subsystems, and materials that make up your community, including the HVAC system, roofs, carpets, exterior and interior walls, calking and sealing, etc.

3. Identify each item's life expectancy, determine its current age, project the expected life remaining, and estimate the likely cost, scope and timing for future repair or replacement.

4. Insert this information into a spreadsheet that lists potential repair and maintenance details vertically with five-year planning columns spread horizontally.

5. Insert budgetary cost estimates into this matrix.

You now have the basis for a simple, effective, pragmatic and prioritized capital investment program.

Typical shortcomings in many older assisted living communities across the United States include:

- Very small studio or alcove units

- No kitchenettes

- No showers in the individual living unit

- Shared bathrooms for semi-private occupancy of unrelated residents

- Limited space in community/common areas in older buildings; space that is now desperately needed to serve the growing needs of both the professional staff and the aging residents

- Insufficient size or ambiance of dining areas. Some communities only offer self-service buffet lines; but with aging assisted living residents and competitive threats, full table service may now be an imperative.

Coupled with these typical functional deficiencies are areas of deferred maintenance that can significantly impact efficient operations.

Do Not Procrastinate Important Decisions

Many sponsors judge these problems by monitoring the relative degree of *existing* resident satisfaction. This approach can be dangerous and misleading because the mindset of the existing residents in these aging facilities represents a good news/bad news situation.

The good news is that many existing residents living in sub-par living units (by today's competitive standards) are generally quite happy and content. Formal resident panels indicate a surprisingly high degree of existing resident satisfaction in these aging communities. While many are aware of and have visited the newer competitors, they still prefer their "home". Some are even paying premium prices for relatively low ambiance and impaired functional utility.

The bad news is that these positive attitudes are probably masking the true reaction of the important replacement market; the long-run life blood of any assisted living community. Prospects and their loved ones visiting these communities are generally more critical in terms of first impressions with things such as aesthetics, cosmetics, ambiance and functional design shortcomings. They see an aging facility serving an older, frailer community of residents. Sales and marketing trends indicate that new prospects tend to self-select themselves in a way that leads to an increasingly older and frailer profile of new residents into that type of community.

The professional staffs of these communities start to recognize these subtle changes when their previously strong waiting lists start to soften resulting in a decreasing inventory of serious, qualified prospects. Stabilized occupancy begins to decline and marketing momentum eventually stalls.

Many owner/operators and Boards of Directors may be reluctant to make relatively expensive, progressive capital improvement decisions, hoping that the downward spiral will level off to a plateau of acceptable performance. However, experience clearly indicates that such an operational, marketing and financial miracle is unlikely to occur in many of these aging communities. Capital improvement efforts should be implemented as a consolidated, strategic initiative rather than taking a fragmented, band-aid approach.

Obsolete Locations

Many communities are now asking the strategic question, ***"Will our current assisted living campus and community be an acceptable, appropriate and competitive option for seniors in five to ten years?"***

Some sponsors are relocating their campuses from a changing, demographically obsolete and sometimes deteriorating neighborhood to a location that will better serve their future needs. Others are studying the viability of adding an additional campus to serve the expanding needs in their primary market area. This additional campus strategy can typically take two approaches: 1) a new campus including the full continuum of living arrangements or 2) a well-conceived satellite location usually specializing in one or more living arrangements or medical service delivery systems.

Financial Reserves for Future Capital Expenditures

Many sponsors ask, *"I'm planning a new project, how many capital investment dollars should I reserve annually?"* Adequate capital replacement reserves must also be put aside for any new project. "Adequate" generally means approximately $225 to $250 per unit or bed annually starting the second year of operation, or approximately 1.5 to 2.0 percent of operating revenues. Keep in mind that these factors are for new communities; older buildings could require considerably higher annual reserves. These assessments, which are usually treated as normal operating expense line items, should not be confused with your monthly maintenance department's operating budget for normal scheduled and preventive maintenance and routine minor repairs.

Must you constantly pony up for upgrades? No, but you'll probably pay an even higher price if you don't. A community with five to seven years of deferred maintenance in the five key areas noted in this chapter might have to ultimately invest at least $250,000. The cost of borrowing these funds would be about nine percent, totaling approximately $23,350 a year. In an 80-unit community, this would add about $320 per year to the cost of each occupied unit. To recover this return, you would have to increase monthly fees by about $30 per resident.

Special market niche applications should also be carefully considered during a total renovation and expansion effort. This would include purpose-built applications such as special Alzheimer/dementia units, possible space for a home health agency and fresh approaches to rehabilitation and adult day care.

One of the most effective ways to gradually make changes on an existing campus is to have a master plan that addresses the *total concept,* but implements the necessary changes in a *phased* manner. The plan could include a unit-by-unit upgrade or retrofit by attrition – as the units become vacant. This approach minimizes the impact on existing residents and even allows for a two-tiered pricing strategy as the newer, more state-of-the-art living units become available to future residents.

Many communities find that they must change their pricing and service delivery policies, but are concerned about existing resident reaction. To defer such changes indefinitely is not viable. Using the "new and improved" attrition upgrade strategy opens the gateway for reasonable changes in pricing and service delivery policies. The future viability of the community is gradually re-established. This approach involves a number of challenges, however, it can be very effective in the long run.

Approximately 10 to 15 percent of older communities across the United States may no longer be able to adequately serve future residents or be truly competitive in the marketplace. And the term "older, functionally obsolete community" may not necessarily mean one that has been operating for 15 to 20 years. Some five-year-old communities may face serious obsolescence

Investing for Improvements

and deferred maintenance challenges that threaten their future viability. This is especially true in market areas that now have newer, state-of-the-art competition and a finite number of available age and income qualified senior prospects to sustain the stabilized occupancy of all communities in the market area.

In an old TV commercial for the Fram automobile oil filter, a cagey auto mechanic stood by a smoking engine and held up a filthy oil filter as he said, *"You can pay me now or you can pay me later."* Like skimping on an oil filter change, deferring needed repairs or replacements can be penny-wise and pound-foolish for senior housing sponsors. "Later" can be very expensive.

THE TOP FIVE AREAS OF CAPITAL IMPROVEMENTS

1. **Enhanced first impressions of the community**
2. **Improved impressions of the building exterior**
3. **Rejuvenation of the interior public spaces**
4. **Back-of-the-house improvements**
5. **Individual living unit enhancement**

SECTION THREE

Financial Considerations;

Capital Costs and Operating Expenses

CHAPTER 13

DEVELOPING A REALISTIC CAPITAL BUDGET
The Lifeblood of a Successful Project

Assisted living is an attractive growth industry that can deliver significant financial rewards. But some new owners and sponsors are in for a financial wake-up call due to their erroneous capital cost projections and their unrealistic financial performance expectations. Those who want to attract favorable start-up financing and stay in business long term must start by taking a long, hard look at their basic numbers.

In order to demonstrate typical capital budgeting, this chapter contains specific dollar figures for a typical 80-unit project and the figures are expressed in 1998 dollars, representing national averages. Remember, industry financial guidelines are helpful, but relying solely on these rules of thumb to specifically estimate your new assisted living project's financial performance can be dangerous. Each development is unique, with costs and overall financial performance varying from project to project, region to region. Projecting the financial performance of your new project means carefully evaluating two basic areas of cost; the initial capital budget and ongoing operating expenses. This chapter deals with capital costs.

Top Ten Elements of a Capital Budget

A complete and realistic capital budget includes more than just the costs of developing the project. **The capital budget should include all the significant expenditures necessary to bring your project to stabilized occupancy of at least 93 percent in a reasonable time frame.**

A typical capital budget consists of at least ten major cost elements: 1) land and site development; 2) hard construction; 3) project design and development; 4) furniture, fixtures and equipment; 5) interest accrued on construction debt; 6) a comprehensive sales and marketing program; 7) occupancy/fill-up reserve funds; 8) financing and underwriting fees; 9) a project contingency fund and 10) a debt service reserve fund equal to one year's debt service payments (for tax-exempt bond financing).

Typical Capital Costs

Figure 13-1 summarizes the top ten elements of assisted living capital costs. A new freestanding assisted living community typically has an all-inclusive project cost of $85,000 to $125,000 per unit – total, all-in project costs divided by the number of units. To many, these costs may seem relatively high – until one realistically considers *all* of the necessary hard, soft and intangible costs of bringing the project to 93 percent stabilized occupancy. Several key cost variables are usually location sensitive, such as developed land values and hard

FIGURE 13-1
SENIOR LIVING CAPITAL COST INDICES AND BENCHMARKS[1]

Element of Capital Cost	Assisted Living	Independent Living
1. Raw Land	$5,000 - $9,000 /Unit	$6,000 - $10,000 /Unit
2. Site Development	3,500 - 5,000	4,000 - 6,000
3. Hard Construction (Bricks & Mortar)	50,000 - 70,000	70,000 - 100,000
4. Furniture Fixtures & Equipment	4,000 - 5,500	4,500 - 6,000
5. Design & Engineering	1,200 - 1,800	2,000 - 3,000
6. Development Fee	1,800 - 3,600	3,000 - 6,000
7. Accrued Construction Interest	3,000 - 4,000	4,000 - 5,500
8. Working Capital/Fill-up Reserve Fund	4,000 - 6,000	5,000 - 6,500
9. Sales & Marketing	3,500 - 4,500	4,000 - 5,500
10. Debt Service Reserve Fund [2]	5,500 - 8,500	7,500 - 11,000
11. Financing/Underwriting	1,500 - 2,000	1,600 - 2,100
Average Total (All-In) Cost Per Unit	$85,000 - $125,000	$115,000 - $165,000

Moore Diversified Services, Inc.
Moore Institute Data Base

[1] Indices and benchmarks reflect approximately 75% of current (1998) industry comparables; the remaining 25% can either be above or below ranges indicated herein.
[2] Typically required for tax-exempt bond financing.

Developing a Realistic Capital Budget 117

construction costs. Typical capital cost examples include land ranging between $5,000 to $9,000 per unit and site development costs from $3,500 to $5,000 per unit. Typical densities for senior housing facilities range from 15 to 20 units per acre for an independent living community to 18 to 22 units per acre for an assisted living facility. These densities generally include roadways, site infrastructure, building set-backs, parking, etc. Factoring in spaces for employees, parking requirements are typically 0.75 spaces per unit or slightly lower.

Hard construction costs on a square foot basis can typically range from $85 to $105 per square foot, or approximately $50,000 to $70,000 per unit. This considers both the resident's living area and necessary common spaces. It is important to put some broad categories of capital costs into proper perspective. Land and site development represents approximately 9 to 12 percent of the total project costs; hard construction costs 55 to 65 percent and other soft costs 17 to 20 percent.

Operating Loss Reserve Funds

Assisted living has high fixed operating costs, leading to substantial operating losses during fill-up. The typical fill-up rate ranges between four and seven units per month *net*. The operative word is "net," because units turn over even in the initial stages of occupancy. An 80-unit assisted living community could have a cumulative negative cash flow (after debt service) of $4,000 to $6,000 per unit until the project reaches a break-even (cash flow) occupancy of approximately 80 to 85 percent.

TOP TEN CAPITAL BUDGET COST ELEMENTS

1. Land and site development
2. Hard construction ("bricks & mortar")
3. Project design and development
4. Furniture, fixtures and equipment
5. Interest accrued on construction debt
6. Sales and marketing program
7. Occupancy/fill-up reserve fund
8. Financing and underwriting
9. Project contingency
10. Debt service reserve fund

Initial Marketing Budget

The cost of the sales and marketing activities needed to bring the community to this stabilized occupancy will probably add up to about $3,500 to $4,500 per unit. This includes all collaterals/brochures, program development, media costs, and sales office overhead expenses, plus base compensation and performance incentives for the sales and marketing staff.

The basic strategy of assisted living capital budgeting is to identify and fund all costs associated with developing, financing, marketing and bringing the project to a stabilized occupancy of approximately 93 percent. At that point, the

Developing a Realistic Capital Budget

annual operating budget "kicks in" and funds ongoing operations expenses. This concept is depicted in Figure 13-2.

Accurately determining total project cost is essential, but merely increasing pricing to cover increasing costs could be a dangerous strategy. A project must not become totally cost-driven, pricing itself out of the market or offering consumers too little value for their money.

The goal is to deliver comfortable yet affordable "Oldsmobiles," not extravagant "Cadillacs." A concept called value engineering can decrease or control costs while increasing perceived value.

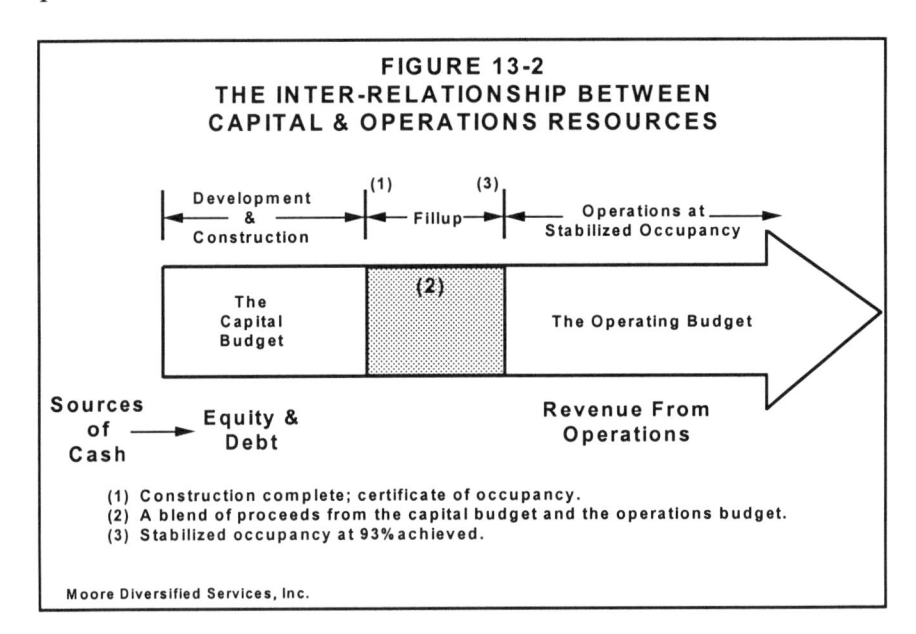

**FIGURE 13-2
THE INTER-RELATIONSHIP BETWEEN
CAPITAL & OPERATIONS RESOURCES**

(1) Construction complete; certificate of occupancy.
(2) A blend of proceeds from the capital budget and the operations budget.
(3) Stabilized occupancy at 93% achieved.

Moore Diversified Services, Inc.

Value Engineering

Value engineering is the pragmatic reduction or control of capital costs without significantly changing the final "look" or operation of an assisted living community. The results of this effort should be largely invisible to the consumer marketplace. Value engineering starts with an exhaustive, but beneficial, review of essentially every line item of capital cost. Through this process, it is not unusual to realize a reduction in total costs of between three and seven percent. Sometimes the value engineering exercise actually *increases* costs – but only when the increase is reasonable and competitive and there is a material and obvious value benefit to the future residents.

Value engineering of capital costs is best implemented using a two-tier process:

- *Tier 1 – Architect/Contractor Driven* – If you are still in the preliminary design phase, ask your development team what it would take to reduce overall costs by 10 percent. If your design and development process is further along, a cost reduction goal of five percent is probably more realistic. They may not reach your total value engineering goals but, more often than not, you'll be pleasantly surprised with the overall results.

- *Tier 2 – Owner/Sponsor Driven* – Now ask yourself, with the help of your professional team, what reasonable trade-offs are you willing to make in an effort to reduce costs? If an 80-unit project with a preliminary cost of $8.0 million ($100,000/unit) could be value engineered by just five percent,

Developing a Realistic Capital Budget

the resultant savings would be $400,000. The savings impact on the reduction of individual monthly service fees would be approximately $46 per unit.

The simple calculations are as follows:

- Preliminary project cost of $8.0 million or $100,000 per unit

- A five percent cost savings realized through the value engineering exercise or $400,000

- Multiplying the $400,000 savings by a 10.1 percent loan constant results in a reduction in annual debt service of $40,400 or $550 per *occupied* unit or approximately $46 per unit per month. Remember, debt service can only be paid by revenues from *occupied* units.[1]

This may not seem like much until you consider the possibility of investing some or all of that savings in other areas having a much higher impact on value. You might also consider lowering the monthly service fee to be slightly more affordable and competitive.

---

[1] Loan constant – a convenient analysis factor which considers the total debt service; interest (9%), principal ($400,000) and term (25 years). See Appendix B for additional loan constant details.

Translating Capital Costs to Pricing

The monthly service fee for assisted living is heavily influenced by three major factors:

1. Paying all necessary operating expenses (See Chapter 14)

2. Covering required debt service or return on investment resulting from the total capital cost of the project

3. Entrepreneurial profit or the funding of other mission objectives

Covering Capital Costs

Assume an 80-unit assisted living project with a total cost of $100,000 per unit at a 75 percent debt-to-equity ratio, a 25-year loan amortization at nine percent resulting in a loan constant of 10.1 percent (see earlier definition):

- **Debt vs. Equity Mix:**

- Debt	$ 75,000 (@ 10.1%)
- Equity	25,000
Total Cost	$100,000

- **Debt service equals:**

  - $7,575/unit/year

  or

  - $630/unit/month

But this is not the whole story. In determining the debt service component to be recovered by the monthly service fee, there are two final adjustments that must be made:

1. *Adjust for occupancy* – Revenue to cover debt service can come from only *occupied* units.

   $$\frac{\$630}{.93} = \$675/month$$

2. *Debt service coverage allowance* – Lenders require a $1.25 to $1.35 for every dollar in debt service to be paid. This means your net operating income per occupied unit (after operating expenses) should be:

   $675 x 1.35 = $910/unit/month

   This is the debt service component of net operating income that must be recovered through the monthly service fee from every occupied unit.

In Chapter 19, this debt service component will be added to the required operating expenses per unit to determine the total monthly service fee for pricing purposes.

CHAPTER 14

REALISTIC APPROACH TO DETERMINING OPERATING EXPENSES

Properly Evaluating All Costs is Critical When Projecting Expenses

In planning assisted living projects, sponsors and operators often underestimate resident acuity and resulting turnover rates, therefore understating operating expenses and setting their prices too low. As a result, their projects suffer from unacceptable operating margins and inadequate cash flow. Ultimately, residents may be in for an unpleasant surprise as prices undergo a necessary, but hefty, increase. But these problems can be avoided if the owner or sponsor starts with a realistic estimate of operating expenses.

Two Key Expense Ratios

Two important ratios can provide guidance when estimating and evaluating assisted living operating expenses:

• *Operating Expense Ratio* – Total cash operating expenses divided by net revenues. For a typical assisted living project, this ratio should range between 58 and 63 percent.

The inverse of the operating expense ratio is the **operating margin.** This is commonly referred to as "EBITDA"; earnings before interest on debt, taxes, depreciation, and amortization. This ratio typically ranges between 37 and 42 percent.

- ***Operating Expenses Per Resident-day*** – I like to evaluate financials in terms of *dollars per resident day.* It's the lowest common denominator. Operating expenses per resident day in assisted living is defined as the total annual expenses (or expenses by major department) divided by the number of residents times 365 days. Resident-day expense ratios can provide an excellent, detailed evaluation of each line item of expense – especially when compared with reliable industry comparables. Total operating expenses per resident-day should typically range between $38 and $48 in most market areas. These costs include basic shelter services and a *realistic* menu of assistance with the Activities of Daily Living (ADLs). The rather broad range of this index reflects significant variables that can exist from project to project, market to market. These variables typically include labor, real estate taxes, utilities, supplies, etc.

Operating Expense Checks and Balances

As a helpful check and balance, the *operating expense ratio* shows the relationship between revenues and expenses while the *expenses per resident-day index* is based solely on operating expenses. If your operating expense ratio appears high or out of line with industry guidelines (58 to 63 percent), the expenses per resident-day index can provide you with general clues to the source of the problem; either revenues being too low or expenses being too high. For example, if your operating expense ratio is 75 percent (high), but your operating expenses are $43 per resident-day (normal), it is likely that your revenues are suppressed.

Estimating Operating Costs - An Overview

With assisted living acuity levels and resident turnover higher than many expected, most experienced operators consider themselves successful if they can hold direct and indirect operating expenses between $1,155 and $1,275 per unit per month. This translates into operating expenses ranging from $38 to $42 per resident-day. When sponsors conduct a detailed operating cost sensitivity analysis, they will discover another challenge – most assisted living operating costs are largely fixed when the doors open and do not vary significantly as a function of occupancies between 75 and 95 percent. Approximately 75 percent of the costs are fixed or only semi-variable, while only 25 percent are truly variable. There is very little variance in the total operations cost of an 80-unit community that has 68 units occupied (85 percent) vs 74 units occupied (93 percent). But because revenues *are* directly variable, the lower occupancy could result in a cash flow differential or deficit of over $150,000 annually.

Labor costs represent at least 60 percent of assisted living operating expenses. Typically, a facility will have approximately .45 to .50 Full-Time Equivalent (FTEs) employees for every resident. An 80-unit community with approximately 36 FTEs in a market with average labor costs can have an annual direct payroll of approximately $720,000. Add up to 30 percent for fringe benefits (vacations, holidays, sick leave and insurance premiums) and payroll taxes and the gross payroll is now about $936,000; or an average of $26,000 per employee.

Putting it All Together - A Snapshot

Figure 14-1 depicts a typical *operating expense budget* in terms of both dollars and per resident-day ratios. Figure 14-2 drops this operating expense budget into an overall *income statement;* showing how all the financial ratios and factors combine for a financially viable community.

<u>Caution</u>: Don't force your budget into my numbers in Figure 14-1! Each community and market area will have a unique operating expense profile. In addition, accounting systems and chart of account formats vary and could impact these benchmarks.

FIGURE 14-1
OPERATING EXPENSE BENCHMARKS

Major Dept./ Cost Center	Annual Operating Expense Budget	Range of Expenses Per Resident-Day[1]
1. Administration	$ 132,500	$ 4.75 to 5.50
2. Activities	33,900	1.45 1.60
3. Assisted Living	224,395	8.00 10.00
4. Plant Maintenance/ Security	101,830	3.50 4.50
5. Food/Dietary	257,970	9.25 12.50
6. Hsekping & Laundry	54,310	1.80 2.40
7. Transportation	21,725	.75 .85
8. Property	122,720	4.00 6.00
9. Marketing & Sales	150,000	3.50 4.00
10. Management Fees	102,670	3.50 4.50
11. Reserve for Replacement	20,000	.75 .90
TOTALS	$ 1,222,020	$ 41.25 to 52.75

CAUTIONS:
1. Each community and market area will have a unique operating expense profile.
2. Accounting systems and chart of account formats vary and could impact these benchmarks.

---

[1] As an example, resident-days for an 80-unit assisted living community would be 80 x 365 days or 29,200 resident-days at 100% occupancy and 27,155 resident-days for 93% occupancy.

Moore Diversified Services, Inc.

FIGURE 14-2
FINANCIAL PROFILE FOR A
TYPICAL 80-UNIT ASSISTED LIVING COMMUNITY
(First Stabilized Year)

	TWO POSSIBLE SCENARIOS	
I. KEY VARIABLES	**ACHIEVABLE**	**LIKELY IN MANY MARKETS**
• Base Monthly Service Fee	$2,000/mo	$2,300/mo
• Expenses Per Resident-Day	$40 PRD	$45 PRD
• Total Cost Per Unit	$85,000	$100,000
II. INCOME STATEMENT		
• Gross Annual Income	$1,920,000/yr	$2,208,000/yr
• Vacancy Factor @ 7%	(134,400)	(154,560)
• Net Revenues	$1,785,600	$2,053,440
• Operating Expenses	(1,086,240)	(1,222,020)
• Net Operating Income (NOI)	$ 699,360 /yr	$ 831,420/yr
• Debt Service[1]	(513,570)	(604,200)
• Cash Flow	$ 185,790 /yr	$ 227,220/yr
III. KEY FINANCIAL RATIOS		
• Debt Service Coverage Ratio	1.36x	1.38x
• Operating Margin	39.2%	40.5%
• Operating Expense Ratio	60.8%	59.5%
• NOI / Unit	$ 8,740	$ 10,390
• Cash Flow / Unit	$ 2,325	$ 2,840

[1] 75% debt, 25% Equity, 9%, 25 years

Moore Diversified Services, Inc.

Figure 14-2 illustrates two assisted living financial scenarios. Note that with reasonable and expected operating expenses, the two scenarios deliver the following financial performance *in the first stabilized year of operation:*

- *Net operating income before debt service;* frequently expressed as "EBITDA" – earnings before interest, taxes, depreciation and amortization – ranges from $699,360 to $831,420. Sometimes it is evaluated as average *unleveraged* cash flow per unit or bed. In this case, unleveraged average cash flow per unit ranges from $8,740 to $10,390.

- *Total annual cash flow after debt service* ranging from $185,790 to $227,220 or $2,325 to $2,840 per unit.

- *Cash return on total investment unleveraged* (*before* debt service) ranges from 10.3 to 10.4 percent; heavily influenced by the *total cost per unit* ($85,000 vs. $100,000).

- *Cash-on-cash return on invested equity* (*after* debt service) ranges from approximately 10.9 to 11.4 percent.

- *The debt service coverage ratio* is in an acceptable range of 1.36x to 1.38x.

Sensitivity of Financial Returns

A review of assisted living financial returns evoke romantic, emotional – and controversial reactions! Most industry experts can't agree on a set of standard indices. Industry surveys are trying to get a handle on this dilemma, but sampling anomalies still exist. Some analysts say there's no way to achieve an EBITDA operating margin *north* of 37 percent. It will probably take several years of market maturity before these numbers really stabilize. However, it is useful to evaluate the *sensitivity* of your community's financial performance.

For example, higher returns could be realized in the example depicted in Figure 14-2 with a modest increase in leverage; setting debt at 80 percent of the project cost. The important debt service coverage ratio would be approximately 1.34x, still acceptable to most lenders.

Other key financial variables include driving down the total cost per unit (where practical) and modestly increasing pricing – assuming that you will remain competitive in your market area.

Cost/Unit and Debt Ratio Sensitivity

Let's *tinker* with the $100,000/unit, $2,300/month scenario illustrated in Figure 14-2. If it were possible to change the total cost/unit and/or modestly increase the average monthly service fee, we would experience dramatic improvement in cash flow and cash return on invested equity – *after* debt service.

	Cash Return on Invested Equity[1]					
Debt/Equity	75%/25%			80%/20%		
Monthly Service Fee	$2,300	$2,400	$2,520[2]	$2,300	$2,400	$2,520[2]
Total (All-In) Cost/Unit:						
• $ 85,000	18.7%	23.9%	27.1%	20.9%	27.4%	31.3%
• $ 95,000	13.5	18.2	21.0	14.4	20.3	23.8
• $100,000	**11.4**	15.8	18.5	11.7	17.3	20.6
Operating Expenses PRD	$45.00	$45.00	$47.00	$45.00	$45.00	$47.00

In the example in Figure 14-2, the unit cost of $100,000 delivered an 11.4 percent cash return on invested equity – assuming a debt-to-equity ratio of 75%/25% and a monthly service fee of $2,300/month. You can achieve a substantial improvement in your returns if key financial factors can be changed. Caution: You obviously can't make these changes in isolation; your lender, contractor and the marketplace may represent significant barriers.

	Annual Cash Flow per Unit After Debt Service[1]					
Debt/Equity	75%/25%			80%/20%		
Mo. Ser. Fee	$2,300	$2,400	$2,520[2]	$2,300	$2,400	$2,520[2]
Total (All-In) Cost/Unit:						
• $ 85,000	$3,975/yr	$5,090/yr	$5,750/yr	$3,545/yr	$4,660/yr	$5,320/yr
• $ 95,000	3,220	4,330	4,995	2,740	3,855	4,515
• $100,000	**2,840**	3,955	4,615	2,335	3,450	4,110
Operating Expen. PRD	$45.00	$45.00	$47.00	$45.00	$45.00	$47.00

[1] 80 units, 93% occupancy, 9%, 25-year mortgage
[2] Represents 5% annual escalation from $2,400/month

In the example in Figure 14-2, annual cash flow per unit was $2,840. This can change dramatically by being able to change the previously mentioned financial variables.

The "Harvesting" Effect

Your financial ratios will also improve with time – assuming you compensate for cost creep and pay attention to operations details. The financial performance in Figure 14-2 reflects the *first full year of stabilized occupancy.* If you increase your fees by five percent and your expenses escalate four percent, your financial return in the second year will increase from 11.4 percent to 14.1 percent, thanks to fixed debt and the power of prudent leverage.

The Classical Financial Break-Even Model

Before you speculate on your future rewards, it is wise to completely evaluate the dynamics of project *lift-off.* Like our space program, the most critical phase of your mission is launching and filling up your project – *without* any catastrophic events!

Figure 14-3 depicts the classical break-even chart applied to assisted living. Chances are you studied the concept in college but never saw a real world, practical application. Now you have.

Realistic Approach to Determining Operating Expenses 134

**FIGURE 14-3
THE CLASSICAL BREAK-EVEN CHART
APPLIED TO ASSISTED LIVING**

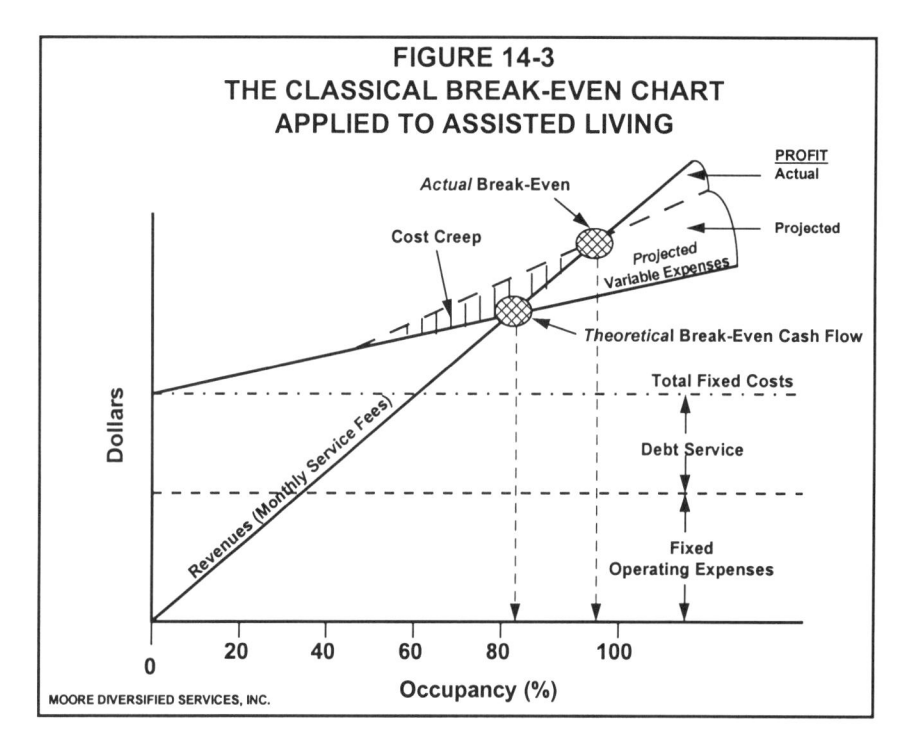

The break-even chart graphically depicts the following important points:

1. Fixed Costs - Certain operating expenses and debt service represent fixed costs facing you every day after you open.

2. Variable Costs - "Ride" on top of fixed costs to establish your total dollar outlay.

3. Revenues - Gradually increase as a function of increasing occupancy (as do variable expenses).

4. Break-Even - That magic milestone and moving target that occurs when revenues equal the sum of fixed and variable costs. This is the point you transition from *loss* (negative cash flow) to profit (positive cash flow).

5. Cost Creep - Is the culprit that *shifts* the actual break-even point; extending losses and requiring higher occupancy before profits and positive cash flow. Some troubled communities *chase* the illusive break-even point – never seeming to come close to catching it.

The break-even concept is not just a cute academic theory; it is the essence of your assisted living financial dynamics!

Some Special Expense Considerations

These considerations include management fees, reserves for replacement and annual expense escalation.

Management fees are an important factor in assisted living. Typically, the management fee collected is approximately five percent of net revenues but can range between four and seven percent. The management fee provides for the overall management and oversight of the community, but does not include many direct costs. Management fees are covered in detail in Chapter 28.

Reserve for replacement – Depreciation (as a non-cash expense) is usually not included in a typical operating statement; the income statement is frequently presented and evaluated on a *cash basis* less depreciation, amortization, interest and tax payments. However, a reserve for replacement fund is created (as contrasted to technically funding depreciation) by assessing a specific dollar amount per unit each year. For a new project, a replacement reserve is created by directly expensing approximately $225 to $250 per unit per year for a new project. These funds are accumulated in a special reserve account and used for future capital investment or replacement. This allocation is in *addition* to the normal operations and maintenance department budget which funds routine and scheduled maintenance of the community.

Annual Escalation – Assisted living financial pro formas typically escalate both revenue and expenses at approximately four percent per year. The actual inflation rate in the senior housing industry over the past five to six years has been approximately 3.5 to 4 percent annually. That is essentially the same rate that owner/operators have increased monthly service fees to their residents. Frequently, there is a positive one point spread between *revenue increases* (five percent) and actual *expense inflation* (four percent).

A Savings of $1.80 is Worth Over $460,000!

This is a pretty provocative statement, but it's true. Consider the following:

- An operating expense savings of $1.80 per resident-day (a decrease of approximately four percent on total expenses of $45 per resident-day).

- Multiply this savings by 27,155 resident-days equals an increase in net operating income of $48,880 per year (80 residents times 365 days, 93 percent occupancy).

- The increased net operating income of $48,880 would be capitalized at 10.5 percent by an appraiser or potential buyer. This results in a $465,525 increase in the imputed value of the community.

- The typical monthly service fee for a resident could be reduced by approximately $55.

This example is a modern day equivalent of the old adage *"A penny saved is a penny earned."* It's obvious that the potential payoff is well worth the cost reduction effort.

The Power of Prudent Leverage

As can be seen earlier in this chapter, average total cost per unit and mortgage interest rates have a significant impact on total returns for your project. *Leverage* is using "other people's money" *prudently* to magnify your financial returns.

Leverage Advantages of Not-For-Profits

In Figure 14-4, I have provided an example on how the *same* assisted living project can experience dramatically different returns when only interest rates or cost of money is considered. Not-for-profits can usually access tax-exempt bond financing at a much lower cost than typical borrowing rates offered to for-profit organizations. In the Figure 14-4 example, the not-for-profit realizes a savings in debt service of approximately $130,000 each year. This cash flow can be used to fund other initiatives or mission objectives.

Seven Ways to Keep Costs Under Control

How are astute operators keeping costs in check? There's no surefire solution, but there are seven strategies that have proven effective:

1. *Reduce both initial capital costs and ongoing operating expenses.* For example, a $5,000 per unit capital cost reduction will lower a resident's monthly service fee by about $40. This would represent about a five percent value engineering cost reduction on a community with an average total, all-in capital cost of $100,000 per unit. A four percent or $1.80 per resident-day operating expense reduction will reduce the monthly fee by $55.

FIGURE 14-4

THE POWER OF PRUDENT DEBT/LEVERAGE

	Individual Assisted Living Unit Annual	
Revenue @ $2,300/mo	$ 27,600 /yr	
Vacancy @ 7%	(1,932)	
Net Revenue	$ 25,668	
Expenses @		
$45 / Resident Day	(15,275)	
Net Operating Income	$ 10,393	
(EBITDA)[1]		
Return on $10,000 Investment	$10,393	
Unleveraged	10.4%	
	For Profit	Not For Profit
Debt Service Payment		
$100,000 / Unit @ 75%		
Debt; 25% Equity		
• Equity $25,000		
• Debt $75,000		
• Debt Constant	@ 10.1%	@ 7.73%
$75,000, 25 years	$ 7,575 /yr	$ 5,795 /yr
Cash Flow:		
Net Operating Income	$ 10,390 /yr	$10,390 /yr
Less		
Annual Debt Payment	(7,550)	(5,795)
Cash Flow	$ 2,840	$ 4,595
Cash-on-Cash Return on		
$25,000 Equity Investment	11.4%	18.4%

Moore Diversified Services, Inc.

---

[1]EBIDTA = Earnings Before Interest, Depreciation, Taxes and Amortization

2. Build a project big enough to optimize operational efficiencies. But take care not to build more units than your marketplace can absorb. This involves a classical trade-off analysis between optimum operational efficiencies and excessive marketplace risk. The optimum size range in many markets is approximately 80 to 100 units.

3. Use the universal worker approach. This involves cross-training your staff in key areas of assistance in daily living activities, food service, and housekeeping. This lowers the number of total employees needed; and reducing payroll by just three FTEs can lower labor costs by approximately $65,000 annually. This could reduce a resident's monthly service fee by about $70 per unit per month in an 80-unit community.

The $65,000 savings would also increase net operating income by the same amount which, when capitalized at 10.5 percent, would increase your project's imputed value by over $600,000.

4. Make capital expenditure decisions that will stand the test of time. "Low-balling" one-time capital costs in the wrong areas can raise operating expenses for the life of the project. This decision involves a classical capital investment versus payback period analysis (see Chapter 16).

5. Make sure the project stands alone and is self supportive. Then – and only then – factor in supplementary income from private subsidies, charitable donations and other mission initiatives. Many not-for-profit board members assume their charitable mission of the past can automatically be projected into the future with their new assisted living community. Assisted living is primarily a private pay business with very limited reimbursement or entitlements at this time (see Chapter 20).

6. *Consider a multi-tier pricing strategy.* Charging a base rate for services needed by most residents coupled with variable or tiered fees for everything else allows each resident to pay for only as much actual assistance as he or she requires (covered in Chapters 15 and 19).

7. *Develop a comprehensive, but flexible, initial financial pro forma.* Make sure that the pro forma can quickly execute a sensitivity analysis and answer a number of "what if" questions: What if your actual expenses are two dollars higher than expected per resident-day? What if occupancy is three percent lower than the hoped-for stabilized rate of 93 percent? What if the project fills up slower than expected?

In short, start your planning with a realistic estimation of the costs you are likely to encounter and don't ever stop looking for ways to operate more efficiently. Facing the need for moderately increasing monthly service fees now may not be pleasant, but it's far better than procrastinating on inevitable decisions – resulting in steep increases to existing residents to adjust for estimating errors or cost creep.

CHAPTER 15

ASSISTED LIVING COST CREEP CAN BE A FATAL DISEASE
Many Sponsors Are in For a $1 Million⁺ Wake-Up Call

Keeping monthly fees affordable is a crucial part of survival, success and profitability for assisted living providers. But equally crucial is the other end of that economic balancing act; ensuring that creeping costs do not infiltrate your profit margin leaving your bottom line bleeding red ink.

Assisted living costs represent a constantly moving target. It is generally recognized that initial fill-up and turnover rates are difficult to predict. But worse yet, the typical assisted living resident suffers from chronic conditions that gradually – but predictably – deteriorate with time. This can result in significant cost creep if increasingly necessary levels of care are provided without corresponding increases in pricing.

The Real World of Cost Creep

The following scenario is being played out hundreds of times daily in assisted living communities all across the U.S.:

Resident aide or Housekeeper: *"Let me give you some additional help today, Mrs. Jones."*

Mrs. Jones: *"Oh, thank you – I just love living here at The Gardens of Westridge."*

Resident aide or Housekeeper: *"No problem, Mrs. Jones, I'm sure you'll feel better tomorrow."*

There are two big problems with this scenario:

1. Mrs. Jones may feel a little better tomorrow – but she has a chronic condition with gradually declining health that will require increasing assistance with ADLs.

2. There are literally thousands of Mrs. Jones' in hundreds of assisted living communities.

Cost creep is the chronic disease afflicting owner/operators. But sound pricing policies can be the miracle drug that can prevent a catastrophic epidemic.

Pricing policies must be flexible to address future costs while remaining understandable, equitable, affordable and competitive

To be sure your price is right, you must first estimate the true cost of operating your community, which typically includes two major components; debt service payments and operating expenses. These elements are discussed in Chapters 13 and 14, respectively. Next, you must develop an equitable pricing policy that communicates value and fairness to the consumer, while being competitive in the local market and delivering consistently favorable financial results. Clearly identifying all costs beyond basic shelter, meals and housekeeping and requiring residents to pay for them as needed is the fairest strategy, not only for the owner/operator, but for residents and their families.

Five Steps to Effective Pricing

1. *Determine your direct baseline costs.* These include the expenses that will be incurred by all residents: food, housekeeping, utilities, maintenance, management and administration, and payment of the underlying debt. Spread these direct costs along with an allocation of other appropriate overhead expenses across the number of units that represents stabilized occupancy – typically 93 to 95 percent.

2. *Develop procedures to periodically measure the assistance required by each resident in performing activities of daily living (ADLs).* This detailed assessment should be an integral part of the initial admissions process. It should also be updated periodically and any time a major change in the resident's condition is observed. The process is analogous to case work-up and monitoring used in nursing.

3. Translate resident care needs into required skill levels. Determine the costs involved in delivering the care. Identify the job descriptions, skill levels and additional time per day needed to deliver care for each individual resident.

4. Develop pragmatic scoring criteria. Each ADL need above baseline costs must be assigned a weight, or score, based on the degree of additional effort required by the staff member and the resulting cost incurred.

5. Translate the scoring criteria into three to five price levels. Segment or group the results of the scoring into three to five definitive categories and assign a cost to each category. Then *load* this cost to take into consideration not only the caregiver's direct hourly wage rate, but also fringe benefits and other reasonable overhead allocation and profit. For example, an additional hour of daily assistance provided by a resident assistant might have a direct salary cost of $8.50 per hour. Adding a 25 percent fringe benefit cost factor and a reasonable allocation for appropriate overhead and profit might yield a total cost to be recovered of approximately $12 to $13 daily for that extra hour of assistance. Figure 15-1 illustrates the impact of cost creep. These costs could easily go to $20 per hour, depending on your actual direct costs and overhead allocation.

Assuming an average of 30.4 days per month, Mrs. Jones, discussed in the earlier example, might be incurring an additional cost of between $12 to $13 per day; $365 to $395 a month, or $4,380 to $4,740 a year. The question is: who's paying for this extra care, you or Mrs. Jones and her family?

FIGURE 15-1

THE IMPACT OF ONE HOUR PER DAY COST CREEP

Base Salary - Resident Aide	$8.50/hr
Fringe Benefits @ 25%	2.10
Subtotal	$10.60/hr
Overhead Allocation and Profit @ 23%	2.40
Total	$13.00/hr

$13.00/Day x 30.4 Days = $395/Month

For Just <u>One</u> Hour of Cost Creep

Moore Diversified Services, Inc.

Financial Impacts of Cost Creep

Many new assisted living facilities say that they offer a fixed monthly service fee of approximately $2,200. This may appear feasible in some markets when you consider that *baseline* operating expenses are approximately $40 per resident-day or $1,215 per month. Debt service payments on a newly developed unit costing $100,000 – with 75 percent leverage or $75,000 in debt at a 10 percent loan constant – will generally average about $910 a month when occupancy and a debt service coverage factor are considered as discussed in Chapter 12. This brings the total cost to be recovered to approximately $2,125 a month. But with Mrs. Jones, a cost creep of $395 a month for additional assistance with ADLs, would yield a total cost of approximately $2,520 per month. Now there is the potential for a negative monthly cash flow of $320 for that specific unit if you had originally priced it at $2,200 per month. This translates to a negative cash flow of $3,840 per year.

If eventually 40 percent of the residents of an 80-unit community receive this level of *uncompensated care,* the results could be:

- Total potential negative cash flow from those 32 units is $122,880.

- Net income shortfall for the project of $151,680. (32 units times $395 cost creep per month times 12 months.)

- A decrease in the imputed value of the project of approximately $1.4 million when applying the 10.5 percent capitalization rate used to determine value as discussed in Appendix C.

> # Cost creep can easily become a $1 million⁺ problem!

As assisted living matures, pricing will become more complex. This is partly because resident acuity levels are much higher than many operators expected and partly because consumers are becoming more sophisticated in evaluating the true value of senior living options. It is therefore more important than ever that pricing policies be flexible enough to address future costs, while remaining understandable, equitable, affordable, and competitive.

It may be necessary for many operators to implement a definitive tiered, a la carte pricing system. This system would typically have a base fee for shelter and core services that would serve the common needs of at least 80 to 85 percent of the resident population. Additional charges would be assessed based on each resident's unique and potentially changing needs as discussed in this chapter. Chapter 19 addresses win-win pricing strategies.

COVERING COST CREEP IS A FIVE STEP PROCESS

1. Determine your baseline costs

2. Develop policies and procedures to measure the specific assistance in daily living required by each individual resident

3. Translate the individual resident care needs into required skill levels and estimate additional costs to deliver this care

4. Develop pragmatic and consistent scoring criteria

5. Translate the scoring criteria into three to five discrete pricing levels

CHAPTER 16

GETTING CREATIVE WITH CAPITAL INVESTMENT

Four Simple Steps That Can Produce Dramatic Results

Investing in ongoing capital improvement is a crucial part of keeping your senior living community in a competitive, "like new" condition. Specific capital improvement strategies are addressed in Chapter 12 and developing a comprehensive capital budget is covered in Chapter 13. But in planning a capital investment strategy, many owners and sponsors either spend money on the wrong things, lose sight of their overall objectives, or pay too much for less than optimum value.

In developing a new assisted living project, there are situations wherein capital expenditure decisions must consider two distinct time horizons. These two time frames are:

- *Short Run* – The Initial Capital Cost Investment Impact

- *Long Run* – The Ongoing Operating Cost of Ownership

To plan effectively, you must weigh the short run capital cost expenditures (immediate capital costs, such as the type of a new heating, ventilation and air conditioning system) against the long run costs of ownership (the ongoing operating costs of such as operating your community; such as maintenance, utilities and insurance). Investing less in capital improvements in the short run can be very expensive over the total ownership period. These cost considerations become very important if the property will be held for more than five years. If you plan to be a short term property owner, be advised that your ultimate sale value can be impacted by a "short run" capital investment mentality. The buyer's due diligence efforts will likely detect flaws in your capital investment planning. Frequently, the least costly capital investment in the short-run can become very expensive over the total ownership period.

The following simple steps should help you make these important trade-off decisions.

1. *Evaluate the payback period and calculate the impact on total project value.* How many years of operation are required for the operational savings/benefits to result in financial break-even or recovery of your initial investment? This can be a simple arithmetic calculation (dividing the initial cost of the capital investment by the estimated annual financial benefit or savings) or a more sophisticated discounted cash flow analysis. Ideally, your payback period should be somewhere between three and five years. From that point forward, there will be a continuing positive financial impact.

For example, assume that a combination of capital expenditure decisions costing a total of $50,000 could save $1,000 a month in operating expenses. That additional $12,000 per year in additional net operating income would pay back the initial investment in about four years. Keep in mind that these annual operating expense savings will likely be realized far beyond the initial payback period, and possibly over the entire useful life of the community.

2. *Estimate the total impact on project value.* To determine the increased intrinsic value of your project, you should *capitalize* the increase in net operating income resulting from the capital investment[1]. The *capitalization rate* is the cash return (percentage) that reasonable buyers or investors would expect to realize on their cash investment; obviously influenced by their perception of relative risk. Appendix C briefly describes the capitalization rate concept.

Continuing with the example from Item 1, that same $12,000 annual savings would also increase the economic value of your community. An investor expecting a 10.5 percent return on his or her cash investment would therefore be willing to invest about $114,000 in order to receive an additional return of $12,000 annually; a 10.5 percent return on cash invested. So with that $50,000 investment, the value of your community is likely to be increased by approximately $114,000.

---

[1] Net operating income equals revenue minus operating expenses (before depreciation, amortization, interest payments and applicable taxes).

3. *Value engineer your capital investments.* This means lowering or controlling capital costs without significantly detracting from the look or operational efficiency of your community. The results of this effort should be largely invisible to the consumer marketplace. This concept is addressed in Chapter 13.

4. *Invest in the "flash value concept."* Flash value is a fairly obscure, but surprisingly simple way of quantifying, and thereby maximizing, perceived value. This concept is defined as follows:

$$\text{Flash Value Index} = \frac{\text{What Consumer Thinks Item Costs}}{\text{Your Actual Cost}}$$

Through consumer testing (focus groups, etc.), you can identify a menu of design features and amenities that exhibit a "flash value index" of greater than two to one. This means that the consumer thinks the item is worth at least twice as much as your actual cost. Then incorporate several favorable flash value items into your project. Typical high flash value items in seniors housing include high-quality wood molding or millwork, walk-in closets, unusual public spaces, and recessed solid-core living unit entry doors. The ideal expected outcome is for the senior and their family to comment, ***"This place sure seems to offer a lot for the money!"***

The "Cap X" Concept

Owner/operators and lenders are also using a relatively new capital investment concept called "Cap X" (for Capital Expenditure) or "reserve for replacement." This is an imputed operations expense line item of approximately $225 to $250 per unit per year allocated and reserved for future capital needs of a routine and generally predictable nature (cosmetic refurbishment, etc.). Some organizations establish the Cap X requirement as 1.5 to 2.0 percent of revenues. This concept is also discussed in Chapter 14.

Capital investment is not just simply spending money for obvious needs. It involves spending the *right amount of money* for the *right items* at the *right time*. This requires prudent capital investment planning that optimizes financial returns to the owner/operator while delivering positive impacts and tangible benefits to current and future residents.

Both of these lofty goals can be accomplished with the help of the four basic capital investment principles that were outlined in this chapter.

Creative Assisted Living Capital Investment
Four Simple Steps

1. Evaluate the investment payback period.

2. Estimate the total impact on project value.

3. Value engineer for cost savings.

4. Invest in *flash value* to enhance perceived value.

CHAPTER 17

THE AGONY AND ECSTASY OF FINANCING ASSISTED LIVING
*Refinancing is Easy – But
Financing New Projects is More Complex*

Thanks to two current trends, most *refinancing* in the 1998 time frame is almost a slam dunk: 1) assisted living as a hot development opportunity and 2) the significant dollars chasing the senior housing and health care sectors. Financing *new* projects is more complex, and frequently more difficult.

Five Favorable Financing Factors

There are five fundamental factors that have caused previously indifferent lenders to quickly focus on assisted living financing: First, a significant in-rush of investor money into the capital markets. With one of the longest economic recoveries on record, consumers in general and baby boomers in particular are saving at historically high rates. Second, reduced lender investment alternatives in other areas such as commercial and industrial real estate ventures. Third, senior housing is now recognized as a more efficient market. There is increased knowledge, empirical performance data and favorable demographics that are attracting the attention of lenders and investors. Fourth, loan characteristics of assisted living are consistent with current lender criteria. Typical assisted living loans are the right size, offer reasonable collateral, provide acceptable exit strategies and lenders feel that the market is reasonably predictable. Fifth, currently (1998), there is reasonable market supply-demand balance. Lenders generally feel that demand is predictable and they are cautiously optimistic that early signs of oversupply conditions are limited to selected markets in the 1998 time frame.

The days of trying to convince your lender, *"If we build it, they will surely come,"* are over. Lenders want to see a definitive plan that identifies and funds *all* costs associated with developing, financing, and marketing your assisted living community; bringing your project to a stabilized occupancy of approximately 93 percent in a reasonable time frame. At the point of stabilization your operating budget will kick in, and there should be sufficient revenues to cover ongoing operating expenses, debt service and entrepreneurial profit.

Five Key Lender Criteria

While almost every page in this book could be relevant when seeking favorable debt and/or equity financing, there are five major due diligence items that most lenders look for. They are:

1. *A realistic capital budget* – Key items of a comprehensive capital budget are discussed in Chapter 13 and Appendix A. Lenders particularly expect to see several items frequently overlooked by the applicant. One of these would include comprehensive working capital reserve planning in the initial capital budget. For example, there will be significant negative cash flow in the early months of fill-up for your new project, as most of your costs are fixed and only about 20 to 25 percent of the operating expenses are truly variable (raw food, some utilities, housekeeping, etc.). A typical 80-unit assisted living community normally takes 10 to 12 months after opening to reach break-even cash flow (after debt service). During that critical fill-up period, the project may experience cumulative negative cash flows in excess of $300,000. This must be funded by the capital budget.

Another area frequently overlooked by borrowers is the cost of early sales and marketing activities needed to initially bring your community to stabilized occupancy. These costs will probably add up to about $3,500 to $4,500 per unit for assisted living. This includes all collateral/brochures, program development, media costs and sales office overhead expenses; plus base compensation and performance incentives for the sales and marketing staff.

Obviously, the ultimate accuracy in your construction cost estimate is very critical and will undergo significant scrutiny by lenders. In 1998, hard construction costs average approximately $85 to $90 per square foot in most areas of the United States. But with current unemployment rates in the two to three percent range, padded contractor and subcontractor bids may give you a major wake-up call and financial heartburn!

From a lender's perspective, the basic strategy of capital budgeting for a new assisted living community is to identify and fund all costs associated with developing, financing, marketing and bringing the project to a stabilized occupancy of approximately 93 percent. At that point, the annual operating budget "kicks in" and there should be sufficient funds to cover both ongoing operating expenses and debt service.

2. *A solid and comprehensive financial pro forma* – A detailed pro forma outline is contained in Appendix A. Simply stated, the pro forma should be complete; detailing both initial capital needs along with how your community will perform over the long run. Lenders must always consider the distasteful prospect of foreclosure; they must envision a graceful exit strategy well before they even approve your loan. Along with other financial safeguards, they want to see a management fee of approximately five percent of revenues along with a reserve for repair and replacement of approximately $225 to $250 per unit annually. These items are considered normal operating expenses. These issues are addressed in Chapters 28 and 12, respectively.

3. *Deliver acceptable factors and ratios* – Initial capital investment ratios are covered in Chapter 13 and ongoing operating ratios are outlined in Chapter 14.

Lenders and investors are very pragmatic risk takers and most of them apply industry benchmarks; "rules of thumb" criteria that influence their decisions. One criteria is the project's debt to equity ratio. Typically, lenders want only 65 to 75 percent of the estimated total cost of your project to be represented by their loan. The rest must be covered by the owner's or investor's equity – most of it in *hard cash*. Another key factor is your project's debt service coverage ratio at stabilized occupancy of approximately 93 percent. For your start-up community, every dollar to be paid in your annual debt payment (including both principal and interest) must be covered by at least $1.25 to $1.35 in available cash, or net operating income realized at stabilized occupancy. This is the cash available after deducting all operating expenses. In addition, tax-exempt bond financing for a not-for-profit organization usually requires that an amount of cash equal to approximately one year's total debt service payments be placed in a restricted reserve account. Figure 17-1 summarizes some of these relevant factors and ratios.

4. *Have a well conceived, pragmatic strategic plan* – That's the central theme of this entire book! But pay particular attention to the first ten chapters.

5. *Assemble an impressive, experienced professional team* – Don't hire the naive "never-say-no feasibility consultant" or the inexperienced architect who wants to learn this business at your expense. Most importantly, decide how you can most cost-effectively operate your community; review Chapter 28 which deals with developing an internal resource versus a third party management contract.

Detailed market feasibility studies and comprehensive financial pro formas must be closely integrated. The market feasibility study's findings (outputs) must drive the financial pro forma inputs. In addition, the pro forma must accurately reflect

FIGURE 17-1
ASSISTED LIVING INDICES & RULES OF THUMB

	Range Covering Approx. 75% of the Market	
	Low	High
I. Lender Criteria		
1. Debt Service Coverage Ratio	1.25	1.35
2. Loan to Value	75%	85%
3. Implied Equity	25%	15%
4. Capital Reserve for Replacement (per unit)	$225	$250
II. Operations/Pricing Criteria		
1. Operating Expense Ratio	58%	63%
2. Operating Expenses PRD	$38-$42	$42-$48
3. Average FTE's per Unit		
• Assisted Living	.45	.55
• Dementia	.50	.60
4. Management Fee as a Percent of Revenues	4.5%	5.5%
5. Percent of Cash Flow Disposable Income Used for Monthly Service Fees	75%	80%
6. Assisted Living Fees as a Percent of Prevailing Private Pay Nursing Rates	75%	80%
7. Operating Margin (EBITDA)	42%	37%
III. Capital Budget Criteria		
1. Total Cost/Unit	$85,000	$125,000
2. Land Cost/Unit	7,000	12,000
3. Marketing Cost/Unit	3,500	4,500

Industry Benchmarks Can Be Both Helpful And Dangerous - Use With Caution

Moore Diversified Services, Inc.

your projected development costs, estimated operating expenses, and expected revenues. As your project progresses, any cost increases or other significant financial changes must be programmed into the pro forma. If the revised pro forma indicates that increased revenues are needed, then obviously service fees must be increased. But first the market feasibility study must be reworked to determine whether the necessary service fee changes are, in fact, acceptable in the marketplace. Refer to Appendix A for more details on market and financial feasibility.

Six Pitfalls Facing the Borrower

Securing a loan means more than just meeting your lender's requirements. The relationship must be balanced and equitable. In drafting the final loan agreement or "terms sheet", you should take care to avoid, or at least be aware of, the following six pitfalls:

1. *Excessive loan cross-collaterization* – Lenders may ask you to pledge other assets on your campus for a long period of time as additional security for your new or refinanced assisted living project. As an alternative, request that this cross-collateralization be eliminated after a relatively short period of demonstrated success with the newly-financed project.

2. *Requiring too much cash equity* – Prudent borrowing or leverage optimizes financial returns for both parties. Currently, the acceptable debt-to-equity ratios range from 65 percent debt and 35 percent equity to a higher ratio of 85/15.

3. *Excessive loan pre-payment penalties* —Many lenders charge a penalty for a fancy term called "yield maintenance" if you attempt to pay the loan off sooner than the agreed-upon term. Try to negotiate a declining scale prepayment penalty clause in which the penalty decreases or "burns off" with time, allowing you to pay off or refinance your loan before the end of the original contractual term.

4. *Personal liability* – Some loans are "nonrecourse," meaning lenders look only to the property being financed for security, while others attempt to secure other collateral, including your personal financial assets. Avoid personal liability, or pledging other unrelated assets, where possible.

5. *Loans that mature or come due before the end of the amortization period* – Some lenders will provide a loan with a ten-year term but structure payments with a 25-year amortization. This means the loan *looks like* a 25-year amortization but actually becomes due in ten years. While this can be a good arrangement, make sure you plan for the 10-year "bullet loan" balloon payment.

6. *Upfront financing costs versus fixed interest rates* – Lower permanent interest rates frequently require higher one-time upfront financing costs, frequently called "points." A point is a one-time charge that equals one percent of the total loan amount. This tradeoff consideration is usually more sensitive for loans of less than $10 million.

Other things being equal, if a loan with lower interest rates (and higher points) would cost you the same as one with higher rates but a lower upfront cost *within five years,* it's generally better to go with the lower interest rate loan.

How much will my loan cost?

The big question, of course, is: *"How much will my loan cost?"* Among the lowest interest rates are those charged for variable rate tax-exempt bonds, which currently (1998) close in the range of five to six percent. Creditworthy borrowers closing on construction loans can typically get interest rates of .5 to 1.5 percent over the prime rate. Other forms of more conventional long-term financing are likely to be 1.5 to 2.5 percent over the yield on similar term treasury bonds; or currently in the **eight** to **nine percent** range. **Caution: These rates could change while this book is being printed!**

Regardless of the type of financing you're after, remember that things always get more complex as you approach the close. But knowing ahead of time what you need and what the lender is likely to ask can make the process *much* easier.

CHAPTER 18

BENCHMARKING ASSISTED LIVING
Not Just an Industry Buzzword, a Sound Business Strategy

Management buzzwords such as "Management By Objectives" (MBO) and "Total Quality Management"(TQM) come and go. Often perceived as vague, complex, or confusing, they fade into the past before most of us understand or appreciate their true application or potential benefit to our operations.

Benchmarking is one recently popularized concept that deserves serious consideration. The concept involves a comparative analysis of industry operating factors, financial ratios, and business practices that answers the question: *"How does my community stack up in comparison to my immediate local competitors and similar operations on a regional and national basis?"* Benchmarking has seen limited application in senior housing, but the concept will eventually become a management imperative for many senior housing organizations.

A number of for-profit companies launched Initial Public Offerings (IPOs) and went public in 1996 and 1997. This influx of cash has brought with it lofty performance objectives and new levels of financial and operations disclosure responsibilities. These companies must provide shareholders, potential investors, and industry analysts with detailed reports on how well they are really running their organizations. Benchmarking and peer industry comparables can provide an early warning system, identifying impending problems if you are not staying ahead of the power curve. If you are successful, the concept provides a good way to demonstrate the sound performance of your operation.

Not-for-profits will find benchmarking useful as well. Too many not-for-profits rationalize significant operational inefficiencies as being the inevitable by-product of fulfilling their missions, when in fact they could implement change and realize *substantial improvements.* Their failure to do so is compromising their effectiveness and impairing their mission objectives. As a result, many boards of directors are asking increasingly pragmatic and penetrating questions. Bond underwriters, rating agencies, and accreditation organizations are also looking for increasingly sophisticated measures of successful performance, which could include benchmarking.

Nine Major Benefits of Benchmarking

There are nine major areas within your operations that can materially benefit from the benchmarking process:

1. Improving your financial position

2. Increasing operational efficiency

3. Developing competitive and creative pricing strategies

4. Positioning your products and services better in the competitive marketplace

5. Coming up with new ways to increase resident satisfaction

6. Introducing new quality of life initiatives

7. Enhancing the perceived value of your services

8. Sharpening public awareness or improving your image

9. Clarifying misconceptions about your facility or campus

Other specialty areas of your operation that could benefit from benchmarking include accounting, housekeeping, routine and preventive maintenance, sales and marketing, and overall capital investment planning. Perhaps the best targets for benchmarking are the things that cost you the most money; particularly those that directly affect the perceived value of your community. Staffing, for instance, represents over 60 percent of total operating costs in assisted living – and adequate staffing ratios are important to residents and their families. Benchmarking can help you set realistic staffing patterns that strike a balance between high operational efficiency and optimum resident satisfaction.

Another good prospect is your food and beverage operation. Not only does meal service account for up to one-third of an assisted living community's operating costs ($10 to $13 per resident-day), but it is usually perceived by residents and their caregivers as one of the most important services offered – and it's the one mentioned most critically in resident satisfaction surveys. For an 80-unit project, a savings of $1.50 per resident-day improves annual financial performance by approximately $44,000 and increases the value of the community by over $400,000, assuming a capitalization rate of 10.5 percent. Food service is an area in which it doesn't pay to cut corners – yet finding a way to improve efficiency could really pay off, if it can be done without hurting quality.

Four Types of Benchmarking

Many senior living campuses are currently complacent in their apparent success; suffering from myopia, tunnel vision or acceptance of the status quo. Many will have their performance challenged in the future and some will not know how to attack the problem. One approach is to use multi-level benchmarking involving a four-step process:

1. *Internal benchmarking* involves comparing similar functions within your own departments and, if relevant, your various campuses. For example, one owner/operator with a portfolio of 20 communities has a food and dietary specialist in the central office whose only job is to microscopically analyze all elements of food costs within the various communities in their portfolio. Differences in one community that appear to be out of line with established internal benchmarks are immediately attacked. He also tracks the entire industry, which brings us to the other kinds of benchmarking.

2. *Benchmarking your direct competition* involves comparing your operations to those of your competitors. This means both direct competitors – other communities offering similar living arrangements and services in your immediate area – and indirect competitors, such as a home health agency that synthesizes many care aspects of assisted living in a home-like environment. You must perform a detailed competitive analysis, evaluating the other operators' strengths, weaknesses, opportunities, and threats. A comparison matrix can collect information on competitive product features, tangible benefits, services, amenities, design characteristics, price, quality, and perceived value in the marketplace. Think like a good investigative reporter; securing facts, remaining objective, and attempting to verify your findings with more than one reliable source. You can also learn about a competitor through "mystery shopping," or posing as a potential customer, and in some states, through accessing public disclosure documents.

3. *Regional and national benchmarking* means taking a more global look at your industry. Much of this information can be obtained through private database companies, which compile information on industry trends, statistics, market factors, financial ratios, pro forma profiles, best practices policies, and staffing patterns. Active participation in leading trade associations and networking at professional seminars can also yield some surprisingly helpful benchmarking information; including the sharing of details that would be considered highly sensitive and proprietary in any other setting! Experienced consultants can also provide guidance and help based on industry data they've collected over time.

4. *Functional benchmarking* involves evaluating other types of organizations that have *functions* similar to yours. For example, you might analyze not only senior living food and beverage operations but other food operators nationally. This would involve what's called a "technology transfer," taking the best appropriate business practices and ideas from other industries and applying them to your assisted living community. Just be sure that the conclusions drawn and lessons learned from other industries really apply to your specific situation.

A wealth of benchmarking information can also be obtained from companies in other industries that have already placed a high priority on best practices. These companies include successful industry leaders, those with a diversity of operational experience and those that have experienced problems, developed corrective action plans, and successfully implemented recovery programs.

When evaluating the information you've gathered, it is important to know what to emulate and what to reject. Successful benchmarking efforts usually involve extracting relevant information based on "best practices" or selected vignettes of an organization's complete strategy.

Benchmarking can sharpen your focus and provide a bridge that links your strategic goals and objectives with desired expected outcomes. Finally, the process will force you to define, position, operate, and price your community more effectively. Some benchmarking indices are contained in Chapters 13, 14 and 19.

SECTION FOUR

Pricing & Affordability

CHAPTER 19

CREATING AN OPTIMUM PRICING STRUCTURE
Win-Win Pricing Strategies for Financial Success

Effective assisted living pricing involves striking a delicate balance between:

- Covering your total costs while delivering acceptable financial ratios

    and

- Being competitive and consumer-driven in your market area

These objectives are at opposite ends of the pricing spectrum; frequently creating significant conflicts. And serious mistakes are being made by many sponsors at both ends of the pricing trade-off spectrum.

The Owner/Operator Perspectives

Sponsors must develop sufficient operating revenues to adequately cover:

- Operating Expenses
- Debt Service
- Debt Service Coverage (Margin)
- Entrepreneurial Profit/Funding Mission Objectives

Sounds simple, but as we observed in Chapter 15, cost creep makes estimating operating expenses a moving target.

The Consumer Marketplace Perspective

The optimum assisted living pricing structure for consumers must demonstrate at least five market-driven attributes:

- Understandable
- Equitable
- Deliver High Perceived Value
- Affordable
- Seamless

The last two attributes represent the biggest pricing challenges. Many senior prospects and their families will have serious initial misconceptions regarding their affordability to live in your community. These misconceptions must be creatively addressed during the sales and marketing process. Many assisted living pricing structures are not seamless. An example is the fact that many seniors are getting two uncoordinated bills at the end of the month. One comes from the owner/operator for basic shelter services (living unit, meals, housekeeping, etc.) and another from a third party home health agency for care.

The Service-Enriched, Value-Added Concept

Regardless of your ultimate pricing structure, you're in a *premium price service delivery business*. If you were to unbundle *everything*, your resulting base pricing would probably drive most consumers into sticker shock! You stand a much better chance of marketplace success by creating value through the effective packaging of an array of *benefits* (not *features*).

PRICING MUST STRIKE A DELICATE BALANCE

Market-Driven	Project-Driven
1. Affordable	1. Covering operating expenses
2. High perceived value	2. Servicing underlying debt
3. Competitive in the marketplace	3. Provide lender safety margins
4. Provide hedge against inflation	4. Cash for other missions
5. Credible and rational	5. Entrepreneurial profit

Covering Capital Costs and Operating Expenses

Pricing is a two step process. The two steps are: 1) cover all your current basic capital costs (debt service) and operating expenses and 2) provide a hedge against future cost creep (defined in Chapter 15).

Creating An Optimum Pricing Structure

Figure 14-2 in Chapter 14 presented an assisted living operating scenario that is likely to exist in many markets in the 1998 to 2000 time frame. This operating scenario drives the development of a pricing strategy:

Cost to be Covered	Monthly Cost	Percent of Total Cost
• Operating Expenses @ $45 PRD[1]	$1,365/mo	59%
• Debt Service Payment	630	27
• Cash Flow/ Entrepreneurial Profit[2]	145 $2,140/mo	7
Vacancy Factor	160 $2,300/mo	7 100%

---

[1] Per Resident Day
[2] Also provides acceptable and required debt service coverage ratio of 1.3x.

If you think you'd like to offer a "more affordable" price in your market area, you first must face the reality of this financial summary. Where can you cut costs? And by how much?

Cost Sensitivity Vs. "Affordable Assisted Living"

Note that operating expenses represent almost 60 percent of the required monthly service fee. Further note that debt service for land and "bricks and mortar", etc. requires approximately 27 percent of the monthly service fee. That figure increases to about 33 percent when the debt service coverage factor (included in cash flow) is considered. This subtle point is often overlooked when well intended organizations chase the moving target of *"affordable assisted living"*. Operating expenses are very difficult to reduce, so most sponsors focus on capital costs. But, if you could reduce debt service payments by as much as 50 percent, you would only reduce the required monthly service fees by $300 to $350 per month or 15 percent; from $2,300 per month to $1,950 per month. This surprises and frustrates organizations when they make this sobering discovery.

The sensitivity of capital costs cuts both ways. These capital costs are relatively insensitive when trying to create *affordability* at the low end, but they become much more sensitive in avoiding *premium pricing* and *acceptable operating margins* at the other end of the pricing spectrum. Remember, at this point in the pricing strategy development, we've covered vacancy factor (seven percent), reasonable profit/positive cash flow, debt service and operating expenses for basic shelter and an array of services offering *reasonable* assistance with the Activities of Daily Living (ADLs). But as Chapter 15 points out, additional cost creep in the near future can increase operating expenses and cause significant erosion of operating margins.

Mitigating the Impacts of Cost Creep

Due to increased resident acuity levels resulting from aging in place, you will inevitability experience *operating cost creep*. Simply stated, the cost for providing assistance with ADLs will grow as all of your residents age in place. And implementing a proactive resident discharge policy will likely cause your annual turnover ratio to soar above the industry norm of approximately 40 percent.

Four Basic Pricing Structures

Several industry leaders have initially taken the position that tiered or a la carte pricing was confusing and not market responsive. But realities of cost creep has changed their minds as they faced the real threats of operating margin erosion.

The four pricing structures are:

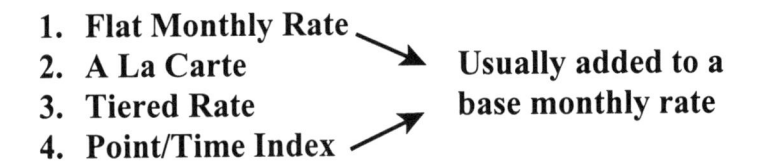

1. **Flat Monthly Rate**
2. **A La Carte** → Usually added to a
3. **Tiered Rate** base monthly rate
4. **Point/Time Index**

1. *Flat Rate* – A basic monthly service fee that varies only as a function of the living unit *type* (studio, alcove, one bedroom). There are no provisions for cost creep except for across the board increases. The main disadvantage is the perception (and the reality) that some residents are subsidizing other resident's higher care levels.

2. *A La Carte* – Charges are added based on a specific service option pricing menu; usually defined on an ADL basis. This approach attempts to bring equity to charges versus care needs of *each* resident. The system does present a challenge to effectively define, implement, track and administer.

3. *Tiered Rate* – This concept basically packages or groups the flat rate plus a la carte charges into definable pricing levels. These levels might be defined as follows for a particular assisted living community:

I – Included in Base Rate:
- Three meals daily
- Daily snacks
- Therapeutic diets
- Weekly housekeeping
- Social, cultural and educational programs
- On-call *occasional* assistance with ADLs
- Scheduled transportation
- Emergency call system
- Health and wellness assessments
- Medication *reminders*

II – Additional $300 Per Month:
- All Level I services
- *Regular* assistance with ADLs
- Assistance with self-managed incontinence
- *Supervision* of medication
- Occasional reality orientation
- Occasional escort service to meals/activities

III – Additional $300 Per Month (from Level II):
- All Level I and II services
- *Frequent* assistance with ADLs
- Assistance with manageable incontinence
- Daily housekeeping
- Medication *administration*
- Escort service to meals/community activities
- Frequent reality orientation

IV, V – There are typically Levels IV and V for residents with additional, more intensive special care needs. These levels are determined for each resident via a professional assessment. Each incremental level of care is an additional $300 per month.

4. *Point/Time Increment Index* – The concept involves a classical "time and motion study" originally developed for the manufacturing industry. A base level of services is provided to each resident. Services and assistance with ADLs above that level are typically delivered and charged in 15 minute increments. An example would be approximately $8.00 for every 15-minute increment per day multiplied by 30 days; resulting in an add-on monthly charge of $240.

Cost creep is here to stay and these costs must be covered by appropriate increases in revenues. This issue has the potential for being a significant industry problem; giving short sighted sponsors an ear drum shattering wake-up call!

Final Check and Balance on Pricing

Two additional guidelines can provide a final check and balance on your overall pricing effectiveness:

- *Assisted Living Pricing vs. Prevailing Nursing Rates* – Assisted living pricing should be approximately 70 to 80 percent of prevailing semi-private nursing rates in your market area. For example, when nursing bed rates are $100/day or $3,000/month, assisted living monthly service fees should average not more than $2,100 to $2,400. You can use the pricing offset to your advantage in sales and marketing; as you honestly and objectively compare your community's capabilities with the nursing alternatives.

- *Consumer Affordability Thresholds* – Seniors can typically spend approximately 75 to 80 percent of their disposable after-tax income for assisted living monthly service fees. This means that their annual after-tax, disposable income must range from approximately $39,000 to $43,000 in order to pay monthly service fees of $2,100 to $2,300 used in the example in Chapter 14. These qualifying incomes may seem shockingly high – until you review the realities of *after-tax* senior incomes covered later in this chapter.

The ultimate pricing challenge that spans the life of your community is to provide the services residents need while covering costs and developing an effective counter-attack for inevitable assisted living cost creep.

Consumer affordability thresholds are sometimes surprisingly high when we take a pragmatic approach to determining a senior's qualifying income. Figure 19-1 shows required qualifying income thresholds when applying the previously mentioned 80 percent assisted living spending criteria coupled with appropriate consideration given to *after-tax* incomes. The figure shows that much of today's private pay market rate assisted living pricing typically requires a minimum qualifying annual pre-tax income of almost $40,000. Nationally about 19.8 percent of all age 75+ seniors meet that criteria.

Other Sources of Income

This situation is alleviated somewhat by three real world factors that exist, but are very difficult to quantify:

- *Liquidated home equity* – Senior's net home equity upon sale typically yields between $100,000 to $150,000 after selling costs. These funds conservatively invested at five percent can result in an increased income of $5,000 per year which can be used to supplement the previously mentioned $40,000 qualifying income threshold.

- *Financial support by family* – There is limited, but growing, anecdotal evidence of this trend. Some industry experts feel that this support could have a significant impact on assisted living affordability in the future.

FIGURE 19-1

MINIMUM QUALIFYING CASH FLOW INCOME REQUIREMENTS FOR A TYPICAL ASSISTED LIVING COMMUNITY

Based on Estimated 1999 Monthly Service Fees

Assisted Living Unit Type	Monthly Fee	Annualized Monthly Fee[1]	Total Annual Cash Flow Requirement After Tax[2]	Required Annual Cash Flow Before Tax[3]
Assisted Living Units:				
• Studio/Alcove	$2,100 - $2,300	$25,200 - $27,600	$31,500 - $34,500	$39,375 - $43,125
• One Bedroom	$2,400 - $2,700	$28,800 - $32,400	$36,000 - $40,500	$45,000 - $50,625

Moore Diversified Services, Inc.

---

[1] Rates based on single occupancy in 1999 dollars.
[2] Assumed 80% of the Seniors' cash flow income can be allocated for assisted living fees.
[3] Assumes an average tax rate of 20%.

- ***Spend-down of existing assets*** – Like nursing home patients, some assisted living residents may be using both their available *income* and some *principal* to pay for assisted living.

Note that the home equity impact – properly computed – can be used when evaluating market feasibility. Family financial support and spend down should not be formally used; but can be considered a "forecasting safety margin."

We tend to take seniors private pay affordability for granted. In fact, as Figure 19-2 shows, income qualified seniors must have a significant savings portfolio in order to afford your community. For example, in order to have a gross, pre-tax income of $40,000, a typical widow must have her Social Security income and over $600,000 earning five percent.

Semi-Private Pricing

Shared occupancy of unrelated individuals is being offered on a limited basis to make private pay assisted living more affordable. When developing semi-private pricing for your assisted living units, you must segment *real estate* costs (shared) from *services and care* expenses; costs that are incurred by *both* occupants. Typically semi-private pricing comes in at approximately 65 percent of the private occupancy rate for the same unit. Stated another way; you should usually yield about 1.4 times the private occupancy rate for shared accommodations. The following example shows these relationships:

FIGURE 19-2

INCOME QUALIFIED SENIORS MUST HAVE AN EXTENSIVE SAVINGS PORTFOLIO

	Gross Pre-Tax Income [1]		
	$30,000	$40,000	$50,000
Widow's Social Security Benefit at $7,700/year • $642 / month	($ 7,700)	($ 7,700)	($ 7,700)
Net Income Needed From Other Sources	$22,300	$32,300	$42,300
Required Savings Portfolio Earnings [2]	Required Savings Portfolio		
• @ 5%	$446,000	$646,000	$846,000
• @ 7%	318,570	461,425	604,285
• @ 9%	247,775	358,890	470,000

Moore Diversified Services, Inc.

[1] Seniors typically have an <u>average</u> tax bracket of approximately 20%. These examples are <u>net</u> after-tax disposable income of $24,000, $32,000 and $40,000 respectively. ($30,000 with 20% tax = $24,000 net.)

[2] Reflects a combination of conventional savings portfolio and pension proceeds (if applicable). Savings portfolio might be increased by an average of $100,000 to $150,000 for a current homeowner selling a home and moving into senior housing.

Private Pay Rates:
- Single/Private Occupancy $2,200/month
- Semi-Private/Shared Occupancy   1,500/month
- Semi-Private as a Percent of Private   68%
- Total Revenue Yield   3,000/month

<u>Caution:</u> Shared occupancy is still relatively rare in new, market rate, private pay assisted living. While the concept does attempt to address the complex affordability issue, anecdotal evidence of broad based marketplace acceptance is still quite limited.

Total Health Care Pricing Spectrum

Figure 19-3 depicts the typical prevailing health care costs (1998 dollars) for a wide spectrum of living arrangements. While each setting satisfies a unique menu of needs, assisted living has the most flexibility to maneuver within the health care service delivery spectrum. When it is an appropriate setting, assisted living is clearly one of the most cost-effective, market responsive options for seniors and their families.

Assisted living could well be the cost-effective missing link between existing entitlements at one end of the continuum (acute, subacute, skilled nursing) and certain aspects of relatively inefficient and costly home care at the other end.

Creating An Optimum Pricing Structure 186

Home care *is* an excellent delivery system, but when the realities of legitimate Medicare cost reduction are addressed, there will be the realization that one hour of care delivered in the home costs approximately the same as a 24-hour day in an assisted living setting. And the current home care entitlement does not include the other significant costs of basic shelter and meals.

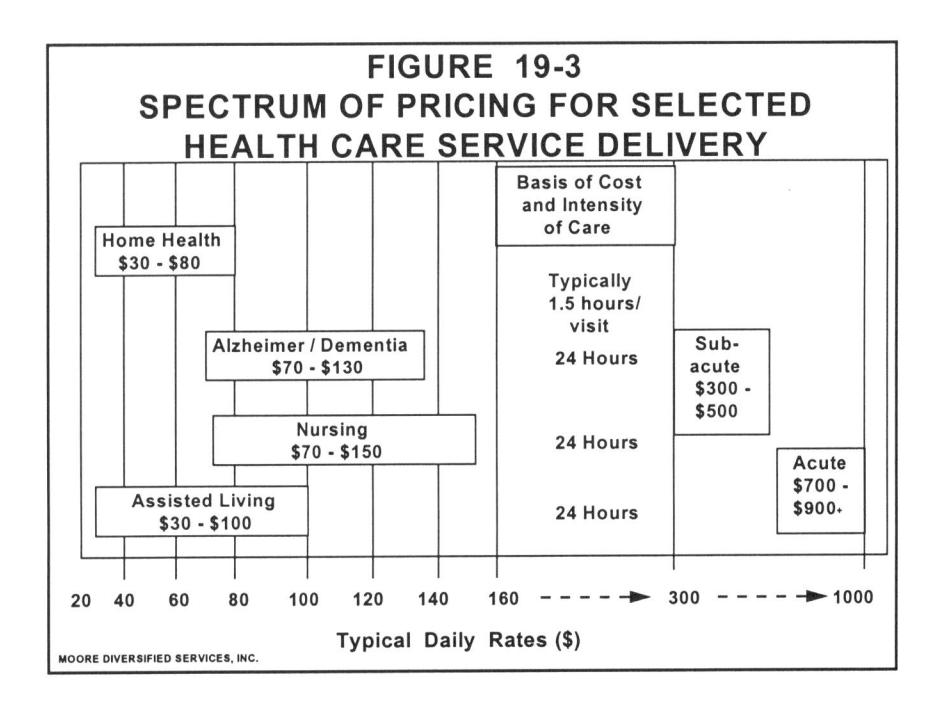

FIGURE 19-3
SPECTRUM OF PRICING FOR SELECTED HEALTH CARE SERVICE DELIVERY

Service	Daily Rate	Basis of Cost and Intensity of Care
Home Health	$30 - $80	Typically 1.5 hours/visit
Alzheimer / Dementia	$70 - $130	24 Hours
Nursing	$70 - $150	24 Hours
Assisted Living	$30 - $100	24 Hours
Sub-acute	$300 - $500	
Acute	$700 - $900+	

Typical Daily Rates ($): 20, 40, 60, 80, 100, 120, 140, 160 ----> 300 ----> 1000

MOORE DIVERSIFIED SERVICES, INC.

Eventually someone will ask the defining question, *"Is it more efficient to deliver care to 80 seniors randomly distributed throughout a 400 square mile county or on a four acre assisted living campus?"*

CHAPTER 20

MYTHS & REALITIES OF SERVING THE GAP INCOME GROUP
Can We Deliver Affordable Assisted Living?

The greatest unmet need in senior housing today is the obvious lack of services and living options aimed at serving seniors with incomes that are moderate but not low enough to qualify for subsidies or government entitlements. Labeled the "Gap Income Group," this sector of the senior market has annual incomes between $12,000 and $25,000. In 2002, these seniors will represent about 28 percent of all the households over age 75 in the United States.

Seniors with reported incomes under $12,000 per year typically qualify for various entitlement programs, such as the HUD 202 and Section 8 seniors housing initiatives. Many seniors with incomes in excess of $25,000 qualify for what has been termed "market rate" assisted living. That means they can afford to pay prevailing rates starting at the lower end of today's senior housing private pay pricing spectrum.

Gap Group Economic Squeeze

The Gap Group is therefore caught in a crack between two other economic classes of seniors – the very low income group who qualify for significant entitlements and the income qualified market rate group who can afford to private pay for a wide variety of senior living options. Trapped between these two economic classes, the Gap Group is significantly underserved and represents *very* large numbers.

Nationally, approximately 30 percent of the age 75+ households report annual incomes of $12,000 or less. The "market rate" group reporting incomes of $25,000 or more represents 42 percent. That leaves 28 percent or approximately 3.1 million aged 75+ households that are largely underserved. Figure 20-1 depicts this economic squeeze. Note these are 2002 demographic projections. The Gap Group represents a total national potential of over 21,000 projects; assuming an average senior housing project size of 150 units and a modest 25 percent

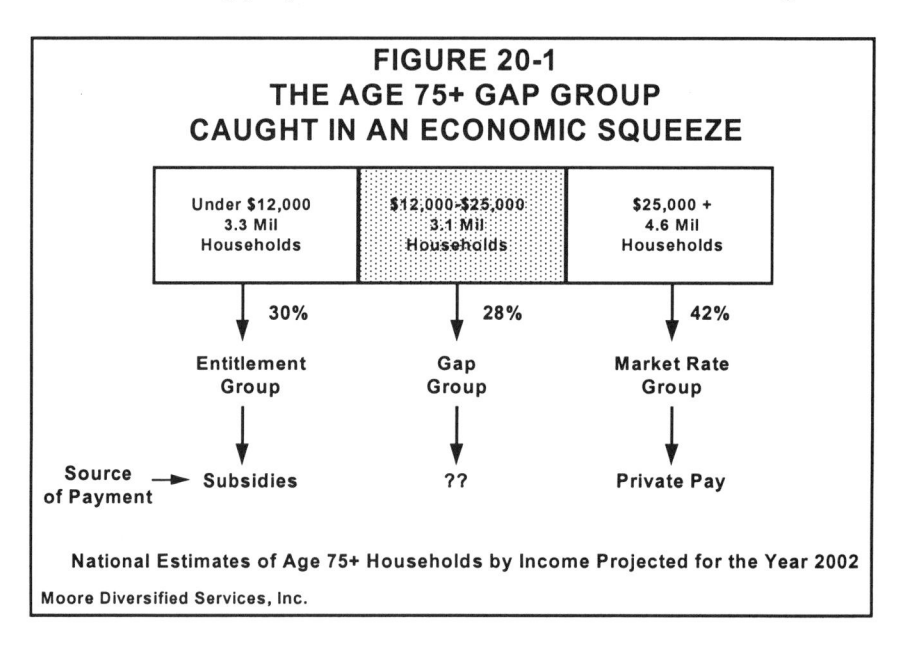

FIGURE 20-1
THE AGE 75+ GAP GROUP
CAUGHT IN AN ECONOMIC SQUEEZE

Under $12,000 3.3 Mil Households	$12,000-$25,000 3.1 Mil Households	$25,000 + 4.6 Mil Households
30%	28%	42%
Entitlement Group	Gap Group	Market Rate Group
Subsidies	??	Private Pay

Source of Payment

National Estimates of Age 75+ Households by Income Projected for the Year 2002
Moore Diversified Services, Inc.

Myths & Realities of Serving the Gap Income Group 189

total market share for senior housing. Figure 20-2 depicts gap group potential in typical major metropolitan areas; while Figure 20-3 shows typical potential in a project's Primary Market Area.

FIGURE 20-2

**THE GAP INCOME GROUP
BY THE NUMBERS (Age 75+)
(Number of Households)**

	Under $12,000 No.	%	$12,000 - $25,000 No.	%	$25,000 - $40,000 No.	%	$40,000 + No.	%
• Total U.S.	3,301,984	30%	3,085,233	28%	1,813,929	17%	2,733,708	25%
• Atlanta	31,122	32	24,086	25	14,979	16	26,504	27
• Boston	43,962	31	41,584	29	22,170	15	35,916	25
• Dallas	24,804	30	19,023	23	12,816	16	26,249	31
• Denver	16,119	26	15,134	25	10,418	17	19,980	32
• Phoenix	30,765	25	31,894	26	23,510	19	37,005	30

Figures for typical metropolitan areas in the year 2002

Source: Claritas

FIGURE 20-3

AFFORDABILITY OF THE GAP GROUP
Typical Primary Market Area

Gross Pre-tax Income	Ability to Pay/ Affordable Service Fee[1] Independent Living	Assisted Living	Number of Households
$12,000-$14,999	$520-$ 650	$ 640-$ 800	2,800
15,000- 19,999	650- 870	800- 1,070	3,200
20,000- 24,999	870- 1,080	1,070- 1,330	3,400

Actual affordability levels of the age 75+ *gap group* fall well below typical senior living private pay pricing requirements.

[1]Assumes a 20% average tax bracket and seniors service fee spending criteria of 65% and 80% of disposable income after-tax for independent living and assisted living, respectively.

Moore Diversified Services, Inc.

Two Major Economic Barriers

There are two primary economic barriers to hurdle when serving the Gap Income Group:

- *Funding initial capital costs through debt service*
- *Covering ongoing operating expenses*

It is amazing how far some well-meaning organizations go in their planning process before actually trying to come to grips with these fundamental economic barriers.

Impact of Capital Costs

Some organizations with existing or donated land feel they are well on the way to realizing an affordable, low income assisted living community. But land costs, depending upon geographical location, typically represent only 5 to 10 percent of the total project's capital costs, thus having only a nominal impact on required monthly service fees.

For example, let's assume you can create an *affordable* project with a very modest total turn-key cost per unit of $65,000; beating the typical capital costs outlined in Chapter 13. The $65,000 figure assumes the total all-in project cost is divided by the number of units. This will require a monthly debt service per unit of approximately $369; assuming a *very low* 5.5 percent cost of capital and perhaps the donated land.

Making required adjustments for five percent vacancy and a debt service coverage ratio (safety margin) of 1.25 increases the debt service per *occupied* unit to approximately $485 per month. If the total cost per unit was $75,000 (still very low by current industry standards), the required debt service per occupied unit is $555 per month – using these best case numbers. Debt service to cover capital costs typically represents only 27 to 33 percent of the total required monthly service fee.

Ongoing Operating Costs

In terms of operating costs, owner/operators have found it extremely difficult to offer basic, service-enriched congregate independent living for a cost per resident-day under $25, or $760 per month. Add these operating expenses to the previously discussed debt service cost of $485 per month and it's easy to see a cost floor for *very basic independent living services* of approximately $1,245 per month.

Assisted living operating costs could be $40 a day or approximately $1,215 per month. Adding the debt service payment of $485 per month and the total monthly service fee is now $1,700. Simply stated, serving the Gap Group is frequently limited by the inability to effectively cover ongoing operating expenses, *even when* land and bricks and mortar costs are reduced significantly. Figure 20-4 provides a summary of Gap Group cost-affordability hurdles.

Despite these obstacles, progressive sponsors across the country are hard at work attempting to break down these formidable economic barriers. They are fighting the battle on five fronts: 1) reduced initial capital costs, 2) creative, lower cost financing, 3) revenue enhancements from other sources, 4) permanent reduction in operating costs and 5) subsidies.

Reducing Capital Costs

Capital costs are being reduced through donations of land and sometimes through cash and in-kind contributions involving

Myths & Realities of Serving the Gap Income Group 193

the reduction of costs for the facility. Aggressive "value engineering" and the use of donated in-kind professional services are also typical initial capital cost reduction strategies.

FIGURE 20-4

CRACKING THE AFFORDABILITY NUT

	Total (All-In) Cost/Unit - Best Case		
	$65,000	**$75,000**	**$85,000**
• Debt Service (@ 5.5%, 30 yrs) Per Occupied Unit [1,2]	$388/mo	$445/mo	$505/mo
• Debt Service Coverage Factor@1.25x	97	110	125
Subtotal	$485/mo	$555/mo	$630/mo
• Operating Expenses @ $40 PRD[3]	$1,215	$1,215	$1,215
Minimum Req'd MSF[4]	$1,700/mo	$1,770/mo	$1,845/mo

[1] Assumes 95% occupancy
[2] Optimum debt service; 5.5%, 30 years, 100% financing
[3] PRD = Per Resident Day
[4] MSF = Monthly Service Fee (Best Case)

Moore Diversified Services, Inc.

Creative Financing

Low interest loans and tax credit incentive programs help; but remember the big nut to crack rests in the area of operating expenses. Debt service represents only about 27 to 33 percent of the monthly service fee requirement.

Permanent Reduction in Operating Costs

Delivering affordable assisted living involves the long-run challenges of attempting to reduce operating expenses which are incurred by the community in perpetuity. Reducing capital costs and deploying creative financing must be combined with lowering day-to-day operating expenses; *without* major compromises in services provided. In terms of operating cost reduction, progressive organizations have made substantial progress in lowering recurring operating expenses through property tax abatement or elimination, the selected use of volunteerism, utilizing the universal worker concept and the advantages of ongoing in-kind service donations.

Others have considered the careful unbundling of selected services. Unbundling is a tempting strategy that does reduce costs, but it can also create other major problems for the seniors being served. Large numbers of low-income seniors have escalating needs for assistance with the activities of daily living and no funds to pay for additional help. This situation will only intensify as time goes on, so it is not practical to provide affordable senior housing in the long run by merely striping away services to reduce costs.

Five Revenue Enhancement Strategies

There are five primary revenue enhancement strategies that can be pursued:

1. *Double Occupancy of Unrelated Individuals* – While normally a dangerous assumption for market rate senior housing, double occupancy is working at the lower end of the economic spectrum in private pay assisted living. A moderately priced assisted living unit charging market rates of $1,900 to $2,100 per month for single occupancy, can typically offer that same unit for $1,200 to $1,400 per month for double occupancy. While not the optimum living arrangement for most seniors, this option is being explored by more and more communities as a practical alternative to serve the growing needs of those seniors with modest incomes. But note, this is a *very* tricky business strategy. See Chapter 19 for more details.

2. *Blending the Rent Roll* – The blended rate approach typically involves lowering the rates on 20 to 30 percent of the units in an assisted living community while modestly increasing the rates of the remaining 70 to 80 percent of the living units. In this manner, the rent roll retains a *revenue neutral* status while at least 20 to 30 percent of the units, in fact, serve the Gap Group. The downside to this scenario is the sobering fact that market rate residents are partially subsidizing members of the Gap Group; the sponsor is shifting the burden to those seniors who can afford to pay more. This also requires the establishment of a pragmatic means testing screening process to determine which residents are legitimately qualified for the below market rate unit.

3. *Endowments for Reducing the Monthly Service Fee* – Endowments or buying down the rates, is a concept whose time may have come, especially for not-for-profits. In order to reduce the monthly service fee for a Gap Income Group senior by $500 per month, an endowment of approximately $86,000 earning an average seven percent annual after-tax return is required. The endowments would obviously have to be increased if the interest income was taxable. Reducing the rate by $750 per month would require a tax-free interest earning endowment of approximately $128,600. "Buying down" the rate by $750 per month for 25 units would require a tax-free, interest earning endowment of $3.2 million. Figure 20-5 provides some typical endowment scenarios.

While these numbers may seem significant, many communities are gradually building endowments in order to better serve the Gap Income Group seniors in the future. Much of this endowment money frequently comes from existing affluent residents of the community who either provide endowment funds while still living or as part of their estate.

A variation of this strategy is to establish a "Family Member Matching Challenge" as in this example: A not-for-profit sponsor tells a family they can offer their loved one a "scholarship" of $300 per month *if* the family can provide an equivalent amount. This stretches available endowment funds and provides motivation and incentives for family financial participation.

FIGURE 20-5
BUYING DOWN THE MONTHLY SERVICE FEE

Desired Reduction in MSF[1]	Per Unit Endowment Required At Various After-Tax Savings Rates		Total Endowment Required To Cover 25 Assisted Living Units
	7%	5%	
• $ 500/mo	$ 86,000	$120,000	$2.2 mil - $3.0 mil
• $ 750	129,000	180,000	3.2 - 4.5
• $ 1,000	170,000	240,000	4.3 - 6.0

[1]MSF = Monthly Service Fee

Moore Diversified Services, Inc.

4. *Spend-down of Liquidated Home Equity* – A modest-income senior selling a home with net sale proceeds of $75,000 can place the proceeds in a portfolio earning approximately five percent after taxes, which would come to $3,750 a year. This would lower the senior's qualifying income threshold for a community requiring a threshold of $30,000 down to $26,250. In a typical primary market area, this would increase the number of qualified 75+ households by approximately five percent.

A senior could also spend-down the newly acquired home equity at a pace that (statistically) does not exceed their expected life (see Chapter 21 for a more complete discussion).

5. *Cash Flow from Other Projects* – A sponsor may tap into one of a growing number of private-pay business opportunities on their campuses to help underwrite another part of the community's overall mission. For example, an effectively designed and properly operated 80-unit assisted living facility on a retirement community campus, with independent units and access to skilled nursing care, can yield approximately $3,000 per unit of annual cash flow. This adds up to a gross potential of $240,000 in annual residual cash, some or all of which can then be dedicated to serving economically disadvantaged seniors.

Life is Full of Trade-Offs

There is one market dynamic that can assist greatly in developing Gap Income Group strategies. A consumer's level of discretion, selectivity and sensitivity regarding the acceptance of available options decreases as a function of decreasing income. Simply stated, consumers of varying economic status must accept tradeoffs based on their relative affordability. This in no way makes low-to-moderate income seniors second class citizens. Rather, it is the economic reality of the marketplace that these seniors can be effectively served with selected tradeoffs that might not otherwise be acceptable to higher income seniors who can afford a more upscale community.

In the future, not-for-profit communities do not have to give up their mission, but they have to rethink the way their funds are allocated. And that means working harder and smarter to deploy nontraditional strategies and initiatives.

Figure 20-6 presents the big picture of assisted living affordability.

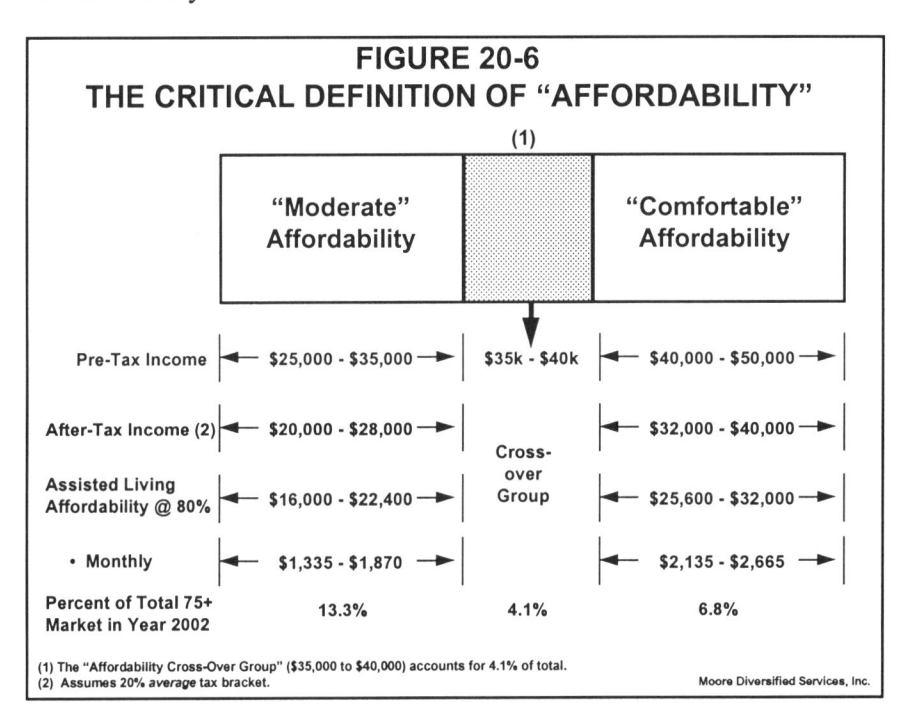

FIGURE 20-6
THE CRITICAL DEFINITION OF "AFFORDABILITY"

	"Moderate" Affordability	(1) Cross-over Group	"Comfortable" Affordability
Pre-Tax Income	$25,000 - $35,000	$35k - $40k	$40,000 - $50,000
After-Tax Income (2)	$20,000 - $28,000		$32,000 - $40,000
Assisted Living Affordability @ 80%	$16,000 - $22,400		$25,600 - $32,000
• Monthly	$1,335 - $1,870		$2,135 - $2,665
Percent of Total 75+ Market in Year 2002	13.3%	4.1%	6.8%

(1) The "Affordability Cross-Over Group" ($35,000 to $40,000) accounts for 4.1% of total.
(2) Assumes 20% average tax bracket.

Moore Diversified Services, Inc.

When the impacts of aging-in-place intensify and reach crisis levels, the Gap Income Group will be recognized as a huge economic and social challenge. Breaking down the existing economic barriers with creative solutions that will stand the test of time are difficult to achieve but, if accomplished, will result in one of the biggest breakthroughs in effectively serving seniors in the new millennium.

CHAPTER 21

FINDING NEW WAYS TO PAY

Creative Uses of Home Equity Can Lower the Qualifying Income Bar and Increase Assisted Living Affordability

Caution – The concepts outlined in this chapter have not been universally accepted by either the industry or the consumer marketplace. But we must find new approaches to solving old problems by sometimes "stepping outside the box." Use the ideas and concepts herein with *extreme caution* – perhaps initially on a limited, experimental basis.

The great majority of the assisted living communities developed in the U.S. over the last ten years are private-pay. Most residents must rely on their Social Security and interest earned on their lifetime savings – after-tax annual incomes – to pay the bills. Some may get help from their adult children or other relatives. But other methods of payment must be found if the industry is to continue and sustain its rapid growth rate and serve more than the 30 to 35 percent of age 80+ seniors who, currently, can realistically afford to private pay for assisted living.

In order to have enough money to pay for other discretionary purchases, a senior should spend no more than 80 percent of their *after-tax income* on assisted living's monthly service fee.

At today's rates that rules out approximately 65 to 70 percent of seniors aged 80 and over. But many of those same seniors could afford assisted living if the industry were to follow the lead of private pay nursing homes or CCRCs; introducing options like properly planned spend-down or partially refundable entry fees.

The Case for Mrs. Barker

Consider Mrs. Barker, an 83-year-old widow living alone in a home she's owned for 30 years. A recent heart attack and osteoporosis have taken their toll and left her frail, occasionally forgetful, and in need of assistance with the activities of daily living. She has a modest after-tax income of $22,500 a year, or $1,875 a month. Figure 21-1 summarizes Mrs. Barker's situation.

After considerable homework and soul-searching, her son Roy concludes that *The Gardens at Westridge* assisted living community is the most suitable place for her – and she reluctantly agrees. But 80 percent of her after-tax income is only $1,500 per month; The Gardens charges $2,500 per month for basic services and a reasonable array of assistance with the activities of daily living.

Roy and his mother look at other options. She could move in with him and his wife, find a more modest rest home (perhaps with semi-private accommodations) or stay in her current home (at relatively high risk) accessing intermittent home health services. Ultimately, she might go to a nursing home and spend down the assets she and her husband had accumulated over a

Finding New Ways to Pay 202

lifetime. And then she would become a Medicaid recipient. All of these options strike Roy and his mother as pretty bleak. Figure 21-2 summarizes the situation.

FIGURE 21-1
MRS. BARKERS' CURRENT SITUATION

- 83-Year-Old Widow:
  - "Statistical" Life Expectancy: 6 Years
- Lives Alone in Her Home of 30 Years:
  - Current Home Value: $110,000
  - Mortgage paid off
- Current Health Condition:
  - Recent Heart Attack & Advancing Osteoporosis
  - Somewhat Forgetful & Frail
  - Needs Assistance With Approximately 3 ADLs
  - Considering Moving to an Assisted Living Community
- Current <u>After-Tax</u> Income of $1,875/Month, or $22,500/Year:
  - Social Security ($900/Month)
  - Savings Portfolio of $235,000 (earns $975/mo. at 5% after-tax savings)
- Can Afford to Spend 80% of Her After-Tax Income for Assisted Living:
  - $22,500 x .80 = $18,000/Year, or $1,500/Month

Moore Diversified Services, Inc.

The Plan

Roy runs some numbers and comes up with a plan. His analysis assumes that his mother's Social Security income of $900 a month will increase at only two percent per year, the after-tax interest rate on her existing savings portfolio of approximately $235,000 will earn five percent, and the required $2,500 per month assisted living service fee in 1998 will likely increase at four percent a year.

Finding New Ways to Pay

FIGURE 21-2

**MRS. BARKER AND HER SON LIKE
"THE GARDENS AT WESTRIDGE"**

The Gardens at Westridge	Mrs. Barker's Current Situation
• 1998 Monthly Service Fee (MSF): $2,500/Month[1]	• A $1,000/Month affordability shortfall
• Annual MSF Escalation: 4%	• Only her Social Security has a modest COLA[2] of approximately 2%/Year

Mrs. Barker's Options Appear Limited

1. Do nothing
2. Access home health on a sporadic basis
3. Try to find lower quality, semi-private Assisted Living accommodations

or . . .

GET CREATIVE!

---

[1]With reasonable allowance for assistance with Activities of Daily Living (ADLs).
[2]COLA = Cost of Living Adjustment
Moore Diversified Services, Inc.

Then he makes the most critical assumption; his mother's reasonable life expectancy. Based on life expectancy tables for a female age 83 and her doctor's assessment of her current health, Roy chooses a life expectancy of six years, knowing obviously that his mother could either die sooner or outlive her statistical life expectancy. He then pulls out his laptop and develops a computer model that answers the question: *"What additional principal assets, put to work as a declining balance fund earning five percent over eight years, could cover the gap between the required $2,500 assisted living monthly service fee and the $1,500 that represents 80 percent of his mother's after-tax income?"*

Roy further realizes that he must factor in future inflation. He finds that the answer is approximately $100,000. Fortunately, Mrs. Barker owns her home free and clear and its market value is approximately $110,000, so upon sale, she would net approximately $100,000 after selling costs (see Figure 21-3). Roy rationalizes that his mother's $235,000 savings portfolio can still serve as her final estate or act as a financial buffer, while the spend-down of her *new asset* – liquidated home equity – can help pay for an appropriate level of care, independence, dignity and quality of life in her final years.

What Have The Barkers Accomplished?

The following summarizes Mrs. Barker's future prospects:

1. Mrs. Barker optimizes her remaining years – with dignity and optimum independence.

Finding New Ways to Pay

FIGURE 21-3
MRS. BARKER AND HER SON GET CREATIVE

1. The Plan: (in round numbers)
   - Sell Home $110,000
     - Selling Costs @ 9%   (10,000)
   - Net Sales Proceeds $100,000

2. Set-Up a "Declining Balance Fund" to Cover the Gap Between:
   - 80% of Her Current After-Tax Income ($1,500/Month)

   And . . .
   - The 1998 Assisted Living MSF of $2,500

   (This Fund covers the 1998 Gap of $1,000/month)

3. Some Variables to Consider:
   - Fund Earnings: 5% (After-Tax)
   - MSF Annual Increase: 4%

The $100,000 fund will spend down in approximately 8 years (a $150,000 fund will spend down in approximately 11 years).

Moore Diversified Services, Inc.

---

2. Her son lives essentially guilt-free and with reasonable peace of mind.

3. Mrs. Barker's required qualifying income threshold for market rate assisted living has been lowered from $44,000 to $22,500 annually.

4. A largely benign asset (her home equity) is put to work creatively and cost-effectively.

And . . .

Mrs. Barker still retains her original $230,000 savings portfolio for her estate.

If everyone employed this method of a declining balance fund, the market for assisted living would increase by approximately 2.3 million households nationally, and by approximately 23,000 households in a major metro area like Boston. Figure 21-4 depicts Mrs. Barker's spend-down profile.

Increased Savings Portfolio – Another Option

Instead of spending down her $100,000, Mrs. Barker could add it to her savings portfolio. Assuming it earned five percent interest, it would produce an after-tax income of approximately $5,000 a year, or $417 a month. Added to her $1,500 budget, this additional income would allow her to spend approximately $1,917 per month for The Gardens at Westridge. Obviously, this would still leave her short by $583 per month.

Declining Balance Entry Fee Option

Another possibility would be to put her net home equity to work as a CCRC-style declining balance entry fee, which would be partially refundable upon death or move-out. This upfront fee assisted living pricing model is rare in the U.S., but very common in Australia. In exchange for the refundable portion of this entry fee, which amounts to an interest-free loan, the

Finding New Ways to Pay 207

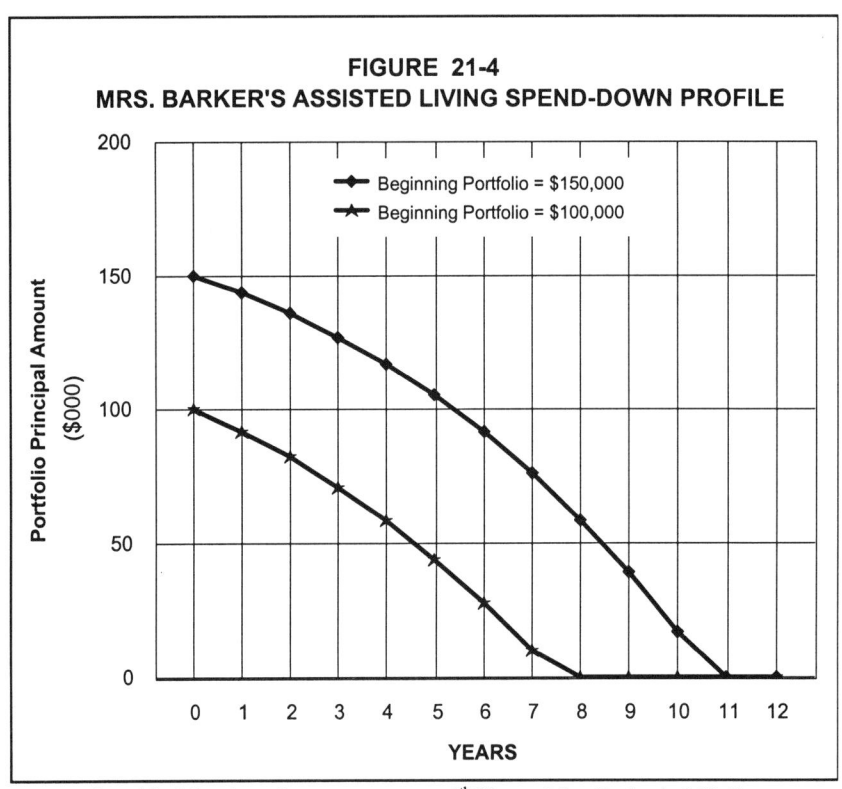

FIGURE 21-4
MRS. BARKER'S ASSISTED LIVING SPEND-DOWN PROFILE

[Graph: Portfolio Principal Amount ($000) vs Years (0-12). Two curves shown: Beginning Portfolio = $150,000 and Beginning Portfolio = $100,000, both declining toward zero.]

Moore Diversified Services, Inc.   6th Year = Mrs. Barker's Life Expectancy

owner/operator could give Mrs. Barker a financial break, deducting the difference between her available income and the monthly service fee from her entry fee, or perhaps even counting her money as "earning" annual interest at his cost of capital.

This option might appeal to potential residents more than the notion of spending down a savings account, as the owner/operator would take on the risk that the resident might outlive her equity. In essence, the community would agree to keep paying the difference between her income and her monthly fee even if the resident spent down her entire entry fee. In Mrs. Barker's case, that would take about eight years.

Such an arrangement would probably be subject to certain state regulations and accounting principles that would require some level of restricted reserve funds. It might encounter some psychological resistance as well. The conventional thinking is that entry fees are not appropriate in assisted living because the average length of stay is only about two-and-a-half years. And adult children tend to be very concerned about liquidity and estate preservation.

Fully Refundable Entry Fee Option

Another innovative, but largely untested, pricing concept in assisted living is aimed at putting the liquidated net home equity asset to work as a fully refundable entry fee; or an interest-free loan to the sponsor owner/operator. While it is true that entry fees in assisted living are relatively rare, it does offer the possibility of yet another approach to addressing affordability. With the refundable entry fee approach, the owner/operator might give Mrs. Barker credit in the form of a reduced monthly service fee for *their* cost of capital (approximately eight percent). In this case, the $100,000 net home equity proceeds would "earn" eight percent as an interest free loan, resulting in an $8,000 per year or $667 per month reduction in the monthly service fees. The reason that this concept would be interest-free is that it is treated as an entry fee and would be within the special tax exemption for seniors. There would likely be state regulations and accounting principles that would require some level of restricted reserve funds.

This approach does not involve spend-down of the principle, but still falls short of bridging the $1,000/month gap. However, it might apply in a number of situations, allowing the senior to "earn" eight percent versus five percent on the liquidated home equity and would be fully refundable upon death or move-out. This concept is summarized in Figure 21-5.

Approach Assisted Living Spend-Down with Caution

The concept of spend-down in assisted living needs cautious and extensive market testing. The prudent approach would be to implement spend-down of the liquidated home equity but not a senior's existing savings portfolio. Significant safety margins should be deployed. Consider offering partially refundable entry fees as a pricing *alternative,* but don't count on it being your sole pricing strategy. These concepts are not without challenges, but their potential to expand the market for assisted living is significant.

FIGURE 21-5
USING REFUNDABLE ENTRY FEES IN ASSISTED LIVING

	Conventional Consumer Savings Approach	Using Proceeds As a 100% Refundable Entry Fee
I. Mrs. Barker sells $110,000 home and realizes net equity after 9% selling costs	$100,000	$100,000
II. Investment return:		
• Pre-tax	6%	8%
• After-tax	5%	8% (Allowable Interest fee loan)[1]
III. Effective increase in after-tax income:		
• Annual	$5,000	$8,000
• Monthly	417 ↓	667 ↓
IV. Increase in Financial Benefit	$3,000/year or $250/Month A 60% benefit	

This approach must be approached with caution – but would materially increase assisted living affordability

---

[1] With owner/operator offering the senior financial credit at their cost of capital (approximately 8%).

Moore Diversified Services, Inc.

Final Caution

To a casual observer, the Barker's story might seem an ideal solution to a family and industry dilemma. But experienced assisted living professionals know it's not that simple. Spend-down is universally accepted and works in nursing homes because the government can be counted on to step in with Medicaid coverage once a resident becomes impoverished, but this is not usually the case in assisted living. Medicaid waivers for assisted living are limited in number, and most owner/operators consider Medicaid reimbursement rates to be too low. Spending down too quickly could leave a senior destitute in the final stages of life. What's more, improper use of spend-down can misrepresent a project's true market feasibility and long-run viability.

SECTION FIVE

Special Market Niches and "Carve-Outs"

CHAPTER 22

SPECIAL CARE ALZHEIMER'S/ DEMENTIA
*A "Carve-Out" Market Niche
Whose Time Has Come*

The impacts of Alzheimer's and other related dementia is devastating for both the victims and their caregivers. It has been labeled by the National Alzheimer's Association as "the disease of the century." Most victims are over age 65, with a surprisingly concentrated number of those afflicted being in their late '70s and early '80s. Because of this, the disease is obviously becoming an integral part of the aging-in-place challenge that is facing both independent living retirement communities and assisted living facilities. The estimated incidence levels of the disease by age cohort vary by reporting agency but appear to be in the ranges indicated below:

Age Cohort	Incidence Level or Percent Needing Assistance[1]
• 75-84	16% - 19%
• 85+	47% - 50%

---
[1] Alzheimer's Disease and Related Disorder Association

In response to this challenge, many progressive assisted living community sponsors are considering the introduction of a special care assisted living; state-of-the-art Alzheimer's living arrangements as yet another component in the complex and growing continuum of care for seniors. For many sponsors, the growing incidence levels of dementia is perhaps the most complex issue they face as they develop effective responses to resident aging in place.

Much has been published about the dreaded disease and the debilitating impact on its victims. Innovative living arrangements are evolving that are striking a delicate balance between reasonable freedom and appropriate security. These specialized Alzheimer's facilities place a high priority on minimizing chemical and physical restraints while attempting to optimize comfort and dignity; lowering the excitement level of the resident.

There is a potential trap as owner/operators accept the reality that Alzheimer's and other related dementia are challenges that cannot be avoided in assisted living. Merely calling an area that has physical security a "special care unit" is not enough. Special care units of the future must address at least three important issues:

1. Recognize a unique care level and market niche
2. Have a *purpose-built* design to respond to special needs
3. Develop strong programmatic content aimed at the unique needs of each resident

The ideal market positioning for the new millennium is twofold: 1) to convince the marketplace that you understand special care and 2) you, in fact, provide *the* special care/Alzheimer's living environment of choice.

Two Market Models

As these special care units become better defined, there will emerge the two basic market models:

- **Residential/Social Model** – For those seniors who are in relatively good physical health, but need sheltered living combined with low to moderate level assistance with the activities of daily living. The physical product is a special design variation of assisted living.

- **Medical Model** – For seniors with more advanced stages of Alzheimer's and other related dementia who also have more complex health problems.

There will be complex market overlaps between today's assisted living models and traditional nursing. These overlaps are addressed in Chapter 1 and illustrated in Figure 1-2. Special care/Alzheimer's units may well become the "carve-out" market niche of the new millennium, but that trend will not evolve successfully without complications and will require considerable attention to necessary details.

The Mind-Set of the Alzheimer's Caregiver

While major emphasis is being placed on the victim, relatively little has been published about the specific market dynamics and the mind-set of the caregiver. But the caregiver is really *the* market. All of the characteristics of the caregiver addressed in Chapter 25 apply, plus other need-driven motivations. Keep in mind, that in many cases, the Alzheimer's caregiver is not an adult child; but the elderly spouse of the victim.

Our focus group research and experience has indicated that there are a number of perceptions, misconceptions, emotions and unmet needs involving the Alzheimer's caregiver:

- *Caregivers have strong need-driven motivations* – The adult children or spouse caregivers of victims clearly demonstrate strong need-driven emotions. They are constantly on a search for options to improve both the quality of *their* life and that of their Alzheimer's victim. In describing their unmet needs in focus groups, caregivers frequently mention that their search for alternatives has delivered less than satisfactory results. However, most are pleasantly surprised when they ultimately become aware of special care Alzheimer's assisted living arrangements that are evolving around the United States.

- *Caregivers complain about delayed diagnosis* – While conclusive Alzheimer's medical diagnosis is complex, many caregivers claim that their loved one's actual condition was diagnosed later in time than was acceptable. This delayed diagnosis creates considerable frustration and hardship on the part of caregivers and their families.

- *Caregivers experience diagnosis denial* – Many caregivers, when actually presented with the initial diagnosis, refuse to admit that this malady could exist in *their* family.

- *Alzheimer's has been described as a closet disease* – The caregiver's initial reluctance to accept the fact that a relative or loved one has the disease, coupled with society's current level of discomfort regarding dementia, has caused individual Alzheimer's situations to be "covered up" for a period of time. Many respondents in focus groups felt that, in retrospect, this phenomenon has a distinct negative impact on effectively addressing dementia in a timely manner; both medically and through service and outreach programs. It has certainly caused family pressures and social problems with friends and neighbors.

- *Caregivers have mixed emotions about support groups* – Most indicate that support groups are clearly helpful in providing emotional support and developing the mental and physical stamina needed to face their tremendous personal challenges. But many comment that support groups do not offer sufficient specific assistance in dealing with the wide spectrum of their unmet needs.

- *Experienced caregivers demonstrate a nursing home frame of reference* – While many caregivers put up a courageous fight to avoid thinking of ultimate custodial nursing care for their loved one, most are aware of the nursing home option. To them, the nursing home is considered a most difficult, expensive and marginally acceptable alternative due to their perceptions and misconceptions of this living environment. For many, this alternative is clearly perceived only as a future reality – and they try to delay the decision as long as possible. With this state of mind, the special care, assisted living option becomes increasingly attractive.

- *Caregivers ultimately display limited guilt regarding difficult decisions* – In retrospect, caregivers report that they experienced surprisingly little long term guilt with regard to the ultimate difficult decision to place their loved one in some form of sheltered living or custodial care. They gradually reached the realization that the decision was both prudent and necessary – both for their loved one and for their own personal health and well being.

Economic Realities

The economic realities of special care/Alzheimer's presents a good news/bad news situation. The good news is that special care units are characterized by being premium priced with good operating margins. You can probably count on a broader primary market area with deeper market penetration because of the strong need-driven response of caregivers and other referral services. The sobering news is that, unlike conventional assisted living, many situations involve two person senior households. In these situations, the decision to move into your special care unit involves incurring the ongoing costs of maintaining two households.

THE MIND-SET OF THE ALZHEIMER'S CAREGIVER

1. Have very strong need-driven motivations
2. Complain about delayed medical diagnosis
3. Initially experience diagnosis denial
4. Describe dementia as a "closet disease"
5. Demonstrate a nursing home frame of reference
6. In a continuing search for options and alternatives
7. Experience limited guilt regarding ultimate difficult custodial care decisions
8. Have mixed emotions about support groups

For many sponsors in the 1980s, it was a traumatic experience to consider and eventually offer what has become known as conventional assisted living within their independent living retirement communities.

But in the 1990s many of these same sponsors are expanding their continuum of living arrangements by offering innovative living arrangements and a wide spectrum of services that will serve the growing needs of both Alzheimer's victims and their caregivers. These new initiatives will also meet the rapidly expanding needs of their independent and assisted living residents as they continue to age in place.

EXPECTED OUTCOMES OF DEMENTIA CARE

- **Minimize excitement levels**
- **Facilitate adaptation to changing needs**
- **Maximize awareness and orientation**
- **Ensure safety and security**
- **Provide opportunities for socialization**

Sources: Moore Diversified Services, Inc.
              Kirby Pines Retirement Community

The newer concepts of special care are emphasizing a special adaptation of the integrated, yet subtly separated, residential/social model of assisted living.

Conclusion

Special care is more residential than it used to be, but less residential than "regular" assisted living.

CHAPTER 23

COMPETING WITH NURSING HOMES FOR MARKET SHARE

The Turf Battle of the New Millennium

For the multi-billion dollar assisted living and nursing industries the big question is, who will win the biggest market share in the future?

Today, the nursing home industry serves approximately 1.5 million seniors. But in recent years, the number of beds has stayed relatively flat while the population of those age 85 and older has continued to grow. As a result, there were 650 beds for every thousand seniors age 85 and older in 1980; today that rate has dropped to approximately 400. Nursing bed census has stabilized at relatively high occupancy levels in most markets.

It is more difficult to estimate the actual size of the fast-growing assisted living industry, but a realistic projection is 300,000 to 400,000 *quality* units. Some Wall Street analysts and trade groups put the number higher – at 700,000 to 800,000 units – but that estimate includes older rest homes in addition to the newer facilities that fit today's more strictly defined state-of-the-art assisted living model.

Myths vs. Reality

As competition heats up between assisted living communities and traditional nursing homes, prepare for the health care turf battle of the millennium. And industry observers, owners, and operators are all speculating on future market share. For a clear view of what's to come, it's essential to first sort out some persistent current myths from future reality.

• *Myth: Growth in assisted living will steal significant market share from the nursing industry.* Assisted living leaders build a compelling case that their predominately residential-social model is a more dignified and cost-effective alternative to traditional nursing. Some also predict that they can steal significant market share from nursing homes, replacing as many as several hundred thousand existing nursing beds over the next five years.

• *Fact: The reality is that resident acuity levels and economic issues will have a significant impact on relative market share.* Average acuity levels have increased dramatically in the past five years for both assisted living and nursing home residents. Assisted living operators are already experiencing higher than expected acuity levels and are compensating for this by offering more ADL assistance – attempting to extend length of stay.

What *is* the optimum setting today for a resident who needs some *nursing-type* care? In the old days, up to 30 percent of existing nursing home residents might have been well cared for in today's assisted living. But that was when the *intermediate level* of nursing care was predominant and average acuity levels were much lower.

Determining what percentage of nursing home residents might otherwise be served in assisted living also depends on their *ability to pay*. Nationally, about 70 percent of the nursing patient days are paid for by Medicaid and eight percent by Medicare; just 23 percent are private pay. In light of rapidly increasing acuity levels and affordability trends, the overlap between assisted living and nursing care has grown considerably. Projections of shifting market share from nursing to assisted living must objectively consider *both* increasing acuity levels and private-pay affordability.

• **Myth: The current and future potential for market-rate, private pay assisted living is significant.**

• **Fact: Many industry professionals are trying to gauge the total existing market for private-pay, market-rate assisted living.** But estimates range broadly, and most are questionable. What is apparent is that the current assisted living industry development pipeline is still catching up with unmet *current* demand. It appears that many age and income qualified seniors who fit the current assisted living need profile are unaware of their options or are still being served in nursing homes. The public companies are filling the assisted living development pipeline at an unprecedented pace; the next 2 to 3 years will determine the actual marketplace supply vs. demand balance.

• *Myth: Today's marketplace mistakes will be "covered" by tomorrow's growth in the 80+ market sector.*

• *Fact: Even if there is substantial new demand for market-rate assisted living, developers must approach the industry with caution.* With resident turnover rates at 35 to 40 percent annually, a large portion of 1999's qualified consumers will simply refill *existing* units rather than absorbing substantial increases in *new supply.*

• *Myth: Special market niches will help expand the assisted living market.*

• *Fact: The market sector to watch as we swing into the new millennium will be seniors in the 80+ age cohort.* So far, at least seven products and services are competing to serve the sheltered living needs of this group: skilled nursing, assisted living, dementia care, independent living, home health, catered living, and supportive living. Catered or supportive living typically allows independent living residents to avoid moving. They can access selected assistance with the activities of daily living; paying for those services as needed on an a la carte basis. As sponsors develop such niches, each is declaring that they will "own" a significant market share.

Though an owner/operator might assume that each sector serves a distinct mutually exclusive need, a closer look reveals that there is considerable market overlap. In addition, hospitals and other providers within vertically integrated networks are rapidly eliminating courtesy referrals to unrelated third parties by offering expanded service themselves; thereby enhancing their own revenues.

As with individual market niches, the services offered by assisted living facilities and nursing homes overlap. Assisted living sponsors contend that their innovative product best addresses future market needs. Traditional nursing home operators, on the other hand, hope to maintain market share given their decades of experience. Realistically, both groups are in for some market turbulence and product and service reshaping. This is depicted in Figure 23-1.

- *Myth: "Affordable" assisted living is a huge market waiting to be tapped.*

- *Fact: I wish this were true, as the need is enormous. Unfortunately, there are critical differences between providing affordable senior housing in the form of existing HUD programs and delivering affordable service-intensive assisted living.* First, consider the challenge of covering recurring operating expenses. Tax credits and other financing incentives work well for essentially service-free, low-income housing, but how can you cover as much as $1,200 per month in ongoing operating expenses? Such costs are largely unavoidable in

Competing with Nursing Homes for Market Share

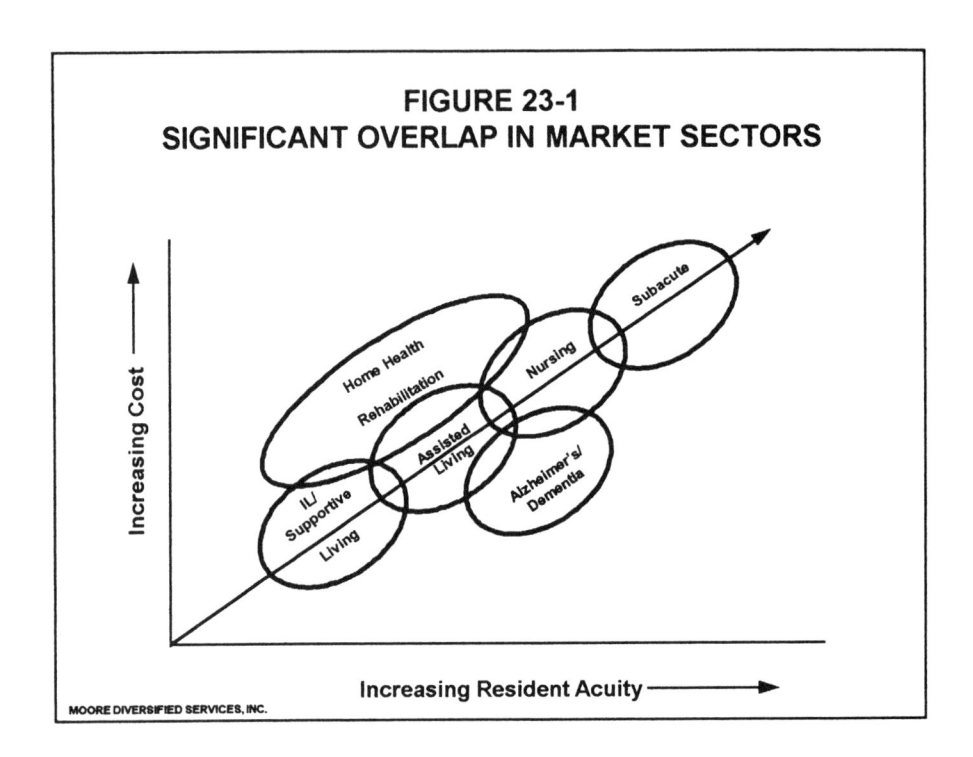

**FIGURE 23-1
SIGNIFICANT OVERLAP IN MARKET SECTORS**

MOORE DIVERSIFIED SERVICES, INC.

assisted living, even if the sponsor has been given the land and building for the project debt-free. For more details, see Chapter 20.

Another factor is market size. Private-pay assisted living typically costs between $1,900 and $2,200 per month – before adding fees for increasing levels of assistance with activities of daily living. Furthermore, these costs can be significantly higher in urban markets. But even at $2,000 per month, a prospective resident must have an annual gross income in excess of $35,000 in order to meet the industry standard criteria of applying no more than 80 percent of their after-tax disposable income to the monthly service fee. Shared occupancy by unrelated residents can lower costs to about $1,400 a month in some markets, but this strategy is being employed only on a limited basis for new assisted living products.

- *Myth: Managed care and government entitlements will soon fund a large portion of the low-to-moderate income assisted living market.* Assisted living is currently a private-pay service. But conventional wisdom is that its cost-effectiveness will lead to widespread entitlements aimed at providing assisted living to low-to-moderate income seniors. Such a change would be necessary in order to realize a large shift in market share from nursing to assisted living.

- *Fact: To date, there are several weaknesses in this theory. First, though Medicaid waivers have generally received good reviews, they are limited in number.* The second concern is whether Medicaid, which is being scrutinized to hold down costs, can afford to provide funding to *two* senior market sectors offering sheltered care and assistance. Medicaid currently focuses on serving only those seniors with relatively high acuity profiles. If a major government entitlement program for assisted living were implemented, would seniors currently ineligible for nursing entitlements "come out of the woodwork" in an attempt to benefit from an expanded entitlement program for this very favorable living arrangement? This is being appropriately labeled by the industry as "the woodwork effect."

Most experienced assisted living industry players concur that strategic planning for assisted living should be primarily on a private-pay basis. Hype and speculation about the possibility of universal entitlements in the future could lead to unrealistic growth planning and expectations for the industry.

How should the industry respond to these evolving trends?

Assisted living sponsors and operators should focus more on measuring *current demand* and place less emphasis on *future growth*, much of which could be consumed by satisfying turnover needs. In order to sustain or increase market share, providers must be able to deal with increased acuity levels, detailed cost controls and realistic pricing.

Nursing home operators must carefully evaluate their options as well, including a careful analysis of the number of existing beds that is appropriate for the future. Many skilled nursing facilities that have more than 120 nursing beds are creating swing wings for subacute care and medical model dementia care. Others are also pursuing a social model assisted living product. Sorting out the myths from reality on these issues still requires a fair amount of speculation. But by ferreting out facts, it's possible to project the market's future potential for both assisted living and nursing.

Two things are sure; the age 80+ population will continue to grow in size and age in a fairly predictable manner. What is less clear is who will really win the turf battle of the new millennium. The assisted living and nursing markets will eventually stabilize – but not without a fair amount of turbulence as the various market sectors find their niche.

CHAPTER 24

BRANCHING OUT INTO THE COMMUNITY

Before Offering Community-Based Services, Answer Five Crucial Questions

The overall health of the assisted living and CCRC market sectors in 1998 has been enhanced by owner/operators implementing traditional strategies which involved increasing their revenues and expanding their range of services. This was usually accomplished by focusing on internal operations issues such as implementing programs to optimize occupancy, adding alternate forms of care to existing campuses, improving departmental efficiency and by renovating common areas and individual living units. Many of these strategies will continue well into the new millennium, but many sponsors are realizing that meeting strategic goals in the future might also include taking a serious look at community-based services and a careful evaluation of outreach services.

These programs benefit both seniors and sponsors; seniors gain access to an array of new services while allowing owner/operators to realize extra income and create strategic "umbilical cords" between the seniors and their campuses. These connections can also make a senior living community more visible; especially to potential future residents.

The Top Ten Community-Based Services

The top ten more commonly offered community-based services are:

1. Home Health Care
2. Homemaker and Companion Services
3. Adult Day Care
4. Meal Preparation/Delivery
5. Personal Emergency Response Systems
6. Transportation
7. Case Management and Geriatric Assessment Center
8. Alzheimer's/Dementia Information Clearing House
9. Rehabilitation and Therapy Clinics
10. Respite Care - on Demand

Some senior living communities are using their food service operations to prepare and deliver meals off campus in a "meals on wheels" concept. Still others are using their own transportation vehicles to transport non-resident seniors, for a reasonable fare, to civic centers, medical practitioners, community events and shopping areas. Respite care (on demand) is being offered as part of Adult Day Care.

Five Important Planning Questions

Not every community has the resources, activity levels or incentives to embark on a formal program of community-based services. Before deciding whether to jump on the community-based services bandwagon, answer these five crucial questions about any service you may be considering:

1. *Is the new initiative really consistent with your mission or strategic plan?* Even a "great idea" will flop if it is incompatible with existing operations or organizational culture. The most frequent incompatibilities with existing operations are in the cost-efficient use of space and staff for the new endeavor. If existing space is already used to its full potential, and if there is no additional staff time available, then the financial rewards may be insufficient to justify the planned venture's new expenses. The optimum community-based services outcome is a synergistic situation that derives additional net income after covering all new costs from otherwise underutilized space or staff time.

2. *What business volume or market penetration is required to make the new service really profitable?* Many times, the business plan and financial pro forma are correctly structured, but the implied input assumptions are either unrealistic or flawed. For example, the financial viability of home care services breaks down into the basic difference between the hourly charge to the client (incremental revenues) and the salary expenses and other direct expenses (variable and fixed costs) incurred. The key question to answer is: *How many visits are required to produce sufficient revenues to cover your fixed monthly expenses and variable costs per visit; yielding an acceptable profit?* The results of this simple exercise can be very revealing.

3. Based on existing and future competition, how likely are you to succeed in the competitive marketplace? Compare your answers to the previous questions with the amount of business you are likely to generate, taking into account both existing and future competition as well as the estimated size of the total target market. The chances are you might find that the total business volume you and your competitors would really need may not be available in your marketplace.

4. Have you identified all of the direct and indirect operations costs associated with the new venture? Many new community-based service ventures fail or are discontinued because of unrealistic estimates of future financial performance; the total operations costs are surprisingly high and the rewards are lower than expected. The initiative may be a well-intended, technical success but the venture fails basic financial tests.

5. Will the new service effectively exploit or utilize existing resources and will there be an acceptable return on required new investment? New investment examples include the space and staff required to support Adult Day Care, the cost of responding to new licensing or certification requirements for a Home Health Agency or the normal but sometimes significant start-up costs of other community-based services initiatives.

Even if the early answers to some of these questions are discouraging, you shouldn't necessarily give up on offering community-based services. Instead, consider forming an alliance with another service provider that would normally be a competitor. For example, a co-venture with a licensed home health agency or rehabilitation service might allow you to expand the range of services you offer without investing a great deal of money. It also allows your provider partner to access your campus, which offers them a guaranteed customer base at a central location.

Ten Steps to Developing the Community-Based Services Financial Model

The following financial model is an approach to quickly determine the preliminary financial viability of your community-based project:

1. Develop a short list or spectrum of services to offer

2. Establish scope and intensity of offering those services

3. Construct an isolated financial pro forma for each individual service (where practical)

4. Determine <u>direct labor</u> concentration[1]

    - Position, titles, skill levels, etc.
    - Number of hours or events billed per calendar period:
        - Week   - Quarter
        - Month   - Year

---
[1] Those actually delivering services for a fee.

5. Identify the fixed cost/overhead structure for the venture

6. Allocate all fixed, indirect and direct costs to the new venture

7. Develop a rationale for any planned write-downs/subsidies:

   - Use of existing resources during start-up without full cost allocation
   - Exploiting unused existing capacity or resource whose cost is already covered
   - Etc.

8. Spread fixed cost/overhead over expected billing hours or events:

   - Uniformly
   - Stratified based on appropriate criteria and rationale

9. Determine "loaded" hourly/event rate (price) which is the sum of:

   - Direct compensation/hour or event
   - All overhead, fixed, and variable costs allocated to each hour or event

10. Set ultimate pricing based on previous steps; including profit/entrepreneurial rewards

This pragmatic process will deliver appropriate financial results if your marketplace assumptions are correct and costs are accurately projected. The use of a sensitivity analysis and added contingency factors can provide effective hedges against future risks.

Going through the community-based services strategic planning process has a number of spin-off benefits. These include, but are not necessarily limited to, the following:

1. Optimizing and leveraging your existing or potential resources.

2. Creating a sharpened, strategic focus for your future operations.

3. Creating potential to expand the continuum of services offered; such as expanding the vertical integrated network.

4. Enhancing your revenues synergistically.

Finally, the resulting service and image "umbilical" between the marketplace and your campus could lay a new foundation for success in the new millennium.

CHAPTER 25

THE ADULT CHILD/ DECISION INFLUENCER

The Sandwich Generation Caught in a Squeeze

The decision influencer was the most overlooked seniors housing and health care market segment of the 1990s. Even if they were not totally overlooked, these adult children certainly were not adequately targeted or properly educated from a marketing perspective. As we approach the year 2000, there is still significant pent-up market potential with this important decision influencer group.

As most experienced assisted living operators now know, adult children between the ages of 45 and 64 are not only the decision *influencers* for their parents, they are frequently decision *makers*. Savvy owners and operators are now selling directly to this crucial market. In order to properly assess and tap this market you must first understand their demographics, past migration patterns, psychographic characteristics and the way psychographics impact the decisions the adult child makes with respect to their parents.

The Age and Income Qualified "Gatekeepers"

Assuming their parents' average childbearing age was about 25, the age 50 to 64 cohorts are the primary decision influencers for the age 75+ senior consumers. It is important to note that the leading edge of the baby boomers started turning 50 in 1996. Already, more than 30 million households are headed by adults between 45 and 64. What's more, in excess of 8 million of these households report annual incomes exceeding $70,000. This figure is significant in light of growing evidence that some adult children are supplementing their parent's income in order to help them private pay for assisted living. This is especially true some time after move-in if the parent gets into financial difficulties. However, this bonus income should not yet be factored into formal market feasibility studies, as empirical information on this important issue is still very limited and not statistically significant.

Important Psychographics

The real key to marketing to these decision influencers is understanding what motivates them. In conducting several hundred decision influencer focus groups, I have discovered that they have a very high propensity to consider and favorably embrace assisted living for their parents – assuming they understand the concept. Many do not.

When we assemble 10 to 12 adult children for a focus group, more than half usually tell a story involving significant concerns about their parent's current health status. Most are concerned about their parent's ability to continue to live independently. These focus group respondents have been screened for only one characteristic; having at least one living parent anywhere in the U.S. The parent's relative health status was *not* a screening criteria. Yet these randomly selected respondents frequently tell stories about the increasing frailty and declining health of their parents. Many express frustration that their parents either fail or refuse to recognize these subtle changes, and most children find it difficult to delicately discuss or counsel their parents about their changing health and declining independence. Many confirm that a role reversal has taken place. As one adult child put it, *"Mom is giving me fits like I'm sure I did to her when I was a teenager."* Another said *"My husband and I are conducting a loving conspiracy in seeking what is best for my mother."*

Decision Influencer Frustrations and Emotions

Caregiver frustrations are summarized in the illustration below:

DECISION INFLUENCER FRUSTRATIONS

- **Observe increasing frailty & declining health**
- **Parents failure to recognize the inevitable**
- **Discussing living options with parents**
- **Parent/child role reversal**
- **Facilitating the difficult move decision**

In discussing this dilemma, most adult children express love, guilt, frustration, a sense of helplessness, and economic concern. These emotions generally peak when the senior and the adult child are geographically distant. This is especially true for those families dealing with Alzheimer's or other related dementia. See Chapter 22 for more details on the Alzheimer's caregiver.

FIVE EMOTIONS OF DECISION INFLUENCERS

1. **Love**
2. **Guilt**
3. **Frustration**
4. **Helplessness**
5. **Economic Concern**

The Sandwich Generation Caught in the Middle

These decision influencers of today are facing other challenges. Because of delayed marriages, many are putting their children through college while also trying to save for retirement and caring for their aging parents. Most are dual income households with both spouses working outside of the home. The number of households facing these multiple challenges will only increase in the future.

Some experts predict the sandwich generation may spend almost as much time and money caring for their parents as they did raising their children. And just about the time they become traditional empty nesters, many face the almost immediate challenge of caring for their parents.

THE GENERATION CAUGHT IN THE MIDDLE

Three Major Challenges

1. **Putting children through college**
2. **Saving for retirement**
3. **Caring for their parents**

Family patterns are changing. Mother does not traditionally move in with married children as in past generations. Seniors tell us consistently that they do not want to move in with their children and become a burden. Most would prefer not living with them, even if invited.

Caregivers and the Work Force

Recent surveys by major employers clearly indicate that an alarming number of their employees, primarily female, are struggling with a caregiver responsibility to the extent that it is affecting their workplace productivity. And the labor force participation rate of females has soared past the 60 percent level in recent years.

In 1998, the Labor Department's Women's Bureau released the results of a study on work and caregiving. Some of their findings were:

1. A significant proportion of American households provides care for an elderly relative.

2. Approximately 72 percent of the caregivers are women and 64 percent work full or part time; 41 percent are also caring for children.

3. More than half reported taking time off from work or coming in later because of caregiver conflicts.

With unemployment rates in 1998 at the lowest level in 20 years, major employers are starting to see similarities between the needs and benefits of senior care and child care. The future of senior care may see some significant involvement in elder care initiatives by Corporate America.

Influencers Can Expand Your Primary Market Area

Certain geographic factors set the stage for adult children playing a very significant role as decision influencers in the marketplace. Their role, properly recognized, can have a major impact on expanding your local primary market area potential by encouraging the migration of seniors who live outside of your area to consider your community.

Migration patterns and mobility trends of the past quarter century have geographically separated many parents from their children. Many of these parents sought the warmer climates of Florida, Arizona and California. Meanwhile, the children went just about everywhere chasing the brass ring and the golden handcuffs offered by Corporate America. In a typical assisted living market area today it is not unusual to discover that many adult children do not currently reside in the city or town where they grew up. To a lesser degree, but certainly significantly, many of their parents have also moved to other locales.

Later in life, there is a basic motivation for a permanent reunion of the aging senior with at least one of the adult children. Trends have indicated that, in many cases, the child takes most of the early initiatives to re-establish that link. Hence, the appropriate label of *decision influencer*.

This geographical displacement between adult children and their parents presents another challenge for influencers and an opportunity for assisted living sponsors. Children are highly motivated to move their parents closer to them as health complications increase. If you are in a metro market that has experienced a significant influx of new employees in the past 10 to 15 years, chances are you can significantly expand your local market by attracting seniors who also did not previously reside in your primary market area. Some seniors will be attracted to your area so they can be near their children. The adult children are the *gatekeepers* but an individual owner/operator who captures only a one-half of one percent of this gross potential could realize a theoretical absorption of 50 units. Obviously, no single community can be filled in this way alone, but the migration potential for assisted living is clearly significant, and frequently overlooked. It is not unusual for a typical assisted living community to have 25 to 30 percent of their residents moving in from outside the community's defined (local) primary market area.

Marketing to the Decision Influencers

To appeal to the adult children/decision influencers, you must develop a credible and ethical market positioning strategy that acknowledges their emotions while addressing their parents' specific needs and concerns. The ideal message to convey is that many adult children have discovered that assisted living is a surprisingly affordable living alternative offering ambience, dignity and maximum independence for parents in later stages of life.

Time-Distance Dynamics

The primary market area for your new assisted living community should be defined or at least heavily influenced by time-distance preferences of adult children. Frequently it is the adult child/decision influencer who really shapes a community's primary market area. Wherever possible, apply the following time-distance rule when defining your primary market area:

> ## Time-Distance Rule
>
> **Working adult children/decision influencers will typically travel up to 30 to 35 minutes from their home or place of employment to visit their parent in assisted living.**

Benefit-driven marketing strategies must offer the best of two worlds, for both the senior and the adult children. This means that assisted living must be designed and positioned in the marketplace for two types of prospects or decision makers; the adult child and the ultimate senior resident. The decision influencer must feel good about supporting and, in many cases, initiating the parent's decision to move. This can best be accomplished by developing strategies aimed at the top five emotions of the decision influencers mentioned earlier in this chapter.

Strategies must be developed with both markets in mind. Market to the seniors in the primary market area using conventional techniques, but also communicate with adult children in the same area using innovative target marketing strategies. The decision influencer's significant role in marketing assisted living to seniors will continue to grow. Properly targeted, the decision influencer can be the center piece and catalyst that enhances all of the other sales and marketing strategies.

SECTION SIX

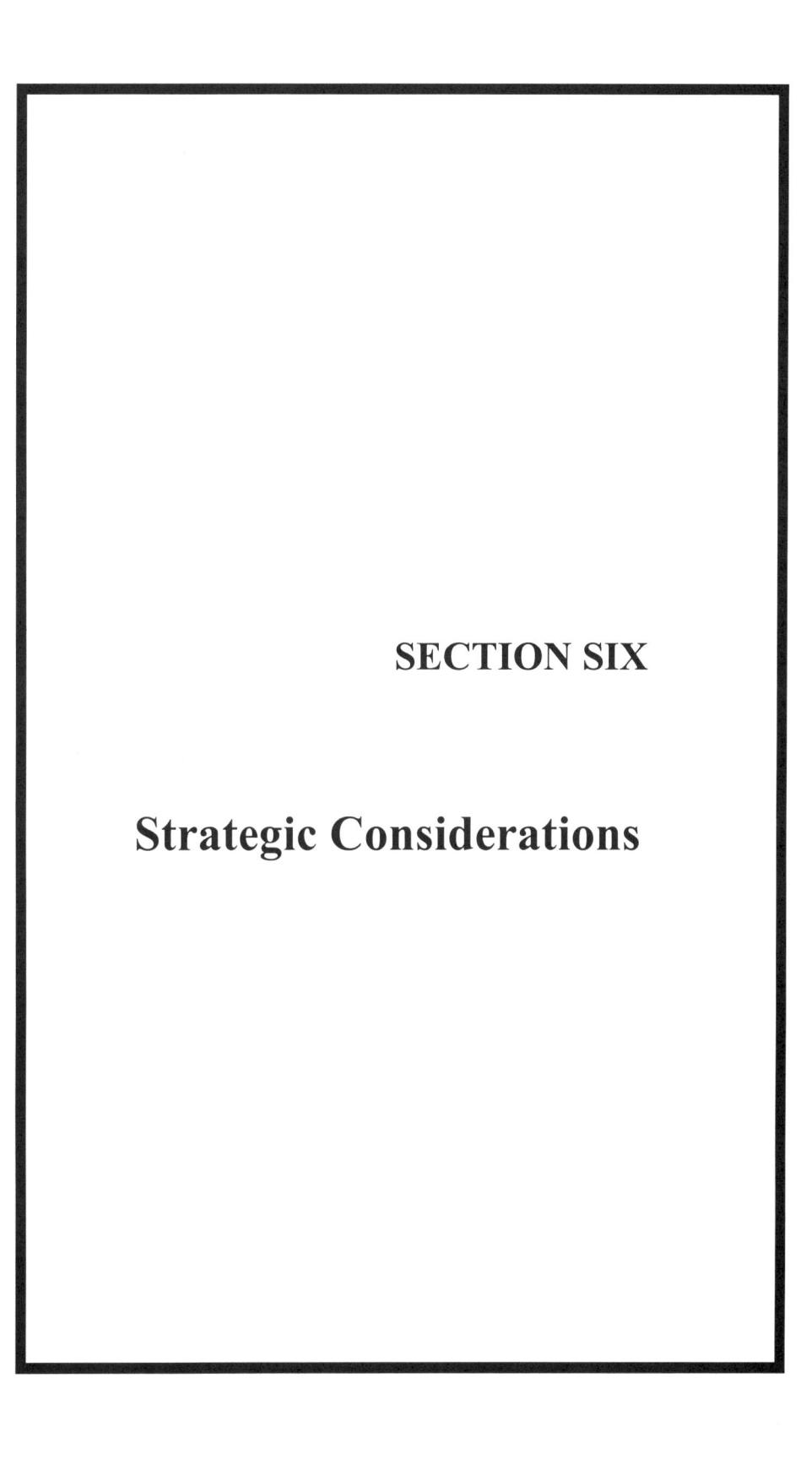

Strategic Considerations

CHAPTER 26

MAKING THE CASE FOR MULTI-FACILITY CONSOLIDATION

Senior Housing Operators Are Finding Strength in Numbers

The consolidation that has taken place in the recent past among senior housing and other health care facilities often consisted of bottom-fishing expeditions, involving the acquisition of marginally performing, troubled properties. These astute bargain hunters have also been assembling significant multi-facility portfolios to achieve economies of scale and what economists would call an optimum *critical mass*. This simply means increased synergy, more efficient operations and increased profits and cash flow.

Since 1996, assisted living companies going public by launching Initial Public Offerings (IPOs) have accelerated the trend to multi-facility operations. These companies have access to significantly lower cost capital (equity raised) and more attractive, less expensive debt. And they must continue to grow significantly in order to deliver on their promise of growing earnings per share.

A multi-facility operation is not automatically more efficient than a single-facility one. For one thing, a chain's multiple campuses must lie within a reasonable geographical area in order for the sponsor to exert effective control. A regional or cluster management concept is evolving wherein a national operator forms cost-effective regions to manage their growing portfolio of properties. Success for a multi-facility operator depends on delivering more value to the residents while yielding more efficient operations leading to increased cash and profits for the operator. This performance satisfies investors in for-profit ventures and allows not-for-profit sponsors to fund expanded mission objectives.

Benefits of a Multi-Facility Operation

A well-planned multi-facility operation yields five major benefits:

1. *Saving money through operating economies of scale* – Some fixed costs are directly related to the operations of an individual facility or campus. But other indirect overhead costs, such as staff training, enhanced marketing strategies, advanced systems and procedures, centralized accounting, human resource development, and professional advisory and consulting services, can be shared by a number of facilities. So an operator with more than one facility can gain financial leverage by spreading significant fixed costs over a large number of revenue-producing units or beds. In addition to spreading overhead costs, multi-facility operators with large scale operations also enjoy increased purchasing power. It is not unusual for companies such as raw food suppliers to provide more attractive pricing to higher volume purchasers.

Let's look at an example of multi-facility operator synergy. A single-facility assisted living sponsor might operate 80 assisted living units. Considering a seven percent vacancy factor and ignoring double occupancy for simplicity's sake, the campus would average 75 occupied units/beds on a given day. Multiplying that number by 365 days yields approximately 27,375 resident days per year.

An astute operator could easily invest $50,000 per year in indirect overhead costs to reduce other costs and increase perceived value and resident satisfaction. Divided by the 27,375 resident days, that $50,000 annual investment pencils out to a cost of $1.80 per resident day, or $55 per month for each resident. But a single-facility operator might think twice about making that investment, or at least passing all of the costs on to the residents. However, if that same sponsor owned or controlled *five* similar communities, the resident days would total approximately 136,875. The same $50,000 per year investment would then cost only 36 cents per resident day, or $11 per month. This would allow the operator to have increased profits, realize higher cash flow, provide higher value for relatively lower monthly rates for the residents *and* pass the added cost on to the residents. While some of the indirect costs might increase modestly by supporting five campuses, such increases will be small considering the 5 to 1 potential savings leverage that would be realized through multi-facility operations.

2. *Maintaining the competitive high ground* – The key marketing strategy today is to dominate market share or at least have a major influence in the marketplace. A sound growth strategy can create significant barriers to entry and, in some cases, actually prevent new competitors from entering local and regional markets. The mere presence of an established, credible multi-facility operator frequently causes other owners, boards of directors or lenders to decide not to take on the risk of one-on-one competition.

3. *Enhancing revenue and cash flow* – Additional incremental cash flow usually comes from two sources; the operational efficiencies mentioned above and internally earned management fees. The larger the operation, the more the operator earns in management fees, which are typically paid at a rate of approximately five percent of adjusted gross revenues. An operator managing five facilities realizes five times the fees of an operator managing only one. What's more, the cost of providing management services to earn these fees rises only incrementally as the number of facilities managed increases. The end result is more net income to enhance the effectiveness of the management operation and increased cash flow to fund other missions or entrepreneurial activities. A multi-facility operator can frequently realize up to 50 percent of their management fees as net cash flow after reasonable management expenses. This of course assumes that the projects are internally managed vs. using outside management companies.

4. *Becoming very attractive as a partner to managed care organizations* – While becoming a managed care partner might not be high on a sponsor's priority list today, such an initiative could become an imperative within the next several years. More and more managed care providers and payors are forming integrated networks. When they ultimately look at senior housing and health care, they will be looking for the same characteristics that make a multi-facility operator successful; critical mass, economies of scale and geographical coverage. Managed care contractors will favor sponsor-owners with the strongest operations, in terms of number of units and beds controlled and having significant geographical coverage.

5. *Securing more flexible and attractive capitalization* – While each project or campus must stand alone financially, investors and lenders are clearly attracted to multi-facility operations. Hence, financiers are more likely to structure a more flexible consolidated financial package for larger scale operations; a relationship that could benefit each and every facility within an operator's consolidated network.

Sponsors can sometimes "cross-collateralize" multiple facilities. This means that their individual facility lending or investing risks are diversified or spread across a number of facilities; creating an effective risk hedged "mutual fund" portfolio of properties. Lenders like this. The most recent trend of Initial Public Offerings (IPOs) is fueled and justified by all of the favorable attributes of a multiple facility operator.

Success Checklist for Multi-Facility Operators

1. **Optimizing Returns Through Operating Economies of Scale**
   - Spread certain fixed costs over more units
   - Staff training/human resource development
   - Enhanced sales and marketing strategies
   - Advanced systems and procedures
   - Centralized accounting
   - Increased purchasing power

2. **Maintain the Competitive High Ground**
   - Dominate the marketplace
   - Control the local and regional "geography"

3. **Enhance Revenue and Cash Flow**
   - Exploit operational efficiencies
   - Realize optimum management fees
   - Exploit the synergy of management service delivery

4. **Become the Optimum Managed Care Provider/ Partner**
   - Form the ultimate integrated network

- Maximize number of units controlled
- Offer maximum geographical coverage
- Provide the widest spectrum of senior services
- Realize critical mass and economies of scale

5. Securing More Flexible and Attractive Capitalization

- Multi-facility operations are more attractive to lenders/investors
- Offers more flexible consolidated financial package for larger scale operations
- Lenders can "cross-collateralize" multiple facilities
- Effectively create risk-hedged "mutual fund" portfolio of diversified properties

Single-facility operators are not necessarily a dying breed, but they do face an uphill battle. Meanwhile, the economic advantages of a multi-facility operation will present an easier pathway to growth and prosperity. Single-facility operators should carefully evaluate future exit strategies; addressing significant personal estate liquidity, ownership transition and overall financial planning strategies. If you are a single-facility operator, don't panic yet; read Chapter 27 to avoid becoming an *endangered* species.

CHAPTER 27

SINGLE-FACILITY OPERATORS FACE NEW CHALLENGES

They Must Maintain a Sharply Focused Attention to Detail

In Chapter 26, I outlined how multi-facility operators have a number of advantages and economies of scale working in their favor. Single-facility sponsors must compensate for these competitive disadvantages by exploiting their own strengths and redoubling their efforts to deploy sophisticated yet practical strategies.

The advantages, opportunities and synergies that can be exploited by multi-facility operators include: 1) saving money through efficient operating economies of scale, 2) maintaining the competitive high ground, 3) enhancing revenue and cash flow, 4) becoming an attractive managed care partner and 5) securing more flexible and attractive financing/capitalization. This led to the obvious question, *"Are single-facility operators a dying breed?"* The answer is no, but they *do* face an uphill battle. Ideally, single-facility operators should strive to be clearly positioned as "the highly personalized assisted living community of choice" in their respective markets.

Five Important Success Strategies

This positioning is achievable, but it is certainly easier said than done. To succeed, providers must aggressively pursue five important success strategies. Executing some of these strategies takes time and money. Operators should set aside approximately four to five percent of revenues, either to pay for third party professional management or to directly invest in the future of their facility. This represents a financial challenge for many, but the payoff can be remarkable. The five success strategies are:

1. *Apply significant entrepreneurial "sweat equity"* – Single-facility sponsors must invest in long hours and frequently defer short-run personal financial rewards in order to enhance and sustain the long-term intrinsic value of their communities. One effective approach is to maintain a state-of-the-art physical plant, making appropriate cosmetic enhancements that deliver high perceived value to both the existing residents and the external marketplace. Many of these enhancements can also result in subtle, yet significant, enhancements that lead to increased operating efficiencies. It is also important to sustain the long run integrity of the physical plant. This means effectively funding depreciation. Most sophisticated operators have a capital expense reserve line item in their annual operating budget, typically set at $225 to $250 per unit per year, which is allocated for future improvements to the physical plant.

Prudent facility expansion can be an effective way to compete with multi-facility operators. Such expansion can benefit from leveraging your current reputation, market momentum and existing base of operations. For example, adding units or beds to existing "core resources" such as the commercial kitchen, laundry and housekeeping operation can be an effective way to compete more effectively with multi-facility operators. Revenue enhancement is also crucial. Bringing in-house certain service delivery systems such as home health care and rehabilitation services, rather than outsourcing them, can produce additional net income. This, of course, presumes the *activity levels* and *case loads* justify taking certain functions internal. The community's pricing structure should be periodically reevaluated. Pricing must be not only equitable to the residents but competitive in the marketplace – and that means delivering superior value for comparable prices.

2. *Maintain hands-on, sharply focused attention to detail* – This is perhaps the most valuable attribute of a single-facility operator, because little things mean a lot in the senior housing and assisted living business. Consumers pay attention to quality and personalized service. Another key factor is value, or how much seniors get for their money. Legitimate value can be a small operator's most significant competitive attribute. By implementing value engineering, or cutting capital and operating costs in areas that have no visual or direct impact on the residents, operators can invest more in areas that yield a higher value to the consumer.

3. Control costs aggressively – One way to do this is by leveraging purchasing power through available cooperative ventures. Some trade associations offer group purchasing power in pharmaceuticals, consumable products, insurance, and other areas, allowing single-facility sponsors to *synthesize* many of the advantages of larger operators.

4. Sustain leading-edge industry knowledge – The private sector and trade associations are starting to offer turn-key product designs, operations manuals, software and packaged sales and marketing programs. Educational seminars, accreditation and certification programs give smaller operators virtually some of the same opportunities as large organizations to stay on top of industry trends.

5. Use outside experts – This may mean retaining a professional management firm or employing individual expert consultants specializing in operations, marketing, or finance. These professionals can provide sophisticated systems and procedures, access to industry comparative data bases and identify the latest trends in successful operational strategies. Benchmarking is an evolving trend that must be addressed and is covered in Chapter 18.

Strategic Checklist for the Single Facility Operator

1. Apply Significant "Sweat Equity"

- Sustain quality physical plant
    - Fund depreciation
    - Enhance operational efficiencies
- Execute cosmetic enhancements
    - Create and sustain favorable resident impact
- Execute prudent expansion
    - Increase number of units
    - Offer services on/off campus

2. Maintain Hands-On, Focused Attention to Detail – Optimize:

- Quality
- Value
- Efficiency
- Resident satisfaction

3. **Control Costs Aggressively**

    - Internal operations
    - Implement universal worker concept
    - Attempt to join cooperatives
        - Trade associations
        - Local/state initiatives

4. **Sustain Leading Edge Industry Knowledge**

    - Educational seminars and certification programs
    - Turn-key/prototype designs
    - Packaged systems and procedures

5. **Use Outside Resources**

    - Industry experts
    - Professional management
    - Industry data bases
    - Trade associations

These strategies can deliver superior quality, high perceived value, a truly personalized touch, high resident satisfaction, and excellent price-to-value ratios. Single-facility assisted living operators need not be a dying breed if they use these tactics. But in a world of industry consolidation, public companies, national chains and the ever-changing state-of-the-art, single-facility operators must promptly and aggressively address the challenges they face.

Should You Consider an Exit Strategy?

A single-facility operator's strategic thought process *must* include the sobering aspect of an exit strategy. I firmly believe that, over the next two to three years, there will be a number of sellers who – today – don't realize they will be sellers. Just as in poker, ***"There's a time to hold 'em and a time to fold 'em."*** This will not necessarily be a distress-driven decision. Community values are peaking, the industry is consolidating and motivated buyers and lenders currently have deep pockets. When you combine these external market factors with your personal financial and estate planning, you may eventually see a win-win situation on the horizon. There is a distinct window of opportunity to explore meaningful and prudent exit strategies.

CHAPTER 28

MANAGING ASSISTED LIVING
Internal Resource or Third-Party Contract?

Consistent and effective management is one of the most important and critical elements driving the success of both new and existing assisted living communities. In theoretical business terms, determining the management structure of an assisted living community is a classical "make or buy" decision taught in leading business schools for the last 50 years. In today's terms, it is a strategic decision with two options:

- Build a permanent internal resource
- Outsource to a qualified third party firm

Short-run, the decision to engage an external third party management company appears relatively easy, but the long-run view introduces a number of variables suggesting that the "make or buy" decision is far more complex. And it is the long-run view of total assisted living management needs that is critical to the future success of both senior living communities and professional management companies in the new millennium.

The possible selection of an external management company should be viewed as a beneficial, value-added strategy – both short-run and long-run. When evaluating the pros and cons of going internal versus entering into a third-party management contract, many issues must be considered. The initial issues that come to mind as potential disadvantages of engaging outside expertise are losing autonomy of direct control and incurring more costs. But a closer look at this important decision leads to identifying the top five project management needs to be satisfied – and the possible rationale for considering a contractual arrangement.

Top Five Project Management Needs

These top five needs are:

1. Extensive industry-comparable database

2. Sophisticated, yet practical systems, procedures, and controls

3. Potential for delivering ongoing economies of scale that directly benefit the community

4. The ability to stay on the leading edge of the state-of-the-art in an ever-changing industry

5. Cost-effective, consistent, focused and continuous creative input

These and other objective criteria should really drive the critical internal versus external project management decision.

In the case of a new or start-up community by a sponsor with limited industry experience, the lender or underwriter may require the retention of a nationally recognized management company. Yet, in spite of their obvious strengths and advantages, some apparently sound third party management companies fail to deliver full potential to their clients. There are typically four potential weaknesses that must be avoided in any selection decision:

1. The lack of consistent, ongoing involvement and oversight by the same key individuals who initially sold you the contractual relationship

2. Inconsistent quality of contract services and sub-par performance of on-site personnel permanently assigned to the community

3. The inability to effectively communicate and work with the owner, sponsors, and board of directors.

4. They do not get the job done; ineffective sales and marketing results and/or excessive operating costs.

Consistent monitoring and progress reporting systems can serve as effective early warning signals.

Fire the Manager!

Progressive management companies recognize these potential challenges and most work very hard for their clients, trying to avoid what has been termed in the business as the "baseball manager syndrome." This is a frequently erroneous business rule of thumb that says, *"When successful performance is in doubt, fire the manager!"*

Stabilized Occupancy and Ongoing Operations

Management contracts are sometimes terminated when a community reaches stabilized occupancy of 93 percent. The owner normally thinks the job is done. Yet this could be one of the most beneficial periods to actually have a professional manager providing ongoing guidance and leading-edge strategies. Net operating income and cash flow accelerate dramatically beyond break-even occupancy and become extremely attractive if you can operate in that exclusive zone above 93 percent stabilized occupancy. The difference between 93 percent *stabilized* occupancy and 97 percent *optimized* occupancy can frequently justify the *cost* of a professional management company. *Value* would be a more appropriate term.

Ongoing management strategies certainly include a continuation of existing initiatives that were implemented during initial project fill-up. But now these initiatives require increased focus and intensity. The ongoing initiatives include but are not necessarily limited to the following: 1) maintenance marketing; keeping the community full, 2) a detailed capital replacement and cosmetic upgrade program with both short- and long-run implementation goals, 3) execution of the fine points of subtle, but effective, revenue enhancement and expense reduction and 4) sustaining and optimizing resident satisfaction, quality of life and perceived value. Extraordinary management of service, cost, quality and convenience leads to high perceived value by both existing and future residents.

Indeed, management initiatives leading to operational enhancements at or above stabilized occupancy may be difficult to identify and execute, but the pay-offs can be significant. For every dollar earned or saved, the financial value of a community increases by a factor of almost ten dollars[1].

Third-party management companies can appear to be, and sometimes are, very expensive. But the financial pay-off for extraordinary community management puts many of these costs into proper perspective. One of the best ways to evaluate the relative costs of going internal versus using a professional management company is to seek answers to three key questions: 1) What obvious overhead costs would exist under either scenario?, 2) What are the tangible and intangible cost-benefits

---

[1] Net income is typically capitalized using a rate of approximately 10.5 percent; meaning investors are willing to accept (initially) a 10.5 percent return on their investment.

of the potential relationship? and 3) Can existing or restructured internal management realistically achieve the same objectives and performance levels as a professional management company? The final question to ask is how can you *most effectively* provide a wide array of management of services.

Management Fees

Basic management company fees can vary for a number of valid reasons, but typically range from approximately 4.5 to 5.5 percent of adjusted gross operating revenues. The "industry standard" is about 5.0 percent; that is the figure lenders typically look for as an expense line item when they evaluate your financial pro forma or loan package. Management fees of six to seven percent of revenues exist; but only in cases wherein extraordinary benefits and value are delivered to the owner.

Risk sharing incentives are starting to emerge in the industry. Under the risk sharing concept, both the owner and the management company agree on a budget with a defined net operating income (revenues minus expenses) or net cash flow target. If actual performance exceeds budget expectations, the management company receives an added incentive fee. If expectations are not met, the management company's fees are impacted accordingly.

A typical incentive arrangement might be where the additional incentive management fee is 25 percent of any *increase* in net cash flow above the budgeted amount for a definable period (usually one year). Sometimes a management company agrees to subordinate at least some of their earned fees to available cash flow after normal operating expenses and required debt service. Keep in mind there is no free lunch; the practical rules of risk vs. reward factor into all of these negotiated relationships.

Typical Management Services Provided

For newcomers to the assisted living industry, there are frequently some misconceptions and misunderstandings regarding the services actually provided by management companies in exchange for their fees. For example, the third party management company will hire certain personnel and incur certain costs at your community – *in your behalf.* That means these costs are passed through to your normal operating expense budget and are not covered as part of the typical five percent management fee. This is normal, conventional and common throughout the industry. In addition, a new project that has not yet reached stabilized occupancy will require some fixed cash retainers; payments to the management company as they help you bring the project to stabilized occupancy. The amount of these fees vary with the size of the project and other characteristics, but can range from approximately $5,000 to $10,000 per month during the initial start-up phase.

As in any other purchasing or outsourcing decision, it is best to receive competitive inputs from quality management companies with long-standing industry experience and good reputations. You must carefully evaluate a number of important services that are typically included in a comprehensive management contract relationship. Some of them include, but are not necessarily limited to, the following:

1. **Management Services**

    - Provide oversight and expertise
    - Supervise daily operations
    - Implement policies and procedures

2. **Sales and Marketing Initiatives**

    - Develop sales and marketing plan
    - Manage/supervise activities
    - Report status; weekly, monthly, quarterly
    - Deliver appropriate results

3. **Provide Operating Systems and Procedures**

    - Develop   Accounting systems/software,
    - Install   Policy and Procedures Manual,
    - Execute   Residency Agreements, Employee Manual, etc.

4. **Staffing/Human Resources**

    - Develop job descriptions
    - Hire

- Train
- Supervise
- Implement payroll

5. Budgets and Financial Management

- Prepare
- Obtain review and approval
- Perform to budget
- Report status monthly; explain variances
- Prepare billings/collect receivables; disburse payables

6. Financial Management and Controls

- Establish
- Maintain
- Monitor
- Report

7. Monthly Financial Statements

- Develop
- Prepare
- Report monthly
- Compare vs. budget

8. Risk Management

- Recommend adequate insurance coverage
- Keep appropriate insurance coverage in force

These are typical services provided. However, individual management contract terms and conditions can vary over a wide spectrum.

Short-Run & Long-Run Relationships

Some sponsors new to the business will retain a third party management company for their initial project and then gradually develop a strong, permanent internal resource. In these cases, let your management company know in an honest and straightforward manner about your long-run strategic objectives. In order to retain the right quality level of services, you must allow the management company an adequate budget and a reasonable time period to get the job done. You will not get top talent and focused attention if they think you are a "short-term client."

The ideal approach may be a multi-tier strategy involving continuous access to top-level industry expertise and experience, while developing a strong, permanent internal resource base and constantly keeping up with the ever-changing state-of-the-art in the assisted living industry.

Clearly, third-party management arrangements are not appropriate for every situation. But the inherent challenges and potential downsides of such a relationship can be eliminated or neutralized. And the significant advantages can sometimes lead to new levels of superior performance benefitting both residents and sponsors.

CHAPTER 29

"I *WAS* SOMEBODY ONCE"

The Real Issue is Resident Quality of Life . . . Not Just Resident Satisfaction

In my work, I try to *live* in as many senior living communities as possible. So far I've had short stays in over 30 independent and assisted living communities. As I was having dinner one evening with a distinguished senior in an assisted living community he said, **"You know, I was somebody once."** A lady at the next table chimed in, **"The young people who help us are just delightful – but they really don't understand us."** This community had all the right services and amenities. It was also staffed abundantly, and all the staff members knew residents on a first-name basis. Yet, something very important was lacking – a true understanding of seniors' inner emotional needs.

Over the past few years, people who provide senior living environments, from independent living through assisted living and nursing homes, have talked a great deal of talk about developing a *seamless continuum* of care. But our sharp focus on the "continuum" is sometimes no more than a business strategy. The real issue for determining success in the new millennium involves an area where many have accomplished very little; delivering true *quality of life* for residents.

Most seniors define a high-quality life as including a comfortable living environment, relatively good health, independence in their daily routine, the opportunity to express themselves and to experience life satisfaction and fulfillment. These desires can be translated into ten quality of life attributes. Five of these are delivered by any good senior community. They are: 1) health maintenance, 2) security, 3) comfort, 4) peace of mind, and 5) services offering quality, value, and utility. But the next five present some real challenges. Senior housing owners and operators *must* provide ways for residents to: 1) enjoy experiences, adventures and nostalgia, 2) maintain relative independence and control of their daily lives, 3) socialize with others, 4) be intellectually stimulated, and 5) express themselves and enjoy self-fulfillment (refer to Figure 29-1).

A new breed of seniors in the next millennium will expect more from our communities. We all recognize the importance of *demographics,* but we must also recognize seniors' changing *psychographics.* Let's assume the typical seniors considering your community will be 80 years old in the year 2000. As teenagers during the Great Depression and young adults during World War II, they reached maturity during the post-War boom. By the time of the Vietnam War and the rebellions of the 1960s, they were in their forties. By the 1970s, many were members of "The Establishment," and they were nearing retirement age during the boom/bust cycle of the 1980s. All those turbulent times created a series of birthmarks, making many of these seniors more demanding, less complacent, and more pragmatic in their search for self-fulfillment than their predecessors. These birthmarks are depicted in Figure 29-2.

FIGURE 29-1

TOP TEN QUALITY OF LIFE ATTRIBUTES

Seniors are on a constant search for quality of life in the following areas:

1. Experiences/adventures/nostalgia
2. Comfort/peace of mind
3. Security
4. Convenience
5. Quality and value
6. Health maintenance
7. Individual recognition
8. Socialization
9. Intellectual stimulation
10. Self-expression and fulfillment

The Real Issue is Resident Quality of Life . . .
Not Just Resident Satisfaction

Moore Diversified Services, Inc.

FIGURE 29-2

BIRTHMARKS OF AGE 80+ SENIORS IN THE NEW MILLENNIUM

"Birthmark"	Year	Age of Senior
Great Depression	1933	13
World War II	1943	23
Post War Boom	1950	30
Vietnam War/ Rebellions of '60s	1965	45
Boom and Bust of the '80s	1985	65
Prosperity of the Mid '90s	1995	75

A new breed of seniors will expect more from senior living communities.

Moore Diversified Services, Inc.

These birthmarks are further complicated by gender. The men will have experienced the *"gray flannel suit"* era of Corporate America – along with the transition from that period of conformity to a more entrepreneurial time that made modern day pioneers and adventurers popular. The females will have made the transition from being primarily homemakers to joining the skyrocketing numbers of women in the outside work force, making them less passive, more worldly and less apt to settle for someone else's definition of the status quo. To give tomorrow's seniors the quality of life they want, you must seriously consider five initiatives:

1. *Answer the question: What do my residents really want out of the remainder of their lives and how can we best deliver it – even if it involves shared risk?*

2. *Focus clinical and medical care plans more on supporting and enhancing quality of life rather than heavily regimented and institutional medical routines.*

3. *Add an increased emphasis on geriatrics and holistic approaches to wellness and health care to your existing traditional health care procedures, which tend to emphasize just treating health problems.*

4. *Make sure your assistance with activities of daily living truly supports each resident's needs, wants, and capabilities – in a flexible resident-centered manner.*

5. *Focus your operations on the <u>individual</u> resident's daily life, not a general group setting high-tech care plan.*

It may not be easy to determine how well your efforts are working, but it's important to try. Resident satisfaction surveys are useful, but they frequently don't tell the whole story. Many respondents soften their assessments, fearing retribution from management if they criticize their communities. Providers must learn to monitor another vital sign of each resident – paying close attention to how well each resident's quality of life needs are really being met.

If one were able to inventory and make use of the aggregate knowledge, experience and resources that exist with seniors in a typical senior living community, the results would be staggering. The unique capabilities, intellect and inner drives of these seniors that were developed over a lifetime of productive work and community contribution suddenly do not fade away as they "retire" and move into senior living communities. But sadly, in many cases, they are inadvertently suppressed – never surfacing again during the autumn years of their lives. Senior living communities have a tremendous opportunity (and responsibility) to provide a truly stimulating lifestyle for the senior.

Resident panels, focus groups and satisfaction surveys all indicate that most seniors report being generally happy living in a retirement communities. But these results do not necessarily mean that they have achieved *optimum* self-fulfillment.

The primary obstacles to improving quality of life will be creativity and cost. Implementing the new quality of life discipline will require increased staff time and innovative programming strategies, which would increase operating expenses. But there could also be financial advantages. In the long run, increased quality of life may lead to decreased institutional health care needs and related costs. Although this is only a theory, it's a plausible one that deserves to be tested.

Providers who don't take resident privacy, dignity, optimum independence, and the seniors' search for self-fulfillment seriously may pay for it in the end. In the not-too-distant future, a new breed of seniors may demand key quality of life elements, seeking out communities of choice that are truly focused on improving quality of life.

To personalize the quality of life challenge, those of us involved in the senior housing and health care industry might consider ourselves "achievers." By the time we reach 80 years of age, we will probably want to be called *"distinguished achievers."* In order to sharply focus on this complex issue of quality of life, project yourself into the future 30 or 40 years and ask the defining question, ***"What would I really want out of life at age 80?"*** It's safe to say that the answer for many of us would be, ***"Not exactly what I see today."***

The quality of life challenges are tremendous as we attempt to optimize senior's lifestyle in a cost-effective group setting but with individual privacy, dignity, optimum independence and self-fulfillment.

SECTION SEVEN

The Future is Not What It Used to Be

CHAPTER 30

PREPARING FOR A MARKET CORRECTION

"An Ounce of Prevention is Worth (More Than) a Pound of Cure"

It's no news that assisted living has taken off like a rocket and is still on the rise in the late 1990s. But just like the stock market, the senior living industry occasionally overheats and experiences a *correction.* It happened in the late 1980s. Assisted living may be headed for just such a correction between now and the year 2000. As we learned in the 1980s, an industry correction in the senior housing market does not necessarily mean a massive oversupply of product. It is more likely to reflect some owner/operators' misunderstanding of the true characteristics of the marketplace.

Types of Assisted Living Players

The types of players who currently attend overflowing seminars and conferences to gain insight about assisted living, typically fall into three major categories: 1) existing, experienced freestanding assisted living developers and established owner/operators who are completing their continuum and expanding their campuses, 2) owner/operators and administrators of hospitals, nursing homes and other related businesses who see assisted living as a natural extension of what they do and 3) people who have not been directly associated with senior housing or health care, but see assisted living business opportunities from their particular business perspective or company culture. The operative words for that third category are "company culture."

When seasoned professionals attempt to explain assisted living market realities to newcomers, the frequent response is, *"You don't understand – we're going to be different."* Today, it is not uncommon for someone to say, *"We're going to roll out 20 or 30 of these projects each year all over the country."* Sounds like the same story we heard in the 1980s when many relatively new industry players, including some of today's industry leaders, were surprised to discover that their well-intended senior housing strategies would ultimately go against the grain of the marketplace.

One of the most serious threats to the assisted living industry is the entry of well-intended individuals from other business cultures, such as real estate or health care, who fail to adapt their company cultures appropriately. Some of these new players perceive assisted living more as a real estate income property scenario, placing limited emphasis on the crucial component of assisting residents in the activities of daily living. They usually plan to serve non-frail seniors whose needs will be minimal or can be served separately by third party home health intervention. But front line experience with high acuity resident profiles and consistently high turnover rates indicates that this situation-driven position is doomed to fail. Chances are a number of these well-intended owner/operators will be out of the business over the next 18 to 36 months. Isn't that exactly what happened in the seniors housing market in the 1980s?

Foundation for the Future

For serious assisted living owner/operators and sponsors, it is time to secure the marketplace high ground – but making sure that this lofty position is based on a strong, solid foundation rather than a crumbling plateau of erroneous assumptions or short-run thinking. Now is clearly the time to do a thorough evaluation of the direction in which your facility is taking and, if necessary, make corrections. Assuming a full spectrum of best case/worst case scenarios, ask yourself, *"Will I remain viable by continuing to execute my current internal strategies in light of the changing external competitive marketplace?"* If your current operation is somewhat marginal, you can be sure it is likely to get worse as the assisted living market gets more complex.

A Five-Step Evaluation Process

This evaluation can be structured as a five-step process. First, go back to basics: 1) scrutinize your pricing structure, ongoing operating costs, potential for cost escalation or creep, staffing, operating strategies, and sales and marketing plan, 2) then do the same for your competition, both current and anticipated, 3) establish tangible success benchmarks and expected outcomes, 4) look for symptoms of potential problems and prescribe appropriate solutions and 5) finally, establish firm criteria for regular checkups.

The ultimate questions to ask during this process is, ***"Will my project have acceptable performance outcomes over the next five years?"*** If the answer is yes, then ask, ***"What could possibly prevent the continuation of my current successful trends?"*** And finally, ***"What can and should I do to mitigate future potential problems?"***

Answer Five Key Questions

To conduct your evaluation, focus on the following five critical issues:

1. ***Identify four key challenges and opportunities*** likely to affect the assisted living industry over the next five years. Develop new strategies to minimize or neutralize the challenges and exploit the opportunities (Chapter 33).

2. ***Develop a strategic response to ten major industry trends and ten key issues.*** These include: rising acuity levels, increased regulation, complex pricing strategies, market proliferation, the influx of managed care and the cost creep that becomes inevitable as residents become more frail and their chronic needs increase (Chapters 3 and 32).

3. ***Address the ten most important questions assisted living owner/operators face today*** as well as over the next five to ten years, including; what model is best for your needs? What resident profile to expect? How to deliver assistance with ADLs? What initial absorption rates to expect? What staffing levels are needed? What kind of start-up losses to be braced for? How to price your project? (Chapter 6).

4. *Implement an accurate and detailed forecast* of the cost of developing and operating a new project, along with realistic and conservative estimates of current and future operating expenses (Chapters 13, 14 and 15).

5. *Based on the costs you've estimated, create a flexible but fair pricing strategy* that balances project-driven needs with market-driven competitive forces. This means controlling both normal operating expenses and the additional costs involved in serving your residents' growing needs (Chapters 19 and 21).

Preparing for a market correction is simply good business sense. Assisted living is sure to encounter new challenges and opportunities in the near future. If you sharpen your strategic focus now you will survive even if there is a market turbulence. And if there is none, you will truly prosper.

PUTTING IT ALL TOGETHER
ASK THREE STRATEGIC QUESTIONS

1. "Will I remain viable by continuing to execute my current internal strategies in light of the changing external competitive marketplace?"
2. "Will my project have acceptable performance outcomes over the next five years?"
3. "What can and should I do - *now* - to avoid future potential problems?"

Final Checklist

At the risk of being repetitive, I'll end this chapter with yet another of my "top ten." What follows is an outline of ten strategies to consider when you evaluate the issue of market correction:

1. ***Create a Laser Sharp Focused Market Positioning***
    - What business are you *really* in?
    - Watch out for market myopia

2. ***Control as Much of the Referral Pipeline as Possible***
    - Hospitals/subacute care
    - Nursing
    - Rehabilitation
    - Home health
    - Adult children
    - Referral professionals

3. ***Look for Practical Revenue Enhancement***
    - Rehabilitation services
    - Home health satellite
    - Geriatric assessment
    - Adult day care

4. ***Extend the Average Length of Stay***
    - Redefine admission and discharge criteria
    - Be prepared for higher levels of acuity and care

- Proactively address cost creep
- Expand on and encroach on the nursing business

5. *Explore Market Niche "Carve-Outs"*
   - Alzheimer's/dementia
   - Respite care
   - "Catered living"

6. *Create an Optimum Pricing Structure*
   - Understandable
   - Equitable
   - Cover current and future costs
   - Flexible
   - Market responsive

7. *Get Creative with Affordability Issues*
   - Address practical approaches to resident spend-down
   - Value engineer with a passion:
     - Capital costs
     - Operating expenses
   - Explore semi-private accommodations
   - Develop innovative staffing models

8. *Develop a Market-Responsive, Cost-Effective Design*
   - Value engineered
   - High perceived value

9. ***Establish Best Practices and Benchmarking Initiatives***

    - By department
    - Make local, regional and national comparisons

10. ***Correctly Answer the Top Ten Planning and Development Questions***

    - See Chapter 6

Turn to the next chapter if you already have a troubled community.

CHAPTER 31

TURNING AROUND TROUBLED COMMUNITIES
What to Do When Things Go Wrong

This chapter is for those readers who, unfortunately, missed responding to the potential market correction strategies addressed in Chapter 30.

Troubled assisted living projects are likely to plague the industry in the future. They will, in all probability, include both for-profit and non-profit communities. Some newly developed communities are clearly situation-driven rather than being focused on the true needs of and benefits to seniors. Existing assisted living communities in maturing market areas are succumbing to their own aging-in-place challenges and the forces of new, well-conceived competition. Many markets are becoming more complex and individual project primary market areas are shrinking due to market saturation resulting from increasing competition.

Yet, in spite of these challenges, assisted living is still clearly a growing industry – and certainly not one that is mature and on the decline. One of the most significant problems associated with troubled assisted living communities is the lack of early recognition that the facility, in fact, needs help – and change.

Many communities fail for all the wrong reasons. Sometimes fundamental and focused corrective actions are the answer. In other cases, the honest pursuit of a worthy mission for non-profit communities is now incompatible with the way the real world marketplace evaluates the value of, and the need for, their community. Inappropriate site locations and design flaws can be serious and may not be correctable but, for the most part, the majority of troubled assisted living communities can be "saved."

Five Basic Actions to Take

There are five basic actions that must be taken to turn around a community that is experiencing an economic emergency – and these actions are strikingly similar to a medical response to a personal medical emergency.

1. *Stabilize the patient* – Many owner/operators are so caught up in the problem that they cannot find the time to stop and take a fresh objective look at their situation. Problems at a community will not get better without appropriate changes. This usually means implementing pragmatic strategies that make sense. Stabilizing the patient means checking for vital signs and prescribing both short-term and long-term solutions.

2. *Check for vital signs* – These vital signs start to determine the nature of the problem and provide the earliest clues for successful corrective action. Is the age and income qualified market size and depth sufficient? Has a realistic primary market area for the community been defined? Has the market area changed due to the passage of time and the possible encroachment of new competition? What is the level of relevant competition; now and in the foreseeable future? Does the community have a sufficient number of gross potential marketing leads that, properly exploited, can translate into closed sales? Are there serious perceptions or misconceptions in the marketplace that are having a negative impact on the community? What are the specific strengths and weaknesses of the community as well as the strengths and weaknesses of the most relevant competition?

3. *Go back to basics* – One of the most difficult challenges facing owner/operators is their reluctance to change the original plan or pro forma. In many cases, the plan was seriously flawed or the pro forma financially unrealistic. Unless the owner/operator is willing to recognize these flaws based on the current facts at hand, recovery is doubtful. In short, you must break your bad habits.

4. *Prescribe a solution* – Troubled communities need both short-term medication and a change in long-term operating strategies. Negative cash flow for an operating community is similar to uncontrolled bleeding in a patient. The first step in turning around a troubled property is to identify the source of the bleeding and attempt to curtail its flow. While easier said than done, focusing on this critical issue aids materially in developing the long-run changes that are necessary.

For every community there can be up to 50 worthwhile strategies that can be used as part of the turnaround approach. Approximately one-half of these strategies can be implemented with relative ease. The other half are likely to be difficult, painful and expensive; but often necessary for overall health and survival.

5. *Have regular check-ups* – New or revised systems and procedures are typically needed for long-term consistency and quality control. There are a number of fundamental strategies that can be applied to troubled properties. These include enhancing first impressions (cosmetically and physically) and repositioning the facility in the marketplace. In addition, installing systems and procedures associated with cost control, marketing tracking and quality control are sometimes part of the overall corrective action strategy. More severe action such as modifying the physical plant through adaptive re-use/conversion from one product type to another is sometimes the practical solution to an inappropriate product or changing marketplace conditions.

There are situations where formal sales and marketing programs are virtually non-existent. In these cases, a complete marketing effort must be developed to jump start new, qualified traffic to the community, resulting in increased sales potential.

One of the most difficult adjustments that sometimes must take place is the decision to change pricing. In many cases, pricing was clearly situation-driven rather than oriented towards the needs and preferences of the competitive marketplace.

Lost prospects are an excellent source of "miracle cure" information. The two percent of the senior consumers who move into your community are obviously very important – but understanding more about the 98 percent who got away can yield invaluable marketplace intelligence. Properly structured, lost prospect surveys provide a very useful tool in prescribing a success strategy for the future.

Five Cardinal Rules for Success

Successful operators and sponsors across the United States characteristically demonstrate five cardinal rules of success. Applying these rules can be extremely helpful in turning around your trouble property.

1. *Apply benefit-driven market positioning* – Every aspect of your community should be tested by asking the question, *"Is this a true and honest benefit to the resident?"*

2. *Have increased attention to detail* – Successful operators have a passion for details; whether it is optimizing operating expenses, meticulous grounds maintenance or developing a humanistic philosophy to enhance quality of life for the residents. Every aspect of the community must be focused on details; with appropriate systems and procedures to maintain consistency and quality control.

3. *Deliver high perceived value* – Good value can be achieved by selecting the right benefit-driven strategies to deploy and clearly communicating these benefits to your residents and marketplace.

4. Have a motivated, caring and focused staff – Each staff position should truly understand their profession and execute it by striking a delicate balance between the objectives of the owner/operator and the needs to be satisfied and benefits to be delivered to the residents.

5. Really understand the residents – Attempting to walk in the shoes of your assisted living residents can provide useful insights as to how to serve them better. It can also make your community truly unique over your competition while all other factors seem to be similar.

Old Habits are Hard to Break

Just like changing harmful lifestyle habits, troubled communities must adopt permanent changes in operating style. One serious impediment to turning around a troubled property is the "original pro forma trap." Most operators are unwilling to change their original plan, even though it now appears that it was ill-conceived and unrealistic. Success in turning around troubled assisted living properties involves recognizing that the present situation may not be compatible with achieving the original dream.

Measuring the gap between the original pro forma and the current situation can be painfully revealing. It can also provide the courage and conviction to recognize the need for change. Operators who have the business acumen and courage to change are the ones who will be able to turn troubled assisted living properties into bona fide success stories.

CHAPTER 32

THE TOP TEN ASSISTED LIVING ISSUES TO ADDRESS IN THE NEXT 12 MONTHS
A "Back to Basics" Checklist for Success

As we race into the new millennium, assisted living continues to be the hottest area of growth and development in the senior housing arena. Publicity about the robust 85+ population growth trends and senior living options appear almost daily in both the business press and consumer publications. The continued new development activity by both public and private companies has created a very high industry noise level. But aside from all this accelerated activity and communications hype, there are some basic issues that require strategic focus by existing sponsors and operators in order to achieve success and profitability in assisted living. Chapter 33 addresses a game plan for growth; converting four key challenges into sound business opportunities. Here is a simple, but very important, ten point checklist for success as you plan for the future.

1. *Create laser - focused market positioning* – Start by answering the defining question, ***"What business are we really in?"*** If you do this you will avoid a disease called *market myopia*. Think in broad terms when you answer this question, and use terms that are understandable and respond to the needs and concerns of potential residents and their families. Some 50 to 60 years ago the railroad industry contracted the market myopia disease – narrowly positioning themselves as being just *railroads* rather than being in the *transportation business.*

You have at least three attractive options to choose from when positioning your product. The first is to say that, ***"Assisted living is a surprisingly affordable living alternative, offering ambience, dignity and maximum independence for seniors in the later stages of life."*** The second is to point out that, ***"Our assisted living community has a strong, but largely invisible, medical basis as the foundation for our assisted living operating philosophy."*** Third is to assert that, ***"Although achieving high scores on resident satisfaction surveys and third-party facility inspections is very important, our primary concerns are the quality of life of our residents and the peace of mind of their caregivers."*** Chapter 1 addresses market positioning.

2. Control as much of the continuum and the assisted living referral pipeline as possible – If you don't, someone else will. Resident referral patterns can change dramatically as other health care providers enter your turf. Your primary focus for gathering referrals should be hospitals, subacute care units, nursing homes, rehabilitation facilities, home health agencies, adult children, and other referral professionals. If you don't presently own or control many of these referral sources, you'd better expect that some of your current resident origin patterns will change in the not-too-distant future. (See Chapter 7 for additional detail).

3. *Look for ways to enhance revenues* – Most assisted living communities are truly profitable at an acceptable level of performance only when the occupancy rate is at least 93 percent. Although many operators are satisfied with somewhat lower levels, you shouldn't be. And don't ignore the revenue potential of rehabilitation services, geriatric assessment and home health services. Even if it was wise to outsource these services in the past, it might be prudent to take some of these services in-house as resident acuity levels intensify and case loads increase.

4. *Sharpen your resident profile definition* – This will become an imperative in the next 12 to 18 months. With some resident turnover rates exceeding 40 percent, many operators are getting the proverbial wake-up call. They now realize that the assisted living business represents higher acuity care than they had originally bargained for – and providing such care has become absolutely necessary for their continued success. Many sponsors are redefining admission and discharge criteria; resulting in increasing encroachment on the traditional skilled nursing care market sector (where licensing and regulations permit). Owner/operators must be prepared to provide higher levels of care and develop methods to proactively identify and address operations cost creep – the inevitable increase in staffing and operating expenses resulting from higher resident acuity levels.

5. *Explore market niche "carve-outs"* – The more common types of carve-outs include special care Alzheimer's/dementia units, respite care and "catered living", which is a form of assisted living with added flexibility and a la carte service options. If you offer Alzheimer's/dementia care, make it legitimate, coupling appropriate, purpose-built physical designs with special programming and customized resident care plans that have been proven effective.

6. *Create optimum consumer pricing structures* – Make the plans easy to understand, equitable, flexible and market-responsive. Obviously, these pricing structures must be designed to cover both current and future costs while being competitive in the marketplace. Higher acuity levels are leading to operations cost creep, creating a new set of challenges for many owner/operators. These sponsors are reluctantly implementing – or at least considering various forms of tiered pricing to compensate for cost creep. As you revisit your pricing structures, you will likely find that the affordability issue represents a very significant future challenge for your operations. This is covered in detail in Chapter 19.

7. *Get creative with affordability issues* – Strike a delicate balance between the situation-driven financial needs of your project and market-driven dynamics. Affordability will become an increasingly difficult issue to address in the future. Some progressive sponsors and owner/operators are even considering practical and prudent approaches to assisted living spend-down and they are evaluating the practicality of selective use of semi-private accommodations. Some are implementing innovative staffing models including the universal worker approach. You can count on labor being one of the most significant challenges of the future. Staffing can represent over 60 percent of total operating costs and is becoming a scarce commodity at both the entry and upper management levels. Operating costs must be constantly value engineered with a passion. And all of this must be accomplished without major compromises to what the consumer perceives as high value when comparing your costs with the products and services offered by the local competition.

8. *Develop a market responsive, cost-effective design* – This involves balancing long-run operational efficiency with short-run high perceived value in the eyes of the consumer. In the 1999 time frame there are really three major design issues: 1) total project size, 2) design of the public spaces and 3) the mix of studios versus one-bedroom units. While it may appear desirable to maximize the number of units in order to optimize revenue and spread fixed capital and operating costs efficiently, it is equally important to avoid unacceptable marketplace risk by introducing too many units into your competitive market.

Industry experience indicates that the minimum size for a stand-alone assisted living community should be approximately 60 units. This assisted living unit count can be lower if these units are integrated with other revenue producing entities such as independent living, nursing, etc. Elaborate public spaces such as "neighborhoods" or the cluster concept in each wing are nice, but such space can be relatively expensive. These design features certainly facilitate marketing and should be given serious consideration – but their relative cost must also be factored into the decision, particularly as it impacts monthly service fees in a very competitive market.

Assisted living unit design has evolved from modest studios of 275 to 300 s.f. to larger studios or alcove units of approximately 350 s.f. Within the past three years there has also been a definite trend involving the growing demand of one-bedroom units with modest living areas averaging between 450 to 550 s.f. Current unit mixes can include up to a 60 percent concentration of these modest-sized, one-bedroom units. (See Chapter 10 for more details).

9. *Establish best practices and benchmarking initiatives* – Determine how your community really stacks up when compared to both your immediate competitors and similar communities on a regional and national basis. Benchmarking is a relatively new discipline involving a comparative analysis of industry operating factors, financial ratios and overall best practices. The benchmarking discipline can provide an early warning system; identifying impending problems while determining how you rank with your industry peers. This is covered in detail in Chapter 18.

10. *Finally, you must answer five important strategic questions in 1998 and beyond* – These questions are: 1) What business am I really in?, 2) Where do I want my community to be in three years?, 3) How, *specifically*, will I get it there?, 4)

The Top Ten Assisted Living Issues to 297
Address in the Next 12 Months

What could possibly threaten my project in the future? and 5) What should I do now to mitigate that future risk? Implementing these ten initiatives will sharpen your strategic focus, provide a hedge against downside risks and help you realize survival, success and profitability in assisted living as we head for the new millennium.

CHECKLIST FOR SUCCESS
THE TOP TEN ISSUES

1. Market positioning
2. Control the continuum
3. Enhance revenue
4. Sharpen resident profile definition
5. Create niche carve-outs
6. Customize pricing
7. Address affordability
8. Optimize design
9. Establish best practices and benchmarking
10. Answer five strategic questions

FIVE STRATEGIC QUESTIONS TO ANSWER

1. What business am I really in?
2. Where do I want my community to be in 3 years?
3. How, <u>specifically</u> will I get it there?
4. What could possibly threaten my project in the future?
5. What should I do to mitigate that risk?

CHAPTER 33

GAME PLAN FOR GROWTH
How to Turn Four Key Challenges Into Opportunities

In this increasingly complex marketplace, it's becoming harder for providers to achieve survival, growth and profitability. What's more, some sectors of major markets are already approaching an overbuild condition as developers and providers rush to stake their claims in scores of "hot" markets. But savvy assisted living providers who take a realistic look at market trends have a unique window of opportunity to turn four distinct challenges into opportunities – and distinguish themselves from the competition.

Challenge #1: *Resident turnover is higher than expected.* Many owner/operators are surprised to encounter resident turnover of 30 to 40 percent a year. True, some residents live at their communities for extended periods, but the average length of stay is approximately two-and-a-half years. Refilling units vacated by turnover is consuming available demand at a faster pace than most people expected; amounting to the demand equivalent of several "phantom" projects in a typical metropolitan market area.

Opportunity: *Explore ways of expanding your market.* Some owners and operators are extending the resident stays by changing admission and discharge criteria while increasing the intensity of health care services. Others are attempting to lower affordability thresholds. This is difficult because significant portions of assisted living cost structures are largely fixed. Semi-private accommodations have met with mixed success in most markets.

Other owners and operators are considering offering residents new ways to pay, including the option of spending down assets. This is a controversial issue, but one that deserves serious consideration. For more details on this concept, see Chapter 21.

Still others are redoubling their efforts to market to the adult child decision influencer. Such efforts can expand a provider's reach in two ways. First by accommodating those seniors who currently live outside the primary market area and are encouraged by their children to move close to them. Second, by bringing in seniors who fall below acceptable private pay income thresholds, but could qualify through the financial assistance of their children supplementing the senior's income and ability-to-pay resources. For example, in Atlanta's Fulton County there are over 23,000 households headed by adult children between the ages of 45 to 64 with current incomes in excess of $75,000. If just *one percent* either provided some financial assistance to income qualify their parent or attracted a parent back to the Atlanta area, the market would gain 230 new assisted living prospects.

Challenge #2: *Labor is rapidly becoming the most critical assisted living resource and cost issue.* Unemployment is at its lowest level in well over a decade. This does not bode well for the assisted living industry, whose operations, strategies and economics are based largely on the availability of low-cost, entry-level employees. In a typical 80-unit assisted living project, labor accounts for approximately 65 percent of operating expenses, and over 70 percent of the 40 full-time equivalent employees (FTEs) are at or near entry level. Even at entry-level base hourly rates, their average cost, loaded for direct and indirect payroll expenses and fringe benefits, can exceed $20,000 per year.

Labor unions see senior housing and health care as one of their last hopes of stabilizing their declining membership, or even regaining lost ground. Their demands typically include more pay, increased staffing requirements and more benefits. In a market with labor unions, a typical project could grow by three FTEs and result in a wage increase of entry level workers by 10 percent. This would increase operating expenses by approximately $66,000 annually or $2.50 per resident-day. To recover this cost increase at 93 percent stabilized occupancy, the owner would have to increase each resident's monthly service fee by about $75 a month.

Labor unions are not the only force that can cause payrolls to swell. Many assisted living operations are experiencing cost creep resulting from an increase need for assistance with the activities of daily living. As residents age in place, gradually needing more care, labor costs increase (see Chapter 15).

Opportunity: *Fine-tune your operations so you can tolerate increases in the cost of labor.* Recognize these labor threats now and conduct a financial sensitivity analysis of your operation to see how well you can tolerate potential labor cost changes in the future. Look for operational efficiencies and ways to realize economies of scale. Determine how to become financially competitive in your local labor market. Create a positive work culture that enhances employee morale. Finally, consider a pricing structure that can accommodate both cost creep due to aging in place and increased labor costs.

Challenge #3: *Hospitals are diluting assisted living's market share.* More and more hospitals are experiencing declining census and depressed acute care revenues. Hospital CEOs and CFOs see assisted living as a legitimate way to capture revenues they are currently giving away through referrals to other providers. Traditional referral patterns will inevitably change as hospitals create their own continuums, developing not only the so-called social model of assisted living, but possibly offering skilled nursing, home health, and rehabilitation services as well. This is discussed in detail in Chapter 4.

Opportunity: *If you can't beat 'em, join 'em.* Many hospital administrators are smart enough to realize that their acute care business culture may not work as well in the highly competitive, complex assisted living market sector. For example, hospitals who let their traditional culture drive the development of a new assisted living project might green-light construction costs of over $130 per square foot and operating expenses of up to $70 per resident day. With appropriate advice and counsel, these hospital CEOs and CFOs will quickly realize that, to be competitive in assisted living, they need to keep construction costs no higher that $85 to $95 per square foot and operating costs at no more than $40 to $50 per resident day. Joint ventures and synergistic relationships are being given serious consideration by many progressive hospital administrators, who would rather get 50 percent of properly earned assisted living financial rewards than 100 percent of the serious problems they could encounter without a partner who understands the business.

Challenge #4: *How to properly use home health* care. Properly used, home health is a viable way to service ADL needs, but problems are emerging in this high-growth industry. A recent GAO report indicated that a surprising number of Medicare reimbursed home health transactions involved misuse of the entitlements. The "seamless" integration of housing and shelter services provided by the owner/operator and care by a qualified, licensed home health agency is a viable service delivery system. The operative word is seamless.

Some assisted living owners and operators are unrealistically attempting to use home health as their primary method of providing assistance with the activities of daily living. But many are ignoring the added financial burden placed on the senior. Home health in assisted living becomes inappropriate when owner/operators allow home health providers to provide fragmented services at premium prices or by charging extra for things that should be an integral part of a facility's normal spectrum of services to the residents.

Opportunity: *Exploit home health's legitimate strengths – but avoid its weaknesses.* Use home health to augment your own array of services, ensuring that outcomes are competitive, seamless, consistently high in quality, and in compliance with local licensing and regulations.

It's time to get head and shoulders above the increasing assisted living marketplace noise level. Responding to these four challenges now is an excellent way to plan for success in the new millennium.

CONVERTING CURRENT CHALLENGES INTO FUTURE OPPORTUNITIES

The Current Challenge	The Future Opportunity
1. High resident turnover	Extend length of stay, lower affordability thresholds, focus on the adult child
2. Labor; getting scarce and expensive	Prepare today for the inevitable tomorrow
3. Hospitals stealing market share	Get involved in synergistic joint ventures
4. Inappropriate use of home health	Develop care strategies that are seamless and reasonably affordable

CHAPTER 34

THESE MAY BE THE GOOD OLD DAYS

Times Are Good, But it Will Take Work to Keep Them That Way

One of the major questions sponsors and owner/operators are asking privately in boardrooms and publicly at trade association meetings is, *"Can it get any better than this?"* As this book goes to press (July, 1998), assisted living communities and CCRCs across the U.S. enjoy high stabilized occupancies, often in excess of 95 percent. Conventional debt is readily available for growth and expansion, and new sources of equity capital are emerging. Wall Street and the public markets have embraced senior housing – particularly assisted living – as a viable investment option.

But despite these positive signs, the pressure to improve performance is relentless. A number of for-profit assisted living and independent living companies have gone public since 1996 by launching Initial Public Offerings (IPOs). Every 90 days presents a new challenge for these companies as investors and security analysts press the question: *"What have you done for me in this calendar quarter?"* For these public companies, growth and activity is the name of the game as they sweat out the next quarterly earnings report.

The pressure is equally intense for not-for-profits as the senior housing and health care business becomes more complex, making it necessary to do more just to keep up with the changing market. Boards of directors are sharpening their focus on their growing fiduciary responsibilities, and recent refinancing of some communities is putting more pressure on meeting specific bond covenants and overall financial performance ratios. There is also a growing need to generate significant cash flow after operating expenses and debt service in order to fund other missions.

So can it get any better? Probably not – and it could get worse. In fact, it may be time for owner/operators to ask, **"Is my property or portfolio about to hit the wall because of market saturation?"**

At least one early warning sign is already appearing. Relatively long waiting lists for some senior housing communities are thinning out as new competitors enter the market, gradually eroding the traditional back-pressure of senior consumer demand.

When confronted with warning signs, some sponsors offer the rationale that future growth in age and income qualified households will surely rebalance senior housing markets that become temporarily oversupplied. This rationale brings back memories of the 1980s real estate bust, when future inflation was supposed to compensate for any mistakes or overbuilding in real estate markets. Inflation was *not* the answer in 1988, and future senior household growth will *not* be the solution in 1998 and 1999. In many markets, the near-term growth of age and income qualified seniors will likely be modest, sufficient only to refill vacancies in existing units. These refill rates can be high, due to annual turnover rates of 15 to 25 percent in independent living and over 40 percent in many assisted living communities.

So how can you prepare for this brave new world? You must go beyond the question, *"Can it get any better than this?"* Start by asking yourself these six additional questions:[1]

1. *What could happen in the next five years to threaten my assisted living community or portfolio of properties?* Is a major new competitor likely to move into your market, offering better quality, price, or value? Might an oversupply of new units lead to increased vacancies or price wars? If you can imagine any plausible scenario that could create future problems, *now* is the time to implement corrective action to mitigate or eliminate those problems.

2. *Am I really satisfied with my current financial returns?* These returns should be measured in a number of ways: cash flow, cash-on-cash return on investment, return on total equity, return on cost and internal rate of return over a reasonable holding period. For a mature, stabilized project, available cash flow after debt services should be at least 30 percent of the

---

[1] Also see Chapter 5 for five key aging-in-place/resident profile questions.

annual debt payment and cash-on-cash return should be 10 to 18 percent. Total return on equity should be 20 percent or higher, and internal rate of return (for mature, stabilized projects) should be 20 to 30 percent, depending on how long your community's been operating. (See the example in Chapter 14). Don't wait for a financial crisis to emerge; look for ways to enhance your financial positions now.

3. *How does my community stack up against general industry ratios and benchmarks?* Benchmarking, currently a popular corporate discipline, is very useful but must be applied with caution (see Chapter 18). Using broad industry ratios as guidelines can be both helpful and misleading for your specific project. It's not unlike saying: *"My blood pressure is this, doctor. I've never met you before, but is that okay?"* On the other hand, the simplistic rationale, *"we're just different,"* is usually unacceptable and an early symptom of future problems.

In addition to the financial returns outlined above, track your total operating expenses per resident day, which typically range from $27 to $33 for independent living and from approximately $38 to $48 for conventional assisted living. Operating margins after normal operating expenses but before depreciation, amortization, interest payments and taxes should be approximately 48 to 52 percent for independent living and 37 to 42 percent for assisted living. (See Chapter 14 for details.)

4. *Do I have a proactive revolving five-year strategic plan?* The key word here is "revolving." Each year, your five-year plan should be sharpened, refocused, and rolled out for an additional 12 months. This allows you to always keep a clear five-year time horizon in front of you. Key items you should evaluate every year include capital improvements, value engineering, competitive repositioning, net operating income enhancement, increased resident satisfaction, and quality of life improvements.

5. *Do I have an acceptable exit strategy?* This applies to you even if you plan to hold your property indefinitely. Why? The reason is simple. Your long-term holding strategy will not be successful if it doesn't include an acceptable exit strategy.

Simply stated, an exit strategy asks the hypothetical question: *"If I sold my community based on current market conditions, would I be pleased or disappointed by the results?"* If you'd be disappointed, ask yourself an additional question: *"What can I do in the next 12 to 18 months to improve the outcome of this hypothetical transaction?"* The "hypothetical" exit strategy is the acid test for project viability.

6. *Is next year the appropriate time to step outside the box and consider unusual innovation?* Is it time to experiment with some changes that could yield positive results but are not yet fully supported by empirical evidence? Initiatives such as selective unbundling of services or providing expanded assistance with the activities of daily living to residents in independent living units may seem radical, but, like a good farmer or rancher, you can learn a lot by walking your boundaries and fence lines looking for weaknesses and potential problems.

On a scale of 1 to 10, the current success rating of the senior housing and health care industries is about 8.5 (July, 1998). Sustaining this high score will be the most significant challenge sponsors and owner/operators will face as we approach and enter the new millennium. As the senior housing and assisted living business becomes more of a science and less of an art, we can no longer rely exclusively on the past to develop a realistic vision of the future.

I had just completed a series of focus groups at a community in Chicago and, as usual, was headed for another airplane. As I attempted my graceful, but hurried exit, one of the focus group respondents, an 85-year-old man, walked up to me, put his arm around my shoulder and said, ***"You know Jim, the future is not what it used to be. But if we can see the future, we can get there before it happens."*** I thanked him for his wisdom as I left the building. But the significance of his simple comment didn't hit me until I was driving to O'Hare airport

Here was a man, supposedly living a relatively sheltered life, who in one simple statement, outlined how we must approach our industry as we plan for the future. We face some very exciting times in the assisted living industry. And we must anticipate and plan for the future before it actually happens. Failing to believe that the future will be different is perhaps our industry's biggest threat and also our greatest opportunity.

I wish you much success in your assisted living and senior housing endeavors.

Jim Moore, July 1998

APPENDICES

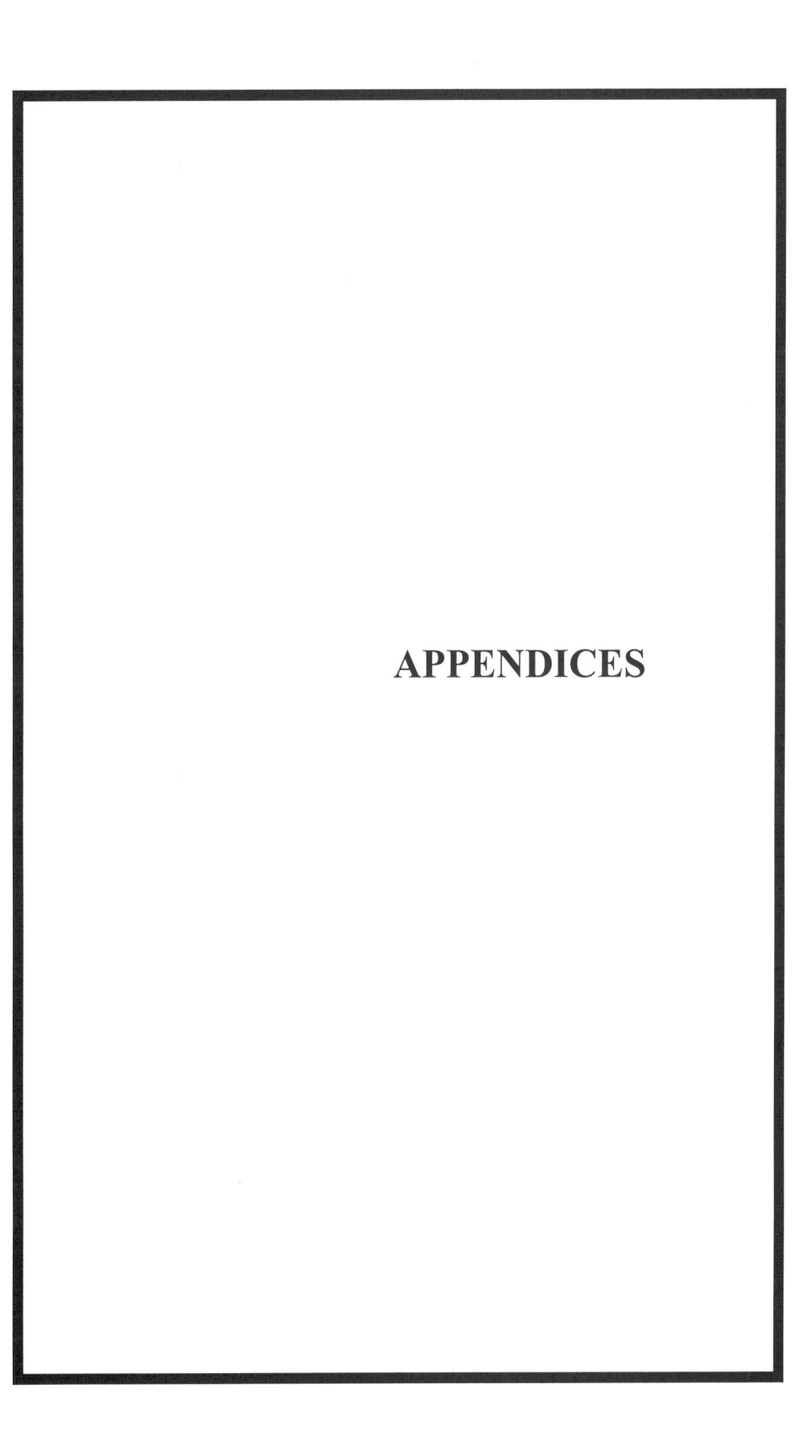

APPENDIX A

OVERVIEW OF MARKET & FINANCIAL FEASIBILITY

An entire book could be devoted to just market and financial feasibility. The purpose of this appendix is to provide the outline or structure for this very important part of the project planning process.

Market and Financial Feasibility As a Closed Loop

Feasibility methodology is gradually evolving from an art to a science. But the process still requires a tremendous application of professional judgement and conventional wisdom. The days of, *"If I build it, they will come"* are over. Some of the classical feasibility analysis mistakes of the 1980s were:

1. Inadequate, improper and erroneous input assumptions
2. Faulty methodology
3. Some theories or hypotheses not supported by sound empirical data
4. Insufficient competitive analysis and field investigations
5. Flawed data analysis and conclusions
6. No direct linkage between market feasibility *outputs* and financial pro forma *inputs*
7. Failure to keep up with the ever-changing market

Overview of Market & Financial Feasibility 311

8. Using the rationale that inflation (growth of senior households) would compensate for any mistakes or overbuilding
9. Relying on incorrect age cohorts, income levels and annual turnover projections, etc.
10. Failure to effectively address "Aging in Place"

Item six is one of the most critical elements of the overall planning process. As Figure A-1 illustrates, market and financial feasibility must be *closely integrated using a closed loop philosophy*. Initially the market feasibility study outputs must drive the inputs to the financial pro forma. The pro forma, in turn, is heavily influenced by the initial design and overall development business plan. Any future changes, such as project cost increases, must be immediately transmitted back to the pro forma. If the pro forma requires increased revenues, the market feasibility study must be reworked to determine if all of these changes and their impacts are still acceptable in the marketplace.

Market Feasibility Study Outline

It is important to have a detailed, definitive work plan for market feasibility; with tangible and specific expected outcomes. The following outline can be used as a guide if you are conducting an in-house market feasibility study or preparing a Request for Proposal (RFP), for engaging a consultant.

Overview of Market & Financial Feasibility 312

FIGURE A-1
HOW THE IMPORTANT FEASIBILITY TASKS ARE INTEGRATED INTO THE BUSINESS PLAN
The "Closed Loop" Between the Competitive Market and Market/Financial Feasibility

WILL THE MARKET ACCEPT REQUIRED MONTHLY SERVICE FEES?

THE COMPETITIVE MARKET
- SIZE AND DEPTH OF AGE/INCOME QUALIFIED MARKET
- WILLINGNESS TO PAY
- ATTITUDES AND OPINIONS

MARKET FEASIBILITY
- MARKET RATES
- TOTAL POTENTIAL REVENUE INPUT

MARKET, FINANCIAL & DESIGN GUIDELINES
PROJECT GO/NO-GO DECISION

PROJECT BUSINESS PLAN
- REQUIRED DEVIATIONS FROM MARKET RATES
- EXCEPTIONS/CHANGES

FINANCIAL PRO FORMA

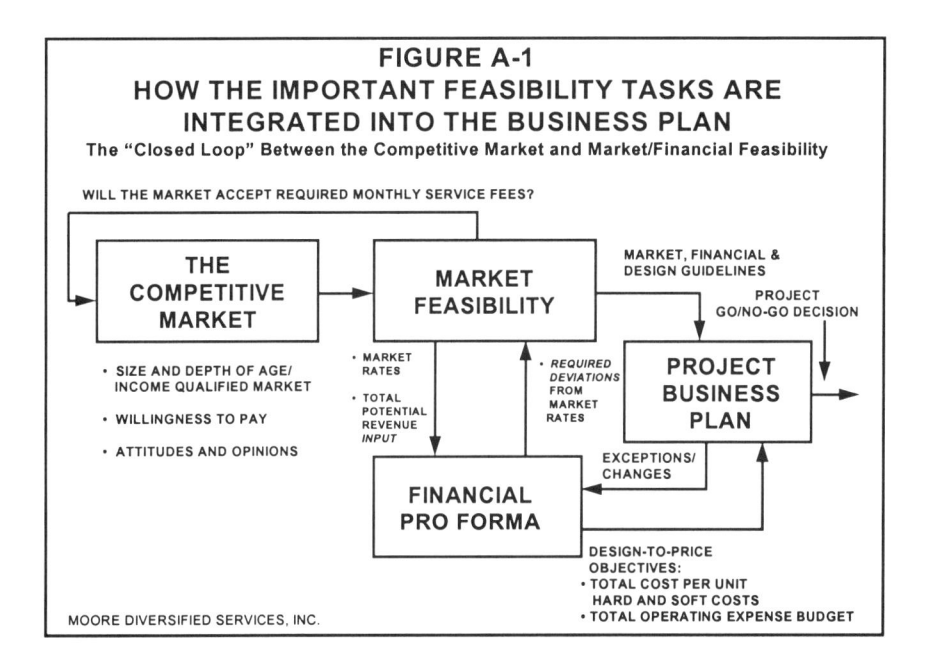

DESIGN-TO-PRICE OBJECTIVES:
- TOTAL COST PER UNIT
- HARD AND SOFT COSTS
- TOTAL OPERATING EXPENSE BUDGET

MOORE DIVERSIFIED SERVICES, INC.

1. *Determine Relevant Market Areas*

- Define the primary, secondary and tertiary market areas
- Estimate impact of population mobility trends on seniors
- Determine impact of decision influencers (adult children)
- Obtain resident origin profiles of competition, where available

2. *Conduct Demographic Economic Base Study*

- Determine total number of age & income qualified households

Overview of Market & Financial Feasibility 313

- Conduct age cohort segmentation and growth projections
- Establish senior consumer qualifying income criteria
- Determine impact of home equity on consumer affordability
- Identify relevant and prudent forecasting safety margins

3. *Conduct Competitive Analysis*[1]

- Assisted living/personal care
- Independent living/congregate care/CCRC
- Special care Alzheimer's/ dementia facilities
- Nursing homes
- Acute care, subacute care
- Home health agencies
- Other senior housing products and services (senior apartments, subsidized elderly housing, etc.)
- Estimate managed care impacts – where relevant

4. *Conduct Specific Site Analysis*

- Subject site description
- Access/egress characteristics
- Drive-by visibility/traffic counts, etc
- Surrounding development/adjacent property owners
- Potential buffers and set-backs
- Appropriate zoning
- Supporting amenities, benefits and features
- Evaluate/rank alternative sites - where applicable

---
[1] Must include both existing and announced projects

5. *Estimate Overall Project Penetration Rates and Market Share*

- By age cohort
- By qualifying income threshold criteria
- Primary versus secondary market area
- Consider annual resident turnover
- Adjust for competitive impacts (existing and planned)
- Weighting of competition – where applicable

6. *Conduct Unit Absorption Scenarios*

- Estimate time to stabilized occupancy (including pre-marketing efforts)
- Adjust for unit turnover during fill-up

7. *Recommend Final Product Mix*

- Unit types
- Number of units/unit mix
- Individual living areas/unit size
- Pricing by unit type
- Consider special market/product segmentation
    - Special care dementia
    - Catered living
    - Etc.
- Identify common area amenities
- Recommend services, amenities, benefits and features

Figure A-2 depicts the typical sequence to follow when evaluating your project's market feasibility.

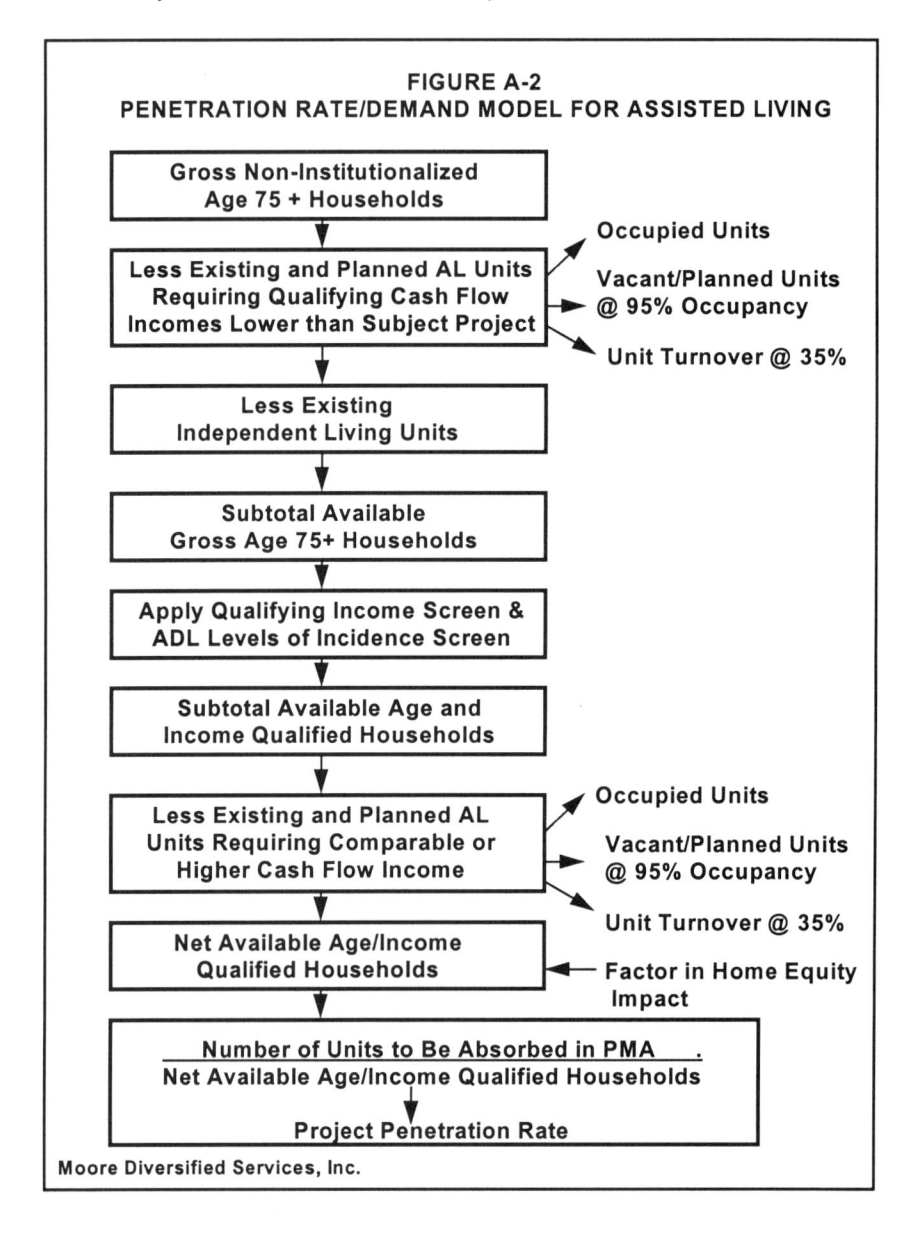

FIGURE A-2
PENETRATION RATE/DEMAND MODEL FOR ASSISTED LIVING

```
          Gross Non-Institutionalized
              Age 75 + Households
                      │
                      ▼                              Occupied Units
       Less Existing and Planned AL Units
         Requiring Qualifying Cash Flow             Vacant/Planned Units
       Incomes Lower than Subject Project           @ 95% Occupancy
                      │
                      ▼                              Unit Turnover @ 35%
              Less Existing
           Independent Living Units
                      │
                      ▼
               Subtotal Available
            Gross Age 75+ Households
                      │
                      ▼
         Apply Qualifying Income Screen &
          ADL Levels of Incidence Screen
                      │
                      ▼
           Subtotal Available Age and
           Income Qualified Households
                      │
                      ▼                              Occupied Units
         Less Existing and Planned AL
         Units Requiring Comparable or              Vacant/Planned Units
            Higher Cash Flow Income                 @ 95% Occupancy
                      │
                      ▼                              Unit Turnover @ 35%
           Net Available Age/Income
             Qualified Households         ◀──── Factor in Home Equity
                      │                              Impact
                      ▼
      Number of Units to Be Absorbed in PMA
      Net Available Age/Income Qualified Households
                      │
                      ▼
             Project Penetration Rate
```

Moore Diversified Services, Inc.

"Bottom-Line" Answers Provided by Market Feasibility

The ultimate outputs of the market feasibility study must answer the following two questions:

1. What percent of the *net* supply of the age and income qualified market (allowing for turnover, competition, etc.) must I capture in order to fill my project?

2. How is the competition doing and is there enough demand elasticity in the market for my project?

3. Is my site really as attractive as I think it is – or am I really situation-driven when I should be market-driven?

4. How fast will my project fill-up – realistically?

5. Does my final product mix meet the following criteria:

    - Responds to market wants and needs
    - Compares favorably with both the existing competition and new potential projects in the future
    - Pricing is consistent with reasonable affordability levels of my target market and offers good value compared to local competition

There is another important question which requires much more analysis: **"Will my market-responsive project concept be financially feasible?"**

Financial Feasibility/Pro Forma Outline

1. *Develop Key Inputs to Realistic and Accurate Capital Budget*

   - Raw land cost allocation
   - Site development costs
   - Preliminary construction cost estimates
   - Contractor general conditions factor
   - Construction contingency
   - Construction interest
   - Development fees
   - Architectural and engineering fees
   - Furniture, fixtures & equipment
   - Legal and accounting fees
   - Financing costs
   - Market and financial feasibility studies
   - Initial absorption/fill-up reserve fund
   - Detailed marketing budget
   - Project contingency

2. *Establish Total Capital/Debt Structure Requirements, Mix and Sources*

   - Equity
   - Debt
   - Other capital sources
   - Credit enhancement

3. *Establish and Plan for Required Lender/Underwriter Criteria*

- Debt to equity ratio
- Debt service coverage ratio:
    - Initial
    - At stabilized occupancy
- Debt service reserve fund
- Cash to debt ratio
- Average debt per unit

4. *Set Design-to-Price Objectives*

- Implement the closed loop concept (see Figure A-1)
- Conduct cost containment/value engineering effort

5. *Project Realistic Operating Expense Scenarios*

- Actual experience (if existing community)
- Industry data base benchmarks
- Specific project analysis

6. *Determine Pricing Options*

- Flat monthly service fee
- Monthly service fee with tiered add-on charges for increased ADLs by:
    - Levels of care/case work-up
    - Additional minutes per day for added ADLs
- Develop preliminary menu of pricing options

Overview of Market & Financial Feasibility 319

- Implement cash flow impact scenarios for various pricing options
- Make final pricing policy recommendations

7. ***Implement Multiple Scenarios of Pricing Options Short List***

- Based on quantitative results of previous tasks
- Insure adequacy of:
    - Net operating income
    - Cash flow
    - Debt service coverage
- Implement computer-driven sensitivity analysis of critical financial variables and assumptions

8. ***Estimate Total Revenues, Expenses, Net Operating Income, Debt Service, Cash Flow and Debt Service Coverage Factor***

- During fill-up
- At stabilized occupancy
- 5, 7 and 10 years in the future

9. ***Conduct Discounted Cash Flow Analysis***

- Use appropriate capitalization and discount rates
- Present value
- Internal rate of return
- Cash flow
- Cash-on-cash return

10. Run a Financial Sensitivity Analysis

- Interest cost at +/- 1%
- NOI sensitivity at +/- 5%
- Fill-up rate at +/- 2 units/month

The critical questions that the completed financial pro forma should answer include, but are not necessarily limited to the following:

1. Have I included *everything* in the capital budget that will provide adequate funds to bring my project to stabilized occupancy?

2. Are there reasonable and adequate contingencies in the pro forma?

3. Are the debt, equity and interest rate assumptions realistic?

4. Will I meet all the criteria likely to be required by lenders?

5. Have I realistically projected revenues and conservatively estimated operating expenses?

6. Will my pricing strategy cover not only my current costs; but also my best estimate of future costs – including potential cost creep?

7. Is the overall project financially prudent; delivering appropriate financial safety margins and entrepreneurial returns – after all expenses and debt service payments have been covered?

The final critical question to ask is, *"Have I updated my market and financial feasibility study to accurately reflect all of the changes that have taken place during the planning and development process?"*

APPENDIX B

MORTGAGE LOAN CONSTANTS

A loan constant is an easy way to estimate the total debt service payment for an assisted living community.

Example:

What is the debt payment per unit for an assisted living community where the average total (all-in) cost per unit is $100,000; with 75% debt ($75,000), 25% equity ($25,000) @ 9% for 25 years?

Referring to Figure B-1:

$75,000 x .101% = $7,575 /year

Or

$ 630 /month

Mortgage Loan Constants

FIGURE B-1
LOAN DEBT CONSTANTS

Interest Rate	MORTGAGE TERM [1] 20 Years	25 Years	30 Years	40 Years [2]
5.00%	7.92%	7.02%	6.44%	5.79%
5.50%	8.25%	7.37%	6.81%	6.19%
6.00%	8.60%	7.73%	7.19%	6.60%
6.50%	8.95%	8.10%	7.58%	7.03%
7.00%	9.30%	8.48%	7.98%	7.46%
7.50%	9.67%	8.87%	8.39%	7.90%
8.00%	10.04%	9.26%	8.81%	8.34%
8.50%	10.41%	9.66%	9.23%	8.80%
9.00%	10.80%	10.07%	9.66%	9.26%
9.50%	11.19%	10.48%	10.09%	9.72%
10.00%	11.58%	10.90%	10.53%	10.19%
10.50%	11.98%	11.33%	10.98%	10.66%
11.00%	12.39%	11.76%	11.43%	11.14%

Moore Diversified Services, Inc.

[1] Based on monthly amortization.
[2] Typical HUD Financing

APPENDIX C

THE CAPITALIZATION RATE CONCEPT

For some experienced operators, the concept of capitalization rates is very familiar and useful. For others, it may be a very foreign technical term. But like loan constants, capitalization rates can play a useful role in your strategic planning.

As used in this book, the capitalization rate ("cap rate") is the annual debt-free (unleveraged) cash return that prudent and experienced investors would expect to realize from a specific investment. Currently cap rates for assisted living typically range from 10.0 percent to 11.5 percent; a 10.5 percent cap rate is used throughout this book.

Example:

In Figure 14-2, the annual unleveraged cash return (net operating income) is $831,420. If an investor expects a 10.5 percent return, what might he or she be willing to invest in order to yield that return?

$$\frac{\$831,420}{.105} = \$7,918,385$$

In a similar manner, you can evaluate the incremental *imputed* increase (or decrease) in your project's value for any situation that would impact net operating income (NOI).

Example:

A capital investment of $50,000 is expected to save $12,000 per year in operating expenses; increasing NOI by a similar amount. How will my intrinsic project value be impacted at a 10.5 percent cap rate?

$$\frac{\$12{,}000}{.105} = \$224{,}285$$

This means that the $50,000 capital investment has increased the intrinsic value of your community by approximately $224,000.

Cap rates are used throughout this book to quantify the impact of certain strategies.